Ten Notable Women of Modern Latin America

Ten Notable Women of Modern Latin America

James D. Henderson, Linda R. Henderson, and Suzanne M. Litrel

ROWMAN & LITTLEFIELD
Lanham • Boulder • New York • London

Published by Rowman & Littlefield
An imprint of The Rowman & Littlefield Publishing Group, Inc.
4501 Forbes Boulevard, Suite 200, Lanham, Maryland 20706
www.rowman.com

86-90 Paul Street, London EC2A 4NE

Copyright © 2024 by James D. Henderson, Linda R. Henderson, and Suzanne M. Litrel

All rights reserved. No part of this book may be reproduced in any form or by any electronic or mechanical means, including information storage and retrieval systems, without written permission from the publisher, except by a reviewer who may quote passages in a review.

British Library Cataloguing in Publication Information Available

Library of Congress Cataloging-in-Publication Data

Names: Henderson, James D., 1942- author. | Henderson, Linda Roddy, 1944- author. | Litrel, Suzanne, author.
Title: Ten notable women of modern Latin America / James D. Henderson, Linda R. Henderson, and Suzanne M. Litrel.
Description: Lanham : Rowman & Littlefield, [2023] | Includes bibliographical references and index.
Identifiers: LCCN 2023026538 (print) | LCCN 2023026539 (ebook) | ISBN 9781538153024 (cloth) | ISBN 9781538153031 (paperback) | ISBN 9781538153048 (ebook)
Subjects: LCSH: Women—Latin America—Biography. | Latin America—Biography. | Latin America—History.
Classification: LCC CT3290 .H464 2023 (print) | LCC CT3290 (ebook) | DDC 920.08—dc23/eng/20230719
LC record available at https://lccn.loc.gov/2023026538
LC ebook record available at https://lccn.loc.gov/2023026539

Contents

Introduction: Latin American Women, Old Perspectives and New	1
Chapter 1: Leopoldina, 1797–1826	13
Chapter 2: Mariana Grajales, 1808–1893	35
Chapter 3: Eliza Lynch, 1833–1886	55
Chapter 4: Clorinda Matto de Turner, 1852–1909	79
Chapter 5: Gabriela Mistral, 1889–1957	101
Chapter 6: Frida Kahlo, 1907–1954	125
Chapter 7: Eva Perón, 1919–1952	151
Chapter 8: Celia Cruz, 1925–2003	169
Chapter 9: Rigoberta Menchú Tum, 1959–	191
Chapter 10: Dilma Rousseff, 1947–	215
Glossary	239
Index	243

Modern Latin America. Public Domain

Introduction

Latin American Women, Old Perspectives and New

I

Latin America is a large and diverse world region, extending from Mexico and the Hispanic borderlands of the United States in the north, southward down to the southernmost tip of South America. The region also includes many of the islands of the Caribbean. The people of Latin America are from all ethnic groups, singly and in racial mix. In the same vein, the histories of Latin America's numerous nations are distinct from one another. Yet Latin America is a region knit together by powerful connecting threads. For example, its people share a Mediterranean culture, meaning they speak languages derived from Latin: Spanish, Portuguese, and French. They share another powerful cultural anchor in their Roman Catholic religion, established among them prior to the Protestant Reformation. Additionally, the region's many Indigenous ethnicities cherish their own enduring, distinct languages and cultural traditions.

Another striking connecting thread exists at the level of historical periodization. Latin America's two principal historical eras, the colonial and the modern, began at clearly definable moments. The colonial era began shortly after dawn on Friday, October 12, 1492. That was when Genoese explorer Christopher Columbus, sailing under the flag of Spain and commanding a mostly Spanish crew, landed on an island in the Bahamas and claimed the New World and its inhabitants in the name of Queen Isabella of Castile. A mere eight years later, in 1500, Portuguese navigators claimed Brazil for Portugal.

About three centuries later, Latin America's colonial period ended and its modern period began over the relatively brief span of fourteen years, 1810 to 1824. During those fraught times women played important, even pivotal roles. At the dawn of Spanish America's independence era, "La Pola," Policarpa Salavarrieta (1795–1817), served as a spy for patriot leaders in the Viceroyalty of New Granada, in northern South America. Her life was snuffed out by the muskets of a Spanish firing squad. Micaela Bastidas Puyucahua (1745–1781) is honored as a precursor of Spanish American independence. Her execution by authorities of the Spanish king was even more ghastly than that of La Pola. Micaela was a coleader, with her husband Tupac Amaru II (José Gabriel Condorcanqui), of an uprising of oppressed Indigenous peoples in highland Peru.[1]

Brazil's struggle for independence stands in contrast to that of Spanish America. Its break with Portugal was relatively quick and bloodless. This was owed in no small part to the actions of the wife of the heir to the Portuguese throne, Pedro da Braganza. The Austrian-born Hapsburg aristocrat Maria Leopoldina came of age in Vienna and traversed the Atlantic to meet her future husband, Pedro. With independence achieved in mid-1824, the royal couple ruled independent Brazil as emperor and empress.[2]

The first century of Spanish America's modern period was marked by ideological struggles between liberals and conservatives. The former wanted the new republics to be democratic in nature, while the latter, in many cases, demanded rule by monarchs, as in colonial times. Throughout the Spanish-speaking Americas, from the first stirrings of revolution until the late nineteenth century, conservatives chafed at the secular character of their liberal-drafted national constitutions. Those were documents full of Enlightenment ideals, chief among them the mandated separation of church and state. This notion was anathema to conservative-minded Roman Catholics, who fought against it for decades. For these and other reasons, liberals and conservatives fought one another in civil wars extending across the breadth of Spanish America. Although these were principally nineteenth-century conflicts, in some nations strife between liberal and conservative factions extended well into the twentieth century.[3]

Over time, Latin American elites found common ground in the cause of economic development. Decades of civil war had left their countries woefully behind the times. Great advances in nations like the United States, Britain, and Germany convinced Latin American leaders that they must set aside their ideological differences and work together in order to achieve progress and prosperity, especially through the export of their countries' natural resources. That is, they became modern by integrating their nations into the world economy under principles known collectively as economic liberalism. Liberal development strategy proved extraordinarily successful—for some. From the mid-1800s onward, monies earned through natural resource export coupled with foreign loans sparked rapid modernization over much of Latin America.

Urbanization moved apace, middle classes grew and diversified, and elites, especially, grew wealthy.

Many women benefited from modernization. It permitted them to expand their traditionally limited social roles by tapping into social networks, friendships, and technological advances of the day. Elite women could and did become schoolteachers, writers, and poets. Unfortunately, poor women benefited little from modernization. In the countryside many farmers—campesinos and campesinas—looked on as their smallholdings passed into the hands of men who turned them into agricultural estates dedicated to the production of export crops. These ranged from sugarcane, henequen, and cotton to coffee and cacao in tropical zones. In temperate parts of South America, wheat and cattle led exports. This spelled trouble in a region that had historically ignored the plight of its least favored citizens. Inequitable modernization touched off revolutionary protest in several Latin American countries. The most striking of these began in Mexico in 1910. In that year the country was ruled by a modernizing dictator named Porfirio Díaz, who was driven from the country early in the Mexican Revolution of 1910–1920. Thanks to its bloody overturning of the status quo, Mexico was able to implement meaningful social reforms. Region-wide protests, often of an overtly revolutionary nature, continued throughout Latin America over the following hundred years. Colombia was the last Latin American country to witness the end of a revolutionary insurgency begun decades before. This occurred in 2010, when the country's Castroite FARC guerrillas (Fuerzas Armadas Revolucionarias Colombianas) laid down their weapons and entered into peace talks with the Colombian government.

Sadly, though, this century of revolutionary striving did not notably improve the lot of poor women in Latin America. Their lack of both money and agency have persisted to the present day.[4]

II

What is the place of women over the entire sweep of Latin American history? In her study of women in colonial Latin America, Susan Socolow found there was little change in the status of women in society. However, by the end of the independence period women had started challenging traditional notions of their rightful place in society. For example, during the years 1823–1824 women in southern Mexico argued that they possessed rights of citizenship equal to those of men. At that same historical moment Argentine women lobbied for publicly funded education for young women. In 1832, Brazilian feminists increasingly demanded these rights and more, in the pages of their newspaper the *Liberal* (*O Liberal*). By the end of the nineteenth century, feminism stood as an established movement not only in Latin America but elsewhere in the world as well.

Latin America's feminist movement took institutional form in 1910 in Buenos Aires at the First International Women's Congress. Delegates to the meeting hailed from Argentina, Uruguay, Paraguay, Chile, and Peru. In the gathering's keynote address, "What Feminists Stand for," Encarnación López, director of the city's Escuela Sarmiento, said,

> The woman [of today] refuses to be bound by the four walls of her home. . . . Instead, she seeks to extend her influence beyond it—whether by contributing to the material improvement of society or through [society's] intellectual elevation by beautifying life through the influence of art [and by] spreading constructive ideas. . . . Who can deny that this movement is beginning to catch on, as women gain awareness of their rights and duties?[5]

The Mexican Revolution of 1910–1917 opened new paths to women seeking fresh ways of asserting their individuality and human rights. Two figures serve to illustrate this. They are Amelia Robles Ávila (1889–1984) and Frida Kahlo (1907–1954). Amelia Robles was the daughter of mescal distiller Casimiro Robles, of Chilpanzingo, Guerrero. In 1910, at the age of twenty-one, Amelia accepted the post of treasurer of the Maderista club of Chilpanzingo, in southern Mexico. Following the assassination of president Francisco Madero, she joined the forces of guerrilla leader Emiliano Zapata—not as a woman but as a man named Amelio Robles. A formal photograph taken around 1915, when Robles was twenty-six, shows him formally dressed in suit and tie and staring fixedly into the camera, his left hand resting on his holstered pistol.[6] A talented warrior, he rose to the rank of colonel in Zapata's army. Notable too was the fact that although troops fighting under Robles's command knew he was born female, none seemed to question that he was now a male.

Following Zapata's assassination in 1919, Amelio Robles led the 315 men under his command northward to join the forces of General Álvaro Obregón, serving with Obregón until the revolution's end in 1920. Amelio Robles returned to his home in southern Mexico, occasionally granting interviews in which he described his exploits during the revolution and living peacefully with his lifelong companion Guadalupe Barrón.[7]

Artist Frida Kahlo illustrates the link between Mexico's revolution and the social reforms won through it. Kahlo was fifteen when, thanks to a mandate contained in Mexico's epochal Constitution of 1917 requiring that education be both free and coeducational, she became part of the first female contingent of students enrolled in the National Preparatory School in Mexico City.

The Preparatoria, as it was known, was Mexico's premier public secondary school. By her senior year Kahlo had fallen in love with and become engaged to student-body leader Alejandro Gómez Arias. Her plan was that following their wedding the two would travel to New York City and live there happily ever after. But Frida's precocious sexuality changed all that. At age eighteen she permitted herself to be seduced by a female coworker and then by one of her father's male colleagues. Hours after the second sexual encounter, she had sex for the first time with her fiancé. Afterward she recounted these experiences to several female friends. When word of this reached Gómez Arias, he summarily broke the engagement. Not long afterward an angry Frida Kahlo confronted Gómez and defended her actions. "It's what EVERYONE does, do you understand?" she said, adding, "I like myself just the way I am."[8] Frida Kahlo's behavior and beliefs were hardly those of a traditional Mexican woman on the verge of marriage.

Both Frida Kahlo and Amelia Robles were children of a modernizing Mexico. Their life experiences anticipated and drove challenges to women's traditional roles. Their break with traditional gender roles eventually became accepted by many people in Latin America and the world.[9]

III

The original edition of this work, *Ten Notable Women of Latin America* (1978), was inspired both by the emerging women's movement and the historiographical turn to the study of gender in history. In the 1970s, few students of Latin American history had read the story of Nobel laureate Gabriela Mistral, whose deep relationships with women inspired and encouraged her work, or of the eighteenth-century adventurer the Nun Ensign who lived her life as a man. By the 1980s a new generation of Latin American specialists took up new approaches to the study of gender in Latin American history. They focused on intersectionality and the way it sheds light on how race and sexual orientation affect women's lives and lived experiences. They also began reading against the grain of source materials and reinterpreting silences in archives. In this way, modern scholars have been able to piece together fragmented archival evidence to employ agency-oriented approaches to their work.[10] In biographical writing, this has meant a gradual turn from portraying women as victims in male-dominated dramas to an examination of ways they maneuvered through sociopolitical and economic challenges of their day.

A present-day problem for Latin American specialists involves the paucity of women's voices in documentary sources, particularly those dating from colonial times. Few women in colonial Spanish and Portuguese America were literate. Fewer still were in a position to wield the pen. Furthermore, while many of the women studied here were lauded during their lives and mourned in death, few from the early period were depicted as having been in command of their own lives.

Through much of the twentieth century, two kinds of writing dominated Latin American women's history within and beyond Portuguese and Spanish America. The first praised heroines of national independence and females notable in the arts. A slightly less common but nonetheless popular biographical approach focused on the unorthodox woman who flew in the face of social convention for romantic or other motives. In recent years, scholars have de-emphasized such "great woman history" in favor of studies dealing with women in groups, arguing that such analysis can give valid insights into day-to-day social problems.[11] Biography, they argue, tends to glorify gifted or unique women while ignoring their mundane sisters. Traditionalists counter that the sociological approach tends to economic and sexual determinism and squeezes the lifeblood from its subject matter. In postmodern scholarship, though, the movement of women—between and within borders, classes, and ethnicities—highlights how some turned both extraordinary and even mundane circumstances to their personal advantage.[12]

This work offers an alternate route to the Latin American past.[13] We not only build on deep secondary source texts from leading scholars but also draw on eyewitness accounts, official records, personal correspondence, art, and prose, from the past two hundred years and more to tell of the ten figures depicted here. These include working and elite women whose fields of action run from Mexico to Argentina, from Peru to Brazil and the Caribbean, and even to the Iberian Peninsula and greater Europe.

Examining these diverse figures enables us to tell the history of modern Latin America through the lens of women's experiences. By understanding the challenges that women faced, we show how they overcame societal challenges and thereby helped shape Latin American history. The actions of the women described here illuminate ways that race, class, and international influences figured in their ambition and life's work.[14]

IV

The first three women figuring in this volume played significant roles in the struggle to achieve national independence. They are Leopoldina da Braganza (1797–1826) of Brazil, Mariana Grajales (1808–1893) of Cuba, and Eliza Lynch (1833–1886), who played a significant role in the life of Paraguay.

Introduction 7

The three figures who follow wielded pen and paintbrush to create new personal and national imaginaries, at the same time pushing literary and artistic boundaries for women. They are Clorinda Matto de Turner (1852–1909), Gabriela Mistral (1889–1957), and Frida Kahlo (1907–1954).

The final four subjects of this work were figures who captured the public imagination and generated both attention and controversy during their lives. They are Eva Perón (1919–1952), Celia Cruz (1925–2003), Rigoberta Menchú Tum (1959–), and Dilma Rousseff (1947–).

Leopoldina de Braganza, a princess of the Austrian House of Hapsburg who crossed the Atlantic to become princess of Portugal, served as regent in her husband's stead and became empress of an independent Brazil. A would-be geologist at age nineteen, Leopoldina traveled to Brazil as the wife of Dom Pedro da Braganza, a prince and son of Portuguese king Dom João IV. She bore her husband six children, one of them the future emperor of Brazil, Dom Pedro II. An avid naturalist who enjoyed hosting and engaging with European and Brazilian figures informed by the Enlightenment, Leopoldina played an important role in Brazil's independence project.

Mariana Grajales, Cuban patriot and free woman of color, was born in Cuba's Oriente (eastern) Province. She bore eleven sons, eight of whom died in Cuba's Ten Years' War against Spain, which was fought from 1866 to 1876. The most famous among her sons was guerrilla leader Antonio Maceo, known to Cubans as the Bronze Titan. Throughout the war Mariana Grajales led female relatives of patriot guerrilla fighters in the field, often while living in jungle encampments and under enemy fire. Cuban poet-warrior José Martí, who fought, and later died at the side of Antonio Maceo, wrote of Maceo's mother that when a patriot fighter was afraid, he looked at Mariana Grajales, kerchief on her head, and ceased being afraid.

Irish-born Eliza Lynch, consort to Paraguayan president Francisco Solano López and the mother of seven of his children, stood at the dictator's side throughout Paraguay's Great War (1865–1870). Also known as the War of the Triple Alliance, this was a tragic conflict pitting tiny Paraguay against much-stronger Brazil and Argentina, seconded by Uruguay. A refugee from the Irish potato famine, Lynch met Solano López in Paris in 1856 and returned to Paraguay with him. Eliza Lynch brought a breath of European culture to the landlocked South American nation. She is regarded today as an honored heroine of Paraguayan history.

The Peruvian feminist, writer, and publisher Clorinda Matto de Turner won fame through novels exposing her country's inhumane treatment of its Indigenous peoples. Matto de Turner was a sharp critic of laxness within the Catholic Church, especially of priests' sexual exploitation of their female parishioners. Matto won recognition as an early voice of Latin American feminism. Driven into exile by Peruvian conservatives, Matto became a leading feminist voice in Argentina, the country that offered her exile late in life.

Gabriela Mistral (Lucila Godoy Alcayaga), of Basque-Indigenous heritage, began her adult life as a schoolteacher in her native Chile. Her greater calling, however, was poetry. Mistral's poetry was unique for its time in that many of her works were written for and about children. During her life the melancholic Mistral served Chile as a diplomatic official in several European countries. She was also a sought-after poet in residence in universities throughout the United States. Mistral won the Nobel Prize for Literature in 1945, becoming the first Latin American woman to do so.

During her convalescence from a bus accident, Mexican Frida Kahlo discovered her talent as an artist. Through her paintings, most of which were self-portraits, she starkly conveyed the existential dilemmas of the female life experience. Kahlo's diverse, frequently surreal self-portraits serve as a window into her physical and spiritual journey. Along with her husband, Mexican muralist Diego Rivera, Kahlo was an adamant Stalinist who believed communism was both a route to improving the human condition and a means of resisting US imperialism. Nevertheless, Kahlo's political engagement never impinged on her creative imagination.

Eva Duarte de Perón, an impoverished girl from rural Argentina, became an iconic figure and driving force for political change in her traditionally male-dominated nation. Having become a well-known radio personality, Eva Duarte gained political power as the wife of general, and then president, Juan Domingo Perón. With her husband, Eva Perón founded her country's Justice, or Justicialist, Party, which become dominant in Argentine politics. Through their membership in that political party, the poor became a force in Argentina's democratic politics. Today Eva Duarte de Perón—"Evita"—is esteemed by disadvantaged Argentines.

Cuban entertainer Celia Cruz, the "Queen of Salsa," grew up in a poor neighborhood of Havana. From there she went on to create music that had global appeal. The Afro-Cuban singer was well known around the Caribbean when Fidel Castro seized control of the island in 1959. Cruz and members of her band despised Castro and his fellow communist revolutionaries. Consequently, they fled Cuba in 1960, eventually relocating to New York City. From the early 1980s until the time of her death, Cruz was a steadfast critic of Castro and his Communist regime. But more importantly, Celia Cruz achieved worldwide fame for her larger-than-life personality and her flamboyant onstage renditions of signature Afro-Caribbean salsa tunes.

By age twenty-one, Rigoberta Menchú Tum had lost her parents and a brother in Guatemala's genocidal war against its exploited Mayan Indigenous minority. Narrowly escaping Guatemala with her life, Menchú Tum fled to Mexico, eventually reaching that country's southern state of Chiapas. During her time in Chiapas, events conspired to make Menchú Tum the leading critic of outrages committed by the Guatemalan military against the country's substantial Indigenous minority. In her role as a lobbyist before the United Nations, Menchú Tum became recognized as a leading voice in defending human rights, especially of Indigenous peoples not only from Guatemala but throughout the world. Her effective lobbying earned her the 1992 Nobel Peace Prize.

Dilma Rousseff began her political career as a Castroite urban guerrilla in her hometown of Belo Horizante, Brazil. The militant student was soon arrested by the military, tortured, put on trial, and imprisoned for three years by Brazil's military regime. Freed in 1983, Rousseff completed her education and over time become a leading Socialist politician in the state of Rio Grande do Sul. In 2010 she became the presidential nominee of Inácio Lula da Silva's Workers' Party. Rousseff went on to be overwhelmingly elected as Brazil's first female president. Reelected in 2014, Dilma Rousseff was soon caught up in the "Car Wash" money-laundering scandal centered on Brazil's Congress. She was impeached and removed from office in 2016. Rousseff remained active in Workers' Party politics as a leading supporter of Inácio Lula da Silva, who was elected to a third presidential term in 2022.

This work conveys both change and continuity in modern Latin America through the lives of ten notable women. Their diverse life stories illustrate the truth that biography extends to ideas, attitudes, and groups, and that history can be fruitfully explored by following the unfolding of a single human life. These biographies underline the humanistic view that individuals have the power to rise above circumstance and the impersonal forces of history by sheer force of intelligence, talent, perseverance, and character.

NOTES

1. The lives of Micaela Bastidas and La Pola are told in chapters 8 and 9 of James D. Henderson, Linda R. Henderson, and Suzanne M. Litrel, *Ten Notable Women of Colonial Latin America* (New York: Rowman & Littlefield, 2022).

2. See chapter 1 of Henderson, Henderson, and Litrel, *Ten Notable Women of Modern Latin America*.

3. In Colombia, bloodshed in conflicts between liberals and conservatives ended only in 1958.

4. A prime example of ongoing burdens borne by disadvantaged women comes from contemporary Brazil. There, in 2020, a domestic worker named Cleonice

Gonçalves became one of the country's first to die of COVID. Cleonice, a diabetic, contracted the disease from her female employer, who had failed to tell her that she had contracted COVID-19 while traveling abroad. The death of Cleonice Gonçalves came quickly and sparked outrage among Brazilians. Their anger led to stepped-up pressure to address the plight of female domestic workers throughout Latin America. A notable leader of this international movement is Mexican Marcelina Bautista. See: Talullah Lines and Jean Gruegel, "Latin American Governments Have Largely Ignored the Risks Facing Domestic Workers During COVID-19," *LSE Latin America and the Caribbean*, December 3, 2020, https://blogs.lse.ac.uk/latamcaribbean/2020/12/03/latin-american-governments-have-largely-ignored-the-risks-facing-domestic-workers-during-covid-19/.

5. "Keynote Speech Presented at the First International Women's Congress of the Republic of Argentina (Buenos Aires), May 18, 1910," in *Women and Gender in Modern Latin America: Historical Sources and Interpretations*, ed. Pamela S. Murray (New York: Routledge, 2014), 125.

6. Gabriela Cano, "Unconcealable Realities of Desire: Amelio Robles's (Transgender) Masculinity in the Mexican Revolution," in *Sex in Revolution: Gender, Politics, and Power in Modern Mexico*, ed. Jocelyn Olcott, Mary Kay Vaughan, and Gabriela Cano (Durham, NC: Duke University Press, 2006), 36.

7. A photo of Robles and Guadalupe Barrón in old age can be viewed on page 39 of Cano, "Unconcealable Realities of Desire."

8. Hayden Herrera, *Frida: A Biography of Frida Kahlo* (New York: HarperCollins, 1983), 54–58.

9. Both Amelio Robles, a transgender man, and the bisexual Frida Kahlo anticipated LGBTQ+ principles. Frida Kahlo was also modern in that she was open about her sexuality. See her paintings *What the Water Gave Me* (1938) and *Two Nudes in a Forest* (1939) for depictions of her while embraced by an unidentified Indigenous woman, in Hayden Herrera, *Frida Kahlo: The Paintings* (New York: HarperCollins, 1991), 126, 127. An indication of the varied directions Latin American women's studies can take is offered in Murray, *Women and Gender*.

10. Merry Wiesner-Hanks, *Gender in History: Global Perspectives*, 2nd ed. (Chichester, UK: Wiley-Blackwell, 2011), 2–9.

11. One example is Susan Socolow's *The Women of Colonial Latin America* (New York: Cambridge University Press, 2000).

12. See, for example, Camilla Townsend, introduction to *Malintzin's Choices: An Indian Woman in the Conquest of Mexico* (Albuquerque: University of New Mexico Press, 2006), especially pages 2–3.

13. The first volume is James D. Henderson, Linda R. Henderson, and Suzanne M. Litrel, *Ten Notable Women of Colonial Latin America* (New York: Rowman & Littlefield, 2022).

14. For a discussion of the term "transnationalism," see Laura Briggs, Gladys McCormick, and J. T. Way, "Transnationalism: A Category of Analysis," *American Quarterly* 60, no. 3 (2008): 625–48, doi:10.1353/aq.0.0038.

REFERENCES

Briggs, Laura, Gladys McCormick, and J. T. Way. "Transnationalism: A Category of Analysis." *American Quarterly* 60, no. 3 (2008): 625–48. doi:10.1353/aq.0.0038.

Cano, Gabriela. "Unconcealable Realities of Desire: Amelio Robles's (Transgender) Masculinity in the Mexican Revolution." In *Sex in Revolution: Gender, Politics, and Power in Modern Mexico*, edited by Jocelyn Olcott, Mary Kay Vaughan, and Gabriela Cano. Durham, NC: Duke University Press, 2006.

Henderson, James D., Linda R. Henderson, and Suzanne R. Litrel. *Ten Notable Women of Colonial Latin America*. New York: Rowman & Littlefield, 2022.

Herrera, Hayden. *Frida: A Biography of Frida Kahlo*. New York: HarperCollins, 1983.

Lines, Talullah, and Jean Gruegel. "Latin American Governments Have Largely Ignored the Risks Facing Domestic Workers During COVID-19." *LSE Latin America and the Caribbean*, December 3, 2020. https://blogs.lse.ac.uk/latamcaribbean/2020/12/03/latin-american-governments-have-largely-ignored-the-risks-facing-domestic-workers-during-covid-19/.

Murray, Pamela S., ed. *Women and Gender in Modern Latin America: Historical Sources and Interpretations*. New York: Routledge, 2014.

Socolow, Susan. *The Women of Colonial Latin America*. New York: Cambridge University Press, 2000.

Townsend, Camilla M. *Malintzin's Choices: An Indian Woman in the Conquest of Mexico*. Albuquerque: University of New Mexico Press, 2006.

Wiesner-Hanks, Merry. *Gender in History: Global Perspectives*. 2nd ed. Chichester, UK: Wiley-Blackwell, 2010.

Chapter 1

Leopoldina, 1797–1826

Portuguese and Spanish Americans won political independence at the same historical moment, but their effectiveness in governing their independent states was remarkably dissimilar. While their Spanish-speaking cousins fought among themselves and broke into political and regional factions, Brazilians created a unified nation that eventually came to dwarf all others in Spanish America. Among the roots of this difference is the important role Austrian princess Maria Leopoldina played in Brazil's independence movement.

Over one hundred years earlier, Portugal and Great Britain had formalized their close relationship in the Methuen Treaty (1703). Through this agreement, the tiny Iberian kingdom came under the thumb of English commercial interests. A century later, when troops of Napoleon Bonaparte swept through and occupied the Iberian Peninsula, Portugal's royal family turned to its British ally to save it from the French invaders. Just in the nick of time, with French troops marching into Lisbon, a British fleet bore Portugal's royal Braganza family away to sanctuary in its South American colony of Brazil. After the fall of Napoleon, the Braganzas hoped to offset Britain's influence by allying themselves through marriage with the Hapsburgs of Austria. Thus did Archduchess Leopoldina of Hapsburg come to leave her beloved Europe for Brazil, where her husband, Crown Prince Pedro of Braganza, awaited her.

Due in large part to this unique history, Brazil's independence struggle was utterly unlike those elsewhere in the Americas. In Spanish America, patriots fought long and hard to free themselves of foreign domination. Prince Pedro I declared Brazil's independence from Portugal on September 7, 1822, and thirty-five days later was acclaimed Constitutional Emperor and Perpetual Defender of Brazil. Brazilian and Portuguese forces engaged in skirmishes for just over a year—but with minimal casualties compared to the bloodshed that marked the wars of Spanish American independence. Other independent states of the Americas struggled to become republics, but Brazil remained a monarchy. On October 12, 1822, people of the former Portuguese colony proclaimed twenty-four-year-old Dom Pedro of Braganza Emperor Pedro I. His loyal and loving wife, Austrian princess Leopoldina, accordingly became Empress Leopoldina. From a distance it seemed to be a story sprung from a fairy tale.

Unlike independence leaders elsewhere in the Americas, Dom Pedro and his royal consort Leopoldina were scions of highest European nobility. He was the Portuguese-born son of the king of Portugal, and she was a daughter of Emperor Franz I of Austria. All other heroes of America's independence struggle were native born—George Washington, Toussaint Louverture, Miguel Hidalgo, Simón Bolívar, and José de San Martín among them.

Brazil's postindependence experience was a far cry from that of nearly all other independent states of the Americas. The Luso-American state remained an empire until 1888, and its history was relatively pacific. Spanish American states experienced existential threats over the course of the nineteenth century. Yet Brazil's complex story of independence—and its aftermath—reflects European power politics and regional conflict that affected Brazilians throughout and beyond the nineteenth century.

Before she traversed the Atlantic and became known as Princess Leopoldina of Brazil, Carolina Josefa Leopoldina Francisca Fernanda of Hapsburg-Lorraine grew up in the conservative household of the last Holy Roman Emperor Francis of the House of Hapsburg. Her privileged life, however, was marked by loss. Leopoldina's mother died when Leopoldina was ten, and then her stepmother, to whom she had become deeply attached, died when Leopolidina was nineteen. Leopoldina also had a close relationship with her sister Marie Louise, from whom she was separated most of her life due to their marriages.

Within the golden walls of Vienna's Schönbrunn Palace, Leopoldina's own placid life belied the uncertain future that awaited her. Protected by Hapsburg power and its centuries-old absolutist traditions, surrounded by her personal servants and ladies-in-waiting, Leopoldina led a tranquil life. Yet though her father, Emperor Francis II (also known as Emperor Franz I of Austria), encouraged her to indulge her tastes, these were not frivolous by any means. Leopoldina was fascinated by the natural sciences, mathematics, history, and travel; she collected coins and medals, studied insects, plants, and animals, read widely, and learned to converse in ten languages. Her devotion to intellectual pursuits was balanced by a love of the outdoors. Every day she rode about the palace grounds, from the ancient Roman ruins down shady promenades where trees towered above clipped hedgerows, and on through thick shrubbery to higher ground behind the fountains. For a few years at least, Leopoldina's life was serene and uncomplicated. It flowed like a gentle Viennese melody. Indeed, music pervaded not only the palace but the city as well, for Leopoldina's Vienna was the Vienna of Haydn, Beethoven, Mozart, and numerous lesser geniuses.

Leopoldina was no fairy-tale princess. Unfashionably studious, her taste in clothes determined by the rigors of frequent horseback riding, Leopoldina was blond and plump, admirably robust, and endowed with the light blue eyes, weak chin, and bowed lower lip that characterized the Hapsburgs. She disliked the trappings of feminine allure such as the long trains, elaborate coiffures, jewels, and rouged cheeks and painted lips that adorned ladies of the court. The devout archduchess felt devotion to beauty was not only time consuming but slightly profane. The formidable Leopoldina avoided worldliness with determination.

In 1810, when Leopoldina was thirteen, her sister Marie Louise married Napoleon Bonaparte of France, who had been Austria's greatest enemy for more than a decade. Stifling her aversion to the upstart emperor, Marie Louise bowed to her father's will and fulfilled her obligation. Napoleon, the "revolution on horseback," had defeated her country three times and was now to be her husband. Four years later, Marie Louise returned to Vienna with her son by Napoleon, the little Duke of Reichstadt. Napoleon's luck had changed. Defeats first in Spain and then, disastrously, in Russia stripped him of power and of the marriage that bound him to Hapsburg prestige.

As soon as Napoleon was in exile and well out of sight, reactionary states took measures to prevent war and form alliances. Austrian diplomat Prince Klemens von Metternich helped organize the Congress of Vienna (1815–1816) to negotiate and maintain a balance of power among states and, it was hoped, continental peace in Europe. The Hapsburgs, like so many other royal families, had long used marriage as a tool of diplomacy, and Leopoldina soon learned of her betrothal to the Duke of Saxony. However, with an offer from Portugal's royal family and the encouragement of Leopoldina's father and Prince Metternich, events soon conspired to deprive the Duke of Saxony of his fiancée.

In late November 1816, a contract was signed arranging the marriage of Leopoldina to Prince Pedro of Braganza, the ruling house of Portugal, whose principal colony was Brazil. While the Portuguese needed an ally to help counter the British, the debt-ridden Hapsburgs hoped to gain access to raw materials and markets to sustain their imperial enterprise. The Hapsburg royal family worried about sending Leopoldina so far away to an uncertain fate as the bride of a husband raised largely in Brazil. But Prince Metternich, Franz's counselor, supported the match because of its financial prospects, and the emperor—after securing Leopoldina's consent—agreed to it.

The Braganzas had ruled Portugal for nearly two hundred years, so there was no question of their legitimacy. But the present ruler, prince regent and soon to be king Dom João VI, father of Pedro, had the dubious distinction of being the only European monarch ever to remove himself, his court, and the entire national government from Europe. The removal occurred in late 1807 as Napoleon Bonaparte's army marched on Lisbon. Rather than submit to French rule, King João loaded the national treasury and thousands of courtiers and government officials on ships provided by Great Britain. Escorted by British warships, they sailed away to Brazil. Stranger still, and much against tradition, once established in Rio de Janeiro, Dom João proved reluctant to return to Europe. He even elevated the Brazilian colony to the status of a kingdom, making it coequal with Portugal.

Portugal's wealth, drawn largely from Brazil, was on full display with the arrival of the Marquis of Marialva, Dom João's special emissary and Portugal's ambassador extraordinary to the Hapsburg court in Vienna. His role was to bring about the proxy wedding of Leopoldina and Pedro. Eager to dazzle the Hapsburgs, he had been instructed to spare no expense during his time in Vienna. This Marialva did with lavishness and flair. On February 7, 1817, the marquis and his retinue arrived with an ostentation that brought throngs of onlookers to Vienna's streets and drew the highest nobility and the emperor himself to inspect them from strategically located balconies. Never had Vienna seen such a lavish embassy.

On the assigned day, in accordance with the most exacting requirements of court etiquette, the ambassador made his formal appearance at court in Hofburg Palace. In the great ballroom he presented Emperor Franz the letter from Dom João that formally requested Leopoldina's hand in marriage. Of all the gifts he brought to court that evening, the most extravagant was a necklace for Leopoldina. It consisted of a miniature portrait of Dom Pedro, surrounded by Brazilian diamonds and topped by a tiny gold crown, supported by a chain made of gold and diamonds. A gasp rose from the court when candlelight caused the diamonds to sparkle. Doubts over Portugal's fondness for Brazil vanished on the spot.

Negotiations over Leopoldina's dowry were carried out by the Marquis of Marialva and Baron von Metternich. The latter's favor was assured by the gift of several ingots of pure Brazilian gold. The bride's dowry was to be 200,000 florins along with a handsome annual allowance of 80,000 florins. But to Leopoldina the most important part of the transaction was Pedro himself. She knew little about him as yet, only that his portrait showed a handsome young man with large dark eyes, curly hair, high forehead, and fine features. In that attractive face Leopoldina thought she saw the reflection of moral superiority, of goodness and kindliness. To her discreet, even timid, questions about his character, she received the most positive answers: yes, he was good-hearted and loved by his subjects; yes, he was an avid student of the natural sciences; yes, he was not only an accomplished musician and composer but a daring horseman as well. Leopoldina was won over by secondhand information and a jeweled portrait.

On the Portuguese King João's birthday, May 13, 1817, Leopoldina wedded his son Dom Pedro, Prince of Portugal, Brazil, and Algarve. An uncle stood at her side, representing her new husband. Marialva offered the celebrants a wedding banquet surpassing anything he had yet shown Vienna. In the Augarten, a large park in the heart of the city, he had built a glass palace, a rotunda with cupola, that would be used only once—in honor of the Hapsburg-Braganza union. On the evening of June 1, two thousand of Austria's highest nobles, the corps of ambassadors to the Hapsburg court, and distinguished officials began to arrive. Greeted by the marquis himself, the guests were treated to sights and sounds that enthralled even the most discerning among them. Thousands of lanterns hung from trees around the glistening palace, and gentle waltzes came from orchestras hidden behind every hedge.

At nine o'clock the royal family arrived, and Leopoldina, dressed in white with Pedro's tiny portrait sparkling at her throat, accepted the first waltz with Marialva. Together they danced to the elegant rhythms so adored by the Viennese while the guests, themselves sparkling with gold, brocades, and gems, looked on. Later, the guests dined on a hundred dishes served on the finest silver, porcelain, and crystal; the royal family ate from plates of solid gold. The Marquis of Marialva further stunned Vienna when, in the days following the banquet, he ordered that the wedding palace be converted to an orphanage and the ornaments be sold to aid the poor of the city. For his unprecedented generosity the people called him king—King Marialva. If young Pedro was anything like his ambassador, Leopoldina was indeed fortunate.

Besides the promise of access to Brazil's natural resources and markets, an incentive for the Austrians to marry into the Braganza family included the opportunity to engage in naturalist and exploratory expeditions. Documenting and disseminating new discoveries would not only benefit Austria for future scientific and trade purposes but also, given elite interest in such knowledge, bring prestige to the empire. Thus members of a Bavarian scientific mission traveled with Leopoldina to Rio de Janeiro. When Leopoldina left Vienna on June 12, she was also accompanied by her three ladies-in-waiting and a cadre of servants, as well as Thomas Ender, the Viennese artist; Dr. Jorge Schaffer, a German-born agent and troubleshooter for the princess; and a librarian to care for her extensive book collection. Accompanied part of the way by

Prince Metternich, the entourage journeyed to Livorno and later embarked on the Portuguese frigates *Dom João VI* and the smaller *São Sebastião*.

During the Atlantic crossing, Leopoldina was entertained by an orchestra contracted by merchants of Rio de Janeiro, and she polished her already excellent Portuguese. She looked forward to meeting her husband and his family, as well she might, since she was still unaware of several disagreeable facts about them. Leopoldina did not know of the continual strife between João and his wanton wife Carlota Joaquina, or of Crown Prince Pedro's relative lack of formal education, or of his constant amatory adventures.

The sight that greeted Leopoldina after eighty-two days at sea was breathtaking. Rio de Janeiro stretched sinuously along the curving beaches of Guanabara Bay, its waterfront unscarred by docks, its sand almost pure white. Behind the city, with its narrow streets and white, flat-roofed buildings, rose the granite peaks Sugarloaf and Hunchback, and smaller hills covered with lush green growth. As a twenty-one-gun salute echoed from the forts around the city, a gilded barge pulled away from the hundreds of small craft in the bay. It approached the ship carrying the royal family: Dom João, Carlota, Pedro, his sisters, and his younger brother Miguel. Leopoldina, on the arm of her protector, the Marquis of Castelo Melhor, boarded the barge and fell into a deep curtsy at the feet of the king, her father-in-law. Dom João raised her gently and kissed her as though she were his own daughter, then presented her to his son. Murmuring words of greeting, Leopoldina gazed for the first time at her husband. She realized immediately that even a portrait surrounded by diamonds could not do him justice: the handsome, magnetic, and athletic prince captured her at first glance.

The artist Jean-Baptiste Debret, part of a French delegation that had arrived in Brazil the previous year, captured the dazzling scenes that followed (see figure 1.1). Leopoldina was to spend one last night on the frigate as it would have been improper for her to disembark prior to the ceremony of nuptial blessing. The next day, November 6, an honor guard formed on the beach at the Royal Pavilion. At eleven o'clock Queen Carlota and the princesses departed the palace and proceeded down Rua Direita to the shore, their six coaches followed by a detachment of cavalry. Dom João, Crown Prince Pedro, and his brother arrived soon thereafter, and the entire family was again rowed out to Leopoldina's frigate, where they found the young bride in a gown of white silk embroidered with silver and gold and sparkling with hundreds of brilliants. A veil of the lightest white silk fell gracefully over her face and blew in the gentle sea breeze.

The royal family, Leopoldina, her ladies-in-waiting, and a bevy of important nobles disembarked with great ceremony. Arriving onshore they entered velvet-draped carriages and traveled slowly through the sand-carpeted streets

Figure 1.1. "Reception of Archduchess Maria Leopoldina by Dom Pedro, the royal family and court on 5 November 1817," Jean-Baptiste Debret (1817). 44.5 cm x 6 9.5 cm, oil on canvas. Museu Nacional de Belas Artes, Rio de Janeiro

between banners emblazoned with the Braganza coat of arms. The air was perfumed by hundreds of flowers and herbs as the procession passed through the three Roman arches built for the occasion by merchants and foreign residents in Rio. At two o'clock they reached the royal chapel on the Palace Square, where the marriage was blessed before cheering throngs. When Pedro took his princess's hand, cannons boomed their salute from the forts around the bay. In the days following her arrival, receptions, concerts, and even a free opera celebrated the marriage. Only then were Pedro and Leopoldina considered adequately wed. They retired to the palace of São Cristovão across the marshes north of Rio.

In the early months of the marriage, Leopoldina and her new husband spent many hours together. Despite the humidity, heat, and constant nuisance of mosquitos, they rode out often, an activity they both enjoyed. They also shared a love of music and theater. Together they attended plays and operas, enjoying performances from the royal box. In the palace of São Cristovão she would often accompany Pedro on the piano while he played any number of instruments.

Brazil captivated the princess. Ever interested in minerology and botany, she found the rich and variegated countryside irresistible, and she explored its fields, forests, and mountains. She often remarked to her companions on the beauty of a tropical flower or a brilliant bird. The Austrian princess was no less interested in the exotic human element of Brazil. Almost four million people, half of them Afro-Brazilian and the rest European and Indigenous, had intermingled to create a whole new palette of human color.

As Leopoldina observed soon after her arrival, the institution of slavery was fundamental to Brazilian society. At the time slavery was coming under attack both in Britain and the United States. But in Brazil, slavery was defended as integral to its economy. Therefore, an elaborate network of laws restricted enslaved people, the half a million free Black, and those of Indigenous and mixed descent from advancing in society, even as the laws preserved the privileges of the Portuguese-born *reinóis* and the *mazombos*, Brazilian-born people of European descent. These groups' privileges were, however, a mixed blessing. Although White people were freed from hard labor on their plantations, they found little to fill long hours of boredom. Wealthy landowners and their families were fed, bathed, and supported by slaves. Urban families sent their slaves out to work as artisans or simple day laborers. Since no man who hoped to rise in society engaged in manual labor, and since there were few schools and fewer cultural diversions in the Brazil of that time, the privileged classes were left to stew in inactivity and ignorance. The only acceptable pastimes for a gentleman were hunting, gambling, and womanizing. Upper-class women were confined to home and church and denied any sort of education.

The Brazilian woman seemed as curious a creature as any of the strange species of fish or fowl Leopoldina found in her new country. No parallel could be found between them and the industrious housewives and wellborn ladies of Austria. Brazilian women of the middle and upper classes were carefully chaperoned and their minds protected from the taint of new ideas—or of ideas generally. They were coaxed into early bloom, married by the age of fifteen, and set to bearing children. If they survived the rigors of motherhood, their fragile beauty soon drowned in layers of fat brought on by shockingly poor diets and gross inactivity. With few demands made on them and with servants to maintain the household, nurse the babies, and watch over the children, women had little to do. They spent their lives seated cross-legged on floor cushions, nibbling convent-baked sweetmeats, and embroidering endless altar cloths. Leopoldina found such an existence unthinkable. On one count, though, she sympathized with her Brazilian sisters. To those who were shocked by the way Brazilian women dressed at home, she pointed out that a light chemise and petticoat, bare legs, and uncorseted bodies were the only sensible attire in a sultry climate. Leopoldina herself wore simple, loose-fitting clothing and refused to cinch in her waist, although an unnaturally tiny waist was the fashion of the day.

In June following her arrival, Leopoldina told her delighted husband that she was expecting a child. The news was doubly welcome to Pedro as he had yet to taste the solemn joys of responsible fatherhood. The months of Leopoldina's pregnancy passed in cheerful anticipation, and on April 4, 1819, the future queen of Portugal was born. The delivery was surrounded by elaborate protocol. When labor began, the entire government—ministers of state, the king's counselors, the diplomatic corps, and other officials—assembled in the palace of São Cristovão. As soon as the baby was born, even before the umbilical cord had been cut, the highest ranking among them crowded into Leopoldina's chamber to welcome the tiny princess. She would, of course, be named Maria, a good Catholic name, since the Hapsburg princesses were all Marias themselves. Leopoldina and Pedro were affectionate parents. They doted on their daughter, and Pedro revealed his modern side by having her vaccinated against smallpox. They found a wet nurse for the baby, but unlike many upper-class parents of the day did not abandon her entirely to the care of servants.

Although the heat, humidity, and constant rains of spring bothered Leopoldina and made her think longingly of "beautiful Europe," she was still reasonably happy. She quickly resumed her active routine after Maria da Glória was born. Every morning before nine she rode out around the palace of São Cristovão or accompanied Pedro to the barracks at Niteroi where, dressed in a blue dragoon uniform, her blond hair pulled back under a cap, and silver spurs clanking on her boots, she reviewed troops with her handsome prince. She had become a popular figure in Rio. Strange though her habits seemed, the Brazilians admired her equestrian skill and respected her intellect.

The frequent trips to Rio and appearances on horseback came to a halt early in December 1819, when Leopoldina suffered a miscarriage that left her weak and depressed. The following July she was again pregnant, but in October she lost the hoped-for child in the fourth month. Frightened by the miscarriages and the ominous possibility that she would never bear a son, Leopoldina withdrew into a cloistered existence, going out infrequently and dedicating herself to sedentary pastimes.

As Leopoldina went into seclusion, Pedro was being drawn into a political whirlwind. Since Napoleon's defeats in 1814 and 1815, defenders of European monarchy had anticipated the return of Dom João to Portugal. A wave of liberalism was sweeping Europe, and monarchists begged the Portuguese king to defend his sovereignty against the threat of democracy. Although shaken by liberal rebellion in Spain and by alarming news of revolt in Portugal itself, Dom João still hesitated to leave his beloved Brazil. For a time, he considered sending Crown Prince Pedro in his place, frightening Leopoldina with the possibility that she might be left behind; but at last Dom João reluctantly consented to return to Lisbon, leaving Pedro to rule Brazil as viceroy and regent.

As revolution rocked the Atlantic world, the idyllic early years of Leopoldina and Pedro's marriage receded from memory. St. Domingue, now Haiti, was the first Caribbean colony to claim independence when in 1804 the Black republic declared national independence. The eastern half of the island, Santo Domingo, remained under Spanish control. Soon, however, Spain's American colonies began their long struggle for independence. In Portuguese America, the presence of Dom João, his family, and the court in Rio de Janeiro inoculated Brazil against liberal republicanism. The king had elevated Brazil from the status of colony to that of a kingdom in 1815. He swept away the monopoly trade rights of Portuguese merchants, opening Brazil to free trade. This helps explain the clashes between Portuguese troops and their Brazilian-born counterparts in the streets of Rio de Janeiro.

When the Spanish Revolution of 1820 brought anti-monarchists to power, the Lisbon Côrtes demanded that Dom João return home. The king agreed but determined that his heir, Prince Regent Pedro, should remain in Rio de Janeiro. This meant that Leopoldina would remain in Brazil and likely never again see her Austrian family. But the continued royal presence gave Brazil a measure of stability not found in Spain's colonies. During this fraught time, Leopoldina anticipated the birth of her second child. Long months of hope came to a happy conclusion on March 6, 1821, with the birth of Prince João Carlos, heir to the thrones of Brazil and Portugal. Two months later, the baby's grandfather boarded the frigate bearing his name, dallied for two days in the hope that something would keep him in Brazil, and finally sailed away, never to return.

In his "Instructions for the Guidance of the Prince Royal as Regent," King João gave Prince Regent Pedro complete authority over Brazil's government and ordered that in the event of the prince's death, the Regency of Brazil should pass directly to the Royal Princess Leopoldina. With that Dom João and the entire Braganza entourage save Pedro and Leopoldina sailed off to Lisbon, but not before stowing riches in the ship's hold. This included chest after chest containing the combined treasure of Brazil and Portugal. Ingots of gold and silver, freshly minted coins, the total assets of Brazil's first and only bank, and even that month's deposits by Rio's charitable institutions—a grand total of 50 million cruzados—left Brazil with Dom João.

Dom Pedro began his rule of Brazil amid clashes between Portuguese troops stationed in Rio and defenders of Brazil's embryonic independence movement. On one such occasion, Leopoldina, then in her eighth month of pregnancy, fled Rio de Janeiro with the royal children to seek safety at the royal plantation of Santa Cruz, west of the capital. Soon after the hot and miserable journey, little Prince João Carlos, the firstborn royal son and heir apparent, not yet a year old, fell seriously ill and died. As Leopoldina wrote to her aunt,

> The poor little one, who had a weak nervous system, caught some sort of inflammation of the liver and, poorly treated, or rather improperly diagnosed, died after two weeks of continuous suffering and a final epileptic siege that lasted twenty-eight hours. I assure you, dear Aunt, that in my whole life I have never known greater grief and that only my religion and the passage of time will console me.[1]

Both Leopoldina and Pedro blamed the Portuguese for the death of their son. Leopoldina's letters home showed increasing signs of strain and bitterness over the ongoing unrest. They also revealed a deep homesickness and disillusionment. She coupled such sentiments with resignation to her duties and assurances that she would carry on as a devoted royal consort and wife.

The departure of the Braganza family left Dom Pedro in a tenuous position. His treasury was bare; only paper money and easily counterfeited copper coins were in circulation. A national sense of insecurity filled the vacuum created by King João's departure. Exports dropped, business was paralyzed, and credit evaporated. No one knew whether Dom Pedro, armed only with native shrewdness and unbounded energy, was equal to the job of governing. Economic disarray, communication made difficult by the size of Brazil, and the increasing popularity of constitutional government were key problems confronting the twenty-two-year-old prince.

Dom Pedro's first acts were calculated to save money. The downtown palace was converted into offices for judicial and administrative personnel, and the royal family moved its possessions to São Cristovão and the plantation of Santa Cruz. Twelve hundred horses had formerly occupied the royal stables; now only 156 remained. In a wise move designed to still criticism, Pedro halved his own allowance before reducing the salaries of government officials.

Leopoldina supported Pedro's economic measures by reorganizing the royal household around slave—rather than paid—labor and by reducing the costs of the palace kitchen that provided meals to an army of staff and guests. She also refrained from complaining about her own finances, even though by that time, after four years of marriage, it was clear that the generous income promised in her nuptial contract would never be paid. Indeed, the only sum she received had been a gift from the Marquis of Marialva while she was still in Vienna. The costs of supporting her personal attendants and of buying books and specimens for her collections had seriously eroded that original sum. And although she spent little on her appearance, she willingly opened her purse to charities and to individuals seeking her help. She had to count on Pedro to refill it, and when his generosity flagged, she found herself absolutely without funds. She wrote to her father for help, and by September 1821 she wrote to the Marquis of Marialva in Paris, promising that she would pay him for the books he had sent as soon as "our pathetic finances are in a state of convalescence."[2] But only by going into debt was she able to pay him back.

The premature death of heir apparent Prince João marked Leopoldina and Dom Pedro in different ways. They both harbored increasing resentment toward the Portuguese, though Pedro was also captured by the revolutionary moment. This concerned the more conservative Leopoldina, who sought stability for her family. "While real Brazilians are good people," she wrote her father in June 1821, "the Portuguese troops are animated with the worst intentions and my husband, God help him, loves new ideas."[3] Fortunately, Pedro had an able ally in the person of José Bonifácio de Andrada e Silva, a gifted politician who worked diligently to tie São Paulo Province to Dom Pedro's government. José Bonifácio had studied in Europe as a youth and remained there many years serving Portugal in various official capacities. In 1819 he returned to his native São Paulo. His intelligence and culture recommended him to Leopoldina, and after his success in calming the south, Pedro hoped he would serve him as minister of state and foreign affairs. José Bonifácio was called to Rio early in January 1822, and Leopoldina, hearing that he was coming, rode out to persuade him to accept the ministry. Her mission was successful.

Leopoldina had long cultivated friendships with intellectually minded people in her native Austria and as princess of Brazil. For this reason, she was the best and perhaps only person who could persuade José Bonifácio to take on the ministerial portfolio. José Bonifácio had been trained in geology, one of her passions, and the two shared a mutual love of natural science. They often conversed in German on this and other topics. In 1820, the circumnavigator, naturalist, and writer Jacques Arago visited Brazil. There, at the court of São Cristovão, he delighted in his exchanges with Leopoldina, appreciating her quick mind and fluent French. He also commented in his later writing that the unaffected Leopoldina met him in worn clothes, uncoiffed hair, dressed "like a real gypsy," greeting him with her customary warmth and plying him with questions about his travels.[4]

Leopoldina's friendship with Englishwoman Maria Graham, later known as Lady Maria Calcott, endured beyond the unrest of revolutionary times. The two women delighted in each other's company, sharing a love of learning and a deep interest in nature. In 1821, the adventurous Maria Graham had journeyed across the South Atlantic with her husband, who served as a captain of the British Royal Navy. Before continuing to Chile, they sailed to Pernambuco, Bahia, and then Rio de Janeiro, where they met the future emperor and empress of Brazil. At the time, the capital city was gripped with tension, but Maria Graham noted Pedro's and Leopoldina's calm demeanor and its effect on their subjects. One night in January 1822 she was at the opera, as was the royal couple. During the performance, the prince received an urgent message: over two dozen Portuguese soldiers were causing trouble in the streets, and in particular harassing the Black residents. As the actors fell silent, and the audience gathered to leave, Pedro moved to the front of his opera box, a very pregnant Leopoldina at his side. He then reassured the audience that there was no trouble, and that they should continue to enjoy the evening. Graham noted his "coolness and presence of mind," and that keeping the elite audience inside the theater likely saved them from potential violence. By the time the opera ended, the streets had been cleared.[5]

From the moment of Dom João's return to Portugal the previous April, the country's increasingly powerful representative assembly, the Côrtes, had tried every means to reduce Brazil to its former subservient position. Displeased by Brazil's advances under the king's care, the Côrtes was now angered by his son's independence of spirit. Dom Pedro responded with hostility to each of the Côrtes's demeaning commands. Knowing his father to be a virtual prisoner of the Côrtes, Pedro ignored it and did as much as possible to help the unhappy João.

Lisbon finally understood the hopelessness of controlling Brazil while Dom Pedro ruled it from Rio. In December 1821 the Côrtes ordered him to return forthwith for the purpose of "completing his education." Leopoldina feared that Pedro would lose Brazil forever if he obeyed, and she used every means to persuade him to stay. In this she was assisted by Pedro's ministers. By January 9, 1822, the efforts of Leopoldina, José Bonifácio, and Pedro's other advisers had the desired result. Dom Pedro answered the Côrtes, saying, "Tell the people that I will stay: *Fico*!" Brazil was just a short step away from severing its ties with Portugal.

Though Pedro had publicly announced his intentions to remain in Brazil, Leopoldina's political and private concerns about the Portuguese continued unabated. "To speak frankly," she wrote her father on January 22, "they are extremely critical and ill-succeeded, and the result could happen that the end is very ugly."[6] She saw that her husband was waffling on declaring independence from Portugal: "He is not as positively decided as I would wish."[7]

Leopoldina soon gave birth to a second princess, Januaria. But she never completely recovered from the loss of her son. Sober by nature, inclined to solitary study, the Austrian princess found it increasingly difficult to shake off her grief, nostalgia for Europe, and loneliness. Circumstance, too, conspired to trap her in melancholy, for as Pedro threw himself increasingly into the swirl of events, Leopoldina was left to her continual pregnancies and domestic concerns without the stimulation his company had provided in the tranquil early years of their marriage. Indeed, constantly afraid of miscarriage, Leopoldina became cautious and introspective. Her debts plagued her too, and with Pedro gone so often she despaired of winning his help. Her personal finances had come to such a state that in early August she received a note from a creditor reminding her of a debt that had fallen due the previous week. With no income of her own, she panicked and wrote her friend Schaffer: "My dear Schaffer, I am grievously embarrassed. Read the enclosed letter; the man says he will make a fuss; for the love of God see if you can satisfy him."[8]

Nationalistic fervor, nonexistent before the Portuguese royal family's arrival in Brazil, was now widespread. Dom Pedro was determined to ride that wave of feeling and emerge as the ruler of the new state. Leopoldina, a child of Austrian absolutism, was not so sure. "Everything here is confusion," she wrote her father late in June, adding:

> My husband, who unfortunately likes anything new, is enthusiastic, and I'm afraid he will pay dearly for it. As for me, they don't trust me, for which I am thankful because I don't have to give my opinion and thus there are fewer arguments. Don't worry because come what may I won't lack anything, since I have my religion and my Austrian principles.[9]

The one consolation Leopoldina found in the midst of the tumult around her was the direction José Bonifácio gave to Pedro's impulses. Amid the revolutionary upheaval and with Spanish America fracturing into multiple states, Bonifácio understood the inevitability of independence and the dangers of setting the large country adrift without a unifying authority. Following his advice, Pedro traveled from one rebellious province to the next, wooing the people with his vision of an independent Brazil united in its allegiance to the crown.

In March 1822 the Brazilian Senate named Dom Pedro *Defensor e Protetor Perpétuo do Brasil* (Protector and Perpetual Defender of Brazil). Dom Pedro then convened an assembly that was to draw up a constitution for Brazil. In August, a popular uprising in São Paulo called Pedro away from Rio, but not before he named Leopoldina regent in his stead. As Leopoldina wrote to her aunt in Vienna, "During his absence I have charge of state affairs, this being the greatest service I can provide to him and Brazil."[10] Accompanied by Lieutenant Castro Canto e Melo, his friend Chalaza the court jester, a secretary, and a pair of servants, Pedro traveled southward at his usual breakneck pace. He had been gone only a few days when Leopoldina received word that the Côrtes in Portugal was planning to send a military expedition to punish Brazil for its rebelliousness and to use force of arms to stop all talk of independence.

Figure 1.2. "Session of the Council of State" (1922), Georgina de Albuquerque. Oil on Canvas, 210 cm x 265 cm. Museu Histórico Nacional, Rio de Janeiro

In Bahia a Portuguese garrison still held out against the Brazilians and, hearing that help was on its way, prepared to attack Dom Pedro's forces. Leopoldina saw that the time had come for Brazil to declare its independence. As seen in figure 1.2, she felt that the Côrtes had no right to override Dom Pedro, Brazil's legitimate ruler. José Bonifácio concurred. Thus the Council of State, presided over by the princess regent, declared Brazil's separation from Portugal. Their letters were then dispatched to Dom Pedro describing the actions of both the Côrtes in Lisbon and the council in Rio. "Pedro," wrote Leopoldina, "Brazil is like a volcano." She urged him to action. With or without him, Brazil would break free from Portugal. "The apple is ripe; pluck it now, or it will rot."[11]

On September 7 court messengers reached the prince regent and gave him the letters from José Bonifácio and Leopoldina. They found him a few hours north of São Paulo at the edge of the river Ipiranga. After hurriedly reading the letters, he strode up the bank to his waiting companions, drew his sword, and shouted, "By the blood that flows in my veins and upon my honor I swear to God to free Brazil." Mounting his horse, he rose in the stirrups with the cry, echoed by his attendants, "Independence or death!"[12]

Pedro was crowned emperor of Brazil on December 1, 1822, yet another elaborate event captured by the French artist Jean-Baptiste Debret. Despite his depiction of pomp and power, Brazil did not gain recognition as an independent state until a few years later. Yet even as diplomatic negotiations for such acknowledgment were underway, Leopoldina wrote letters on the new country's behalf. To her father, she argued for the merits of trade with Brazil, and considered the marriage of her daughter, Princess Maria da Glória, to one of her Hapsburg relatives. After all, the dominant colors of the Brazilian flag were green, for the House of Braganza, and gold, for the Hapsburg Empire.

A second event took place in 1822, one that brought great sorrow to Leopoldina. Shortly before Pedro's celebrated *Grito de Ipiranga*, the Brazilian leader met and fell in love with a twenty-five-year-old beauty named Domitila de Castro. The meeting of the two may have been staged. Domitila's brother, the same Lieutenant Castro Canto e Melo who accompanied Dom Pedro to the south, may have deliberately planned their encounter. Blessed with a lovely smile, perfect silken skin, and a voluptuous body, Domitila found the prince an easy target. By the time Pedro returned to Rio, Domitila was engraved on his imagination. The sight of Princess Leopoldina, again pregnant, carelessly dressed, her brow creased with worry, did little to push Domitila's image from his mind.

Early in 1823, some months after Pedro's elaborate coronation as emperor of Brazil, Domitila arrived in Rio de Janeiro. Unfortunately, Pedro was no longer restrained by the presence of his father King João, who loved and supported Leopoldina. Indeed, Pedro seemed unconcerned, or unaware, of the effect that his actions might have on his wife. Believing that Leopoldina knew nothing of his affair and caring little for what anyone else thought, Pedro went to almost ridiculous lengths to please Domitila.

Leopoldina's third daughter, Paula Mariana, was born in February 1823, eleven months after the birth of Januaria, but the empress continued about her duties. Happily for her, her friend Maria Graham, recently widowed, returned to Rio de Janeiro in March 1823. She rented a house and offered her services as governess to the little princess Maria da Glória. Her offer was accepted. Thus began a relationship that likely sustained Empress Leopoldina through the most challenging times. The Englishwoman noted that motherly duties aside, Leopoldina accompanied her husband on official outings, noting that "their Majesties appear by all accounts to be highly popular." She wrote of "their youth, their spirit," and Pedro's interest in strengthening the country. He was particularly interested in the navy, and together, Pedro and Leopoldina toured the dockyards during the day.[13]

Leopoldina kept her concerns about Pedro's mistress to herself. Soon, however, she came to understand that Pedro's infatuation, already a rich source of gossip all over Rio, was not a brief fling that she could forgive. Rather, it was a full-blown love affair. Leopoldina noted Pedro's impatience with her, his long absences at night, and his moments of preoccupation during the day. News of his escapades reached her, but in public she brushed them aside, preferring to seem ignorant but dignified.

For a year Pedro tried half-heartedly to avoid undue scandal. The problem of Brazil's constitution continued to plague him. While he had promised to support a constitution, he and the constituent assembly of 1823 were soon at odds. The assembly, expressing a dominant mood of Brazil, mistrusted Dom Pedro because he was Portuguese by birth. For his part the emperor found it impossible to work with the representative body. Conflict became so acute that even José Bonifácio and his brothers fell away from Dom Pedro. By November they were in exile. In late March 1824, Dom Pedro, in consultation with a few chosen ministers, wrote Brazil's first constitution. The liberal-minded absolutist proved unequal to the rigors of democracy. Still he kept his promise to give Brazil constitutional rule—but in his own monarchical way.

With a measure of calm restored to Brazil, Pedro turned to matters of the heart. The means he used to hide his affair became ever more childish, more transparent. In public the royal consorts continued to treat one another with apparent affection. But in private, Leopoldina and her husband drifted apart. Far better than he, the empress understood the cost that obvious estrangement would exact, not only from the Brazilian throne but conceivably from the status of kingship in Europe as well. At that moment monarchy everywhere was under fire, and heady experiments in democracy and constitutional government—in the United States, in Great Britain, briefly in Spain—affected nations like a cup of spring wine. Leopoldina knew that the privacy of emperors was afforded no respect by ambassadors from other nations; she knew that the least sign of mortification on her part might jeopardize Brazil's prestige abroad.

She therefore made no public complaint, permitted herself no dramatic outcry, and sent no word of the matter to her father. Bound by ties of marriage and duty to the young nation, the empress chose to suffer in silent dignity. Anyway, Pedro's affair was already the talk of European royalty, and nothing was to be gained by adding to the bulging diplomatic mail pouches. Baron von Mareschal, the Austrian minister, wrote to Vienna, "In spite of the fact that he has a favorite mistress, he has never ceased for an instant to show himself a good husband, and takes advantage of every opportunity to praise the virtues of his consort." Others were less charitable. A shocked British visitor wrote simply, "The Brazilians are not at all correct."[14]

During these years the imperial pregnancies continued, now in pairs. In May 1824 Domitila bore her first child by Dom Pedro, Isabel Maria

Brasileira; the following August, Leopoldina's fourth daughter, Francisca Carolina, was born. In April 1825 Pedro decided to satisfy Domitila's social ambitions by placing her among the ladies who attended the empress at court. Leopoldina agreed reluctantly to accept the affront, and in gratitude Pedro dedicated a sonnet to her, praising her magnanimity and finding parallels between her and other understanding queens of the past. The sonnet did little to help Leopoldina during Domitila's presentation at court. The sight of her husband's favorite, dressed in an exquisite satin robe frosted with pearls, brought into focus the empress's own sad state.

Humiliated by Pedro, in alarming financial difficulties, and once again pregnant, Leopoldina nonetheless conducted herself with dignity even as her trusted relationships fell away. José Bonifácio had already been banished, and then the empress lost another dear friend. Palace intrigue and Dom Pedro's temper forced her English friend Maria Graham to abandon her post in 1825; she returned to England shortly thereafter. The correspondence the two women maintained until Leopoldina's death in 1826 doubtless offered her a measure of consolation.

After her presentation at court, Domitila brought her baby to live at the palace of São Cristovão. In October Pedro awarded her the title of Viscountess of Santos, thereby pleasing his mistress and insulting José Bonifácio, whose family had long been the moving force of Santos. It soon became embarrassingly clear that both the empress and the paramour were to give birth early in December. In this, at least, Leopoldina had a tremendous advantage over her rival: her children were born princes and princesses, while Domitila's were, in spite of her title and new position, bastards. On December 2, the long-awaited prince imperial, Pedro de Alcântara, was born. A week later Domitila suffered through a difficult labor and delivered a weak baby boy, Pedro de Alcântara Brasileiro, who lived only a few months.

Early in 1826 Dom Pedro planned a sea voyage to Bahia and decided to combine work with pleasure by inviting Domitila to go with him. Leopoldina decided to go also, leaving her baby and princesses in the hands of her reliable staff. The weeklong voyage was agony for her, for the pretense at decorum the lovers had maintained in Rio now ceased. One particularly awkward blow was dealt by the ship's captain, who mistakenly addressed Domitila as "your majesty." The poor man realized his error and hid in his cabin for the rest of the voyage.

After returning to Rio, Leopoldina insisted that Domitila move out of the palace. Pedro had no choice but to comply. As compensation for her banishment, he decided to give Domitila a new title and a new villa. Soon Domitila, now the Marquise of Santos, moved into an extravagantly refurbished house on the Rua Nova do Imperador opposite the Boa Vista Botanical Gardens.

The mansion was a true love nest decorated with wrought iron hearts and elaborate murals and equipped with the only modern plumbing in Brazil—this in a society that chose to believe that ladies do not bathe. It was whispered that Domitila put it to good use by taking a bath every day. Between such rumors and the parties she gave in her new residence, Domitila reached the apex of her prestige.

Although he was absorbed by his passion, Dom Pedro found time to devote to his children, watching over their education with infinitely more attention than was ever given to his own and seeing to it that they received the best care possible. Sincerely fond of all his children, he made no distinction between his legitimate and illegitimate offspring. His heart was touched by the stigma attached to Domitila's little daughter, and he ordered her birth certificate changed from "father unknown" to his own name. So that she might suffer less in comparison with his legitimate children, he bestowed on her the title Duchess of Goiás and made certain the entire court understood that she was to be treated with proper respect, according to the strictest protocol. For Leopoldina it was one more in the series of humiliations that had at last become insupportable.

In October 1826, Leopoldina's remarkable forbearance evaporated. Dom Pedro had celebrated his twenty-eighth birthday that month by granting patents of nobility to Domitila's entire family—her father, her brothers, even a distant cousin. To the distraught empress, the court at São Cristovão seemed suddenly filled with people who owed their good fortune to the most despicable of relationships. Deeply worried about the effect of this fact on her innocent children, she asked the Austrian minister to communicate her great unhappiness to Emperor Franz in Vienna; then she confronted Pedro with the demand that he send Domitila far away from Rio. This Pedro refused to do, and the royal couple quarreled violently.

For a brief time after the fight, Dom Pedro tried to be kind to Leopoldina, who was again expecting a child. Then, in late November, he was called away from the capital to Brazil's southern border. Soon after he left, Leopoldina fell ill. On December 2, she suffered a miscarriage and developed a fever that her doctors knew how to treat only by bloodletting. For days she lay burning with fever, anxious about the safety of her children and crying out in delirium that Domitila would stop at nothing to kill the little prince. In moments of clarity, she begged her servants to prevent Domitila from entering the palace, and after being assured that her rival would not be permitted near her or the children, Leopoldina gained a measure of peace. On December 8, somewhat improved, she dictated a letter to her sister Marie Louise:

> For almost four years, my beloved Marie, I have been reduced to the state of greatest slavery by a monster temptress and utterly forgotten by my adored

Pedro. Lately I have received final proof that he has forgotten me completely, mistreating me in the presence of that very one who is the cause of all my afflictions.[15]

As doctors came and went, palace officials posted twice-daily bulletins on Leopoldina's grave condition. Priests led special masses on her behalf, the devout carried images of saints through the streets, and churches filled with the empress's subjects, who prayed that she would recover to guide them once more. But at 10:15 a.m. on December 11, 1826, Leopoldina finally succumbed to puerperal fever. She was twenty-nine years old.

Brazil was plunged into mourning. In the days after Leopoldina's death, the Senate acknowledged her many contributions, and the archbishop of Bahia honored her as a founder of the nation. "I will always be Brazilian in my heart," Leopoldina had written to her father after independence, "as I am determined to fulfill my duties as wife, mother, and for the gratitude of an honorable people."[16] All of Rio de Janeiro turned out for Leopoldina's funeral procession. Artist Jean-Baptiste Debret's last images of the "Mother of Brazil," as she was now called, are not of the woman herself but of her velvet-covered casket, topped by a heavy crown, and the elaborate, solemn convoy.

Pedro remained in Brazil fewer than five years after Leopoldina's death. Rumors swirled that he caused the miscarriage, and he bitterly repented his behavior toward his late wife. He parted company with Domitila and swore he'd never again violate his marriage vows. Yet many attributed Leopoldina's final illness to him. In addition, Pedro's increasingly undemocratic ways further undermined his popularity. He and his second wife, Amelia de Leuchtenberg, were forced to leave Brazil in 1833. Two years later Dom Pedro was dead of tuberculosis, an illness that he contracted during a long but successful military campaign to place his daughter Maria da Glória on the Portuguese throne.

Of Leopoldina's six children, two died before reaching adulthood and two, Maria II of Portugal and Pedro II of Brazil, ruled a combined total of sixty-six years. Pedro II was barely a year old when his mother died, yet he grew to be like her in many respects. A lettered, thoughtful emperor, by 1867 he would press for the abolition of slavery. If she looked down from the heaven in which she so devoutly believed, Empress Leopoldina, the "Mother of Brazil," would have been justifiably pleased with the way her son guided the sovereign nation that she herself had helped create.

NOTES

1. Unless otherwise noted, all translations are by the authors. Letter dated February 12, 1822. Luiz Norton, *A côrte de Portugal no Brasil: Notas, alguns documentos diplomáticos e cartas da Imperatriz Leopoldina* (São Paulo: Companhia Editora Nacional, 1938), 420.

2. Moacyr Flores, "Cartas de Dona Leopoldina," Porto Alegre, Brazil: Instituto Histórico e Geográfico do Rio Grande do Sul (IHGRGS), 2008, 6, https://www.ihgrgs.org.br/.

3. Letter dated June 9, 1821. Norton, *A côrte de Portugal no Brasil*, 441–42.

4. David James, "Jacques Arago and the Imperial Family of Brazil," *The Americas* 5, no. 2 (1948): 222, https://doi.org/10.2307/977808.

5. Lady Maria Calcott, *Journal of a Voyage to Brazil, and Residence There, during Part of the Years 1821, 1822, 1823* (London: Longman, Hurst, Rees, Orme, Brown, and Green, 1842), 182.

6. Norton, *A côrte de Portugal no Brasil*, letter dated January 22, 1822, 449.

7. Lilia M. Schwarcz and Heloisa Starling, *Brazil: A Biography* (New York: Farrar, Straus and Giroux, 2018), 229.

8. Norton, *A côrte de Portugal no Brasil*, letter dated August 4, 1822, 429.

9. Norton, *A côrte de Portugal no Brasil*, letter dated June 23, 1822, 452–53.

10. Bertita Harding, *Amazon Throne: The Story of the Braganzas* (New York: Bobbs-Merrill, 1941), 126.

11. José Theodoro Mascarenhas Menck, *Dona Leopoldina: Imperatriz e Maria do Brasil* (Brasília, Brazil: Cámara do Deputados, 2017), 80–81.

12. Sergio Corrêa da Costa, *Every Inch a King*, trans. Samuel Putnam (New York: Macmillan, 1950), 46. Corrêa da Costa's is but one of several, somewhat differing accounts of that historic moment.

13. Calcott, *Journal of a Voyage to Brazil*, 219.

14. Corrêa da Costa, *Every Inch a King*, 36.

15. Harding, *Amazon Throne*, 157.

16. Paulo D. Ressutti, *Leopoldina: A história não contada. A mulher que arquitetou a independência do Brasil* (Rio de Janeiro: Leya Press, 2017), 245.

REFERENCES

Arago, J., and David James. "Jacques Arago and the Imperial Family of Brazil." *Americas* 5, no. 2 (October 1948): 221–25. https://doi.org/10.2307/977808.

Barman, Roger. *Brazil: The Forging of a Nation, 1798–1852*. Stanford, CA: Stanford University Press, 1988.

Calcott, Lady Maria. *Journal of a Voyage to Brazil, and Residence There, during Part of the Years 1821, 1822, 1823.* London: Longman, Hurst, Rees, Orme, Brown, and Green, 1842.

Corrêa da Costa, Sergio. *Every Inch a King.* Translated by Samuel Putnam. New York: Macmillan, 1950.
Flores, Moacyr. "Cartas de Dona Leopoldina." Porto Alegre, Brazil: Instituto Histórico e Geográfico do Rio Grande do Sul (IHGRGS), 2008, 6. https://www.ihgrgs.org.br/.
Gomes, Laurentino. *1808: The Flight of the Emperor: How a Weak Prince, a Mad Queen, and the British Navy Tricked Napoleon and Changed the New World.* Guilford, CT: Lyons Press, 2007.
Harding, Bertita. *Amazon Throne: The Story of the Braganzas of Brazil.* New York: Bobbs-Merrill, 1941.
Marchant, Anyda. "The Captain's Widow." *Americas* 20, no. 2 (October 1963): 127–42.
Menck, José Theodoro Mascarenhas. *Dona Leopoldina: Imperatriz e Maria do Brasil.* Brasília, Brazil: Câmara dos Deputados, 2017.
Norton, Luiz. *A côrte de Portugal no Brasil: Notas, alguns documentos diplomáticos, e cartas da imperatriz Leopoldina.* São Paulo: Companhia Editora Nacional, 1938.
Oberacker, Carlos H., Jr. *A Imperatriz Leopoldina: Sua vida e sua época, ensaio de uma biografia.* Rio de Janeiro: Conselho Federal de Cultura, 1973.
Publicações do Archivo Nacional (Collected letters of Empress Leopoldina on the centenary of her death). Edited by Alcides Bezerra. Rio de Janeiro, 1927.
Rezzutti, Paulo D. *Leopoldina: A história não contada: A mulher que arquitetou a independência do Brasil.* Rio de Janeiro: Leya Press, 2017.
Schwarcz, Lilia Moritz. "Portraits: Empress Maria Leopoldina of Brazil." In *The Brazil Reader: History, Politics, Culture*, edited by James Green, Victoria Langland, and Lilia Moritz Schwarcz, 158–61. Durham, NC: Duke University Press.
Schwarcz, Lilia M., and Heloisa Starling. *Brazil: A Biography.* New York: Farrar, Straus and Giroux, 2018.
Vieira, Antônio Fagundes. "Funeral da Imperatriz." Vol. 2 of *Revista do Instituto Histórico: Antiquales e memórias do Rio de Janeiro.* Imprensa Nacional, 1927, 358–59.

Chapter 2

Mariana Grajales, 1808–1893

INTRODUCTION

Surveying the ruins of his American empire in the mid-1820s, the Spanish king, Fernando VII, could at least find consolation that Cuba, his richest and only remaining possession across the Atlantic, appeared to be satisfied with its colonial status. Several factors explain Cuba's failure to take up the revolutionary gauntlet along with the other colonies of Spanish America. Throughout years of revolutionary upset, Cuba served as the principal staging point for Spanish soldiers on their way to the mainland. Hence it was always garrisoned with thousands of Spanish troops. Throughout the early nineteenth century and into the 1860s, Cuba experienced an economic boom through its cultivation and export of sugar. That in turn enriched Creole and peninsular landowners and other commercial interests, making them tenacious defenders of the status quo. Burgeoning sugar production brought with it an influx of enslaved people from Africa to work the plantations. In that fact lay a final explanation for Cuban resistance to change. Between 1800 and 1865 some half a million men and women were forcibly transported to the island, and by 1817 the combined enslaved and free Black population surpassed that of Whites. As the Black population grew, so too did White fear of slave revolt. The Spanish minister Calatrava wrote confidently in 1823, "The fear [White] Cubans have of their Black people represents Spain's greatest security in guaranteeing her domination of the island."[1]

Free people of African descent proved most troubling to those who profited from sugar and slavery. Less than half as numerous as White people, they formed an intelligent and ambitious group of artisans and small farmers. Directors of colonial fortunes rightly perceived free Black men and women as a dangerous anomaly in the society they had created, and over the first half

Figure 2.1. Mariana Grajales

of the nineteenth century tried to hobble them by enacting a series of laws limiting their rights as free Cuban citizens.

When dissatisfaction with Spanish rule touched off the Ten Years' War in 1868, many free Blacks joined the revolt and assumed positions of leadership in it. They formed one of the more radical contingents in the revolutionary armies, for in addition to political independence they demanded the immediate abolition of slavery and an end to the racism that they perceived as harmful to Cuba as a whole. Theirs was a sophisticated nationalism that in time broadened to make them an advance guard of Third World anti-imperialism.

There was no middle ground in the Cuban wars of independence. When men joined the revolt, their families were routinely persecuted by the Spanish authorities. Thus women and children often joined the insurgents and traveled with them for years at a time. Far from burdening the armies, they staffed hospitals, operated kitchens, and offered field support that otherwise would not have existed. The best known among these *soldaderas* of the Cuban wars of independence was Mariana Grajales, an iron-willed free Black woman to whom the Spanish referred shudderingly as "the mother of the terrible Maceos" (see figure 2.1).

STIRRINGS OF REBELLION IN THE CUBAN "SLAVOCRACY"

Santiago de Cuba maintained a prison for runaway slaves not far from the neighborhood where Mariana Grajales grew up. As a child she often walked down streets lined with two- and three-room houses until she caught sight of the jail. On days when the Cuban sun poured down on the city as though through a tropical magnifying glass, Mariana watched as the runaway slaves, called *cimarrones*, gathered around the windows of their cells to catch a breath of fresh air. Their faces represented almost every shade on the human palette, from the mahogany of recently arrived Africans to the tan of those whose genes had mingled with those of White people over two or more generations. Many bore scars from the overseer's whip or showed signs of rough treatment at the time of their recapture. Others, their bodies gaunt from fever and poor food, had put up little resistance when they were found and now waited for their masters to claim them. Those faces of despair peering through the bars became for Mariana living symbols of the slave system she grew to hate.

Of all the people who arrived or were forcibly transported to Cuba, the African's lot was harshest, as the *cimarrones* could attest. *Bozales*, newly arrived enslaved peoples, were a common sight in Santiago de Cuba, and it was not until 1820, when Mariana Grajales was twelve, that town fathers protested the custom of leading slaves naked through the streets—a protest lodged not out of concern for the dignity of slaves but in the interests of protecting the free population from so uncivilized a sight. Cuba was almost as inhospitable to the Chinese laborers who came as indentured servants, only to find themselves treated as slaves. At the other end of the color spectrum were White landowners whose wealth came from plantations worked by slaves. Mariana saw them in downtown Santiago de Cuba and caught glimpses of their wives and daughters as they drove by in two-wheeled carriages, fans held gracefully in their hands, dainty feet encased in satin slippers.

Mariana herself was a free woman of mixed heritage whose parents fled to Cuba in order to escape race-related turmoil in nearby Santo Domingo. They lived modestly in Santiago, worked hard, and managed to live decently. Because Spanish colonial laws limited education for Black people, both slave and free, Mariana never attended school, and no one knows whether she learned to read and write. In spite of the handicaps of race and poverty, she grew into a proud young woman who was sure of her own worth in a society that did its best to undervalue it.

When she was twenty-three, Mariana left her father's house to marry Fructuoso Regüeyferos. Marriage to a man of similar background and values was by far the best option available to her. Free union between people of her group was at least as common as marriage, and although women entering such arrangements had few guarantees of support from their men, they were better off than those who fell into the trap of concubinage to wealthy Creoles. Marriage between persons of differing racial backgrounds was prohibited by law, yet the large number of children of mixed parentage proved that the races did indeed intermingle. The seeming availability of women who, unlike the cloistered White ladies of Cuba, were visible in the market and in the streets encouraged men to seek liaisons in classes other than their own. And the fact that there were fewer White women than men—only ten to every twelve or thirteen men—added another motive for cross-class dalliance. Mariana neatly avoided the pitfalls of seduction and instead established a legally constituted home for her children.

Mariana and her husband had four sons—Justo, Felipe, Manuel, and Fermín. After nine years of marriage, Fructuoso died, and at age thirty-two Mariana became a widow and the sole support for her little boys. There was nowhere to go but home, and in 1840 she moved back to her parents' house.

Mariana Grajales did not remain single long after Fructuoso's death. She was, after all, an attractive and respectable widow in the prime of life, and her sons were of an age to begin helping with family chores. Soon after the period of mourning was over, Mariana met a Venezuelan immigrant named Marcos Maceo, a friend of her father's who was a successful small businessman and farmer. Like Mariana, Marcos was biracial and a widower, the father of six children. In 1843, Mariana left her parents' house and moved to Marcos's farm in San Luis, near Santiago de Cuba. Friends and relatives saw the wisdom of the match and approved of it, though it was not sanctified by a formal marriage. Still, the home Mariana and Marcos established was as solid as any household begun with greater pomp and ritual.

Mariana was thirty-five and Marcos some years older when they met. The little girl who stared at *cimarrones* in the prison of Santiago de Cuba had grown into a stalwart opponent of slavery in all its forms. Her feelings were natural for someone of her position and experience. Abolitionist sentiment prevailed among free Black people and people of mixed descent, many of whom had been enslaved or descended from slaves who had bought their freedom through exceptional effort. The line between enslaved and free people, then, was not always clear, and free biracial people like Mariana often maintained social contacts with urban slaves through the godparent relationship and other friendships.

Mariana's fierce beliefs were not shared by Marcos at first. He had tried to stay aloof from involvements since his arrival in Cuba in the 1820s. The wars of independence in Venezuela, where he had fought for the Spanish king against the armies of Simón Bolívar, soured him on war and political strife. Although his brother remained in the king's service in Cuba, Marcos devoted himself to commerce and agriculture. Las Delicias, his farm in the Majaguabo region of San Luis, produced enough sugarcane, sweet potatoes, and fruit to satisfy his large family, plenty of corn husks and stalks to feed his mules, and tobacco for the cash market. In Santiago de Cuba, he owned a three-room house, stuccoed with lime and sand, that had an ample patio with fruit trees growing out back.

Events of 1843 forced Marcos to reconsider his apolitical stance. During that year enslaved people on plantations in Matanzas Province, in north-central Cuba, rebelled against their masters. In groups ranging from a few to two hundred or more, the rebels fought to free themselves and escape to *palenques*—settlements of runaway slaves—deep in the mountains. The rebellions were brutally suppressed, and executions and deaths by flogging were meted out liberally. Such revolts had occurred at regular intervals for decades. Now, however, the slavocracy began to see abolitionist conspiracies at every turn. Captain General Leopoldo O'Donnell, gripped by panic, tried to quell the unrest. Early in 1844 he seized on rumors as proof of a widespread conspiracy led by abolitionists, some of them White, some free Black people. He ordered the supposed leaders of the plot executed, among them a well-known poet, a highly educated dentist, a musician, and a landowner—all middle-class and of African or mixed heritage.

Not content with that perversion of justice, O'Donnell set up a military commission to persecute the non-White population of Cuba. In all, he ordered seventy-eight alleged participants in the "Conspiracy of the Staircase," so called for the stairway-like scaffold on which "conspirators" were flogged to death, to be executed outright. Hundreds of others died of torture, mistreatment, and disease, and a thousand more were imprisoned on the flimsiest of evidence. Only twenty White people were punished; all the other victims were free Black people and, in lesser numbers, slaves. The consequences of the Conspiracy of the Staircase were not lost on Marcos and Mariana. The group of which they were a part had been singled out for persecution. Although the Maceos escaped personal loss, their rights of citizenship were jeopardized.

Beginning in 1844 Captain General O'Donnell enforced a series of measures designed to prevent free Blacks from influencing enslaved men and women. To that end, he gave slaveholders broad power. Meetings of free Blacks were strictly supervised; "disrespect" of Whites became a punishable crime. Enslaved people freed after May 1844 were to be exiled from Cuba, and freedmen who, like Marcos Maceo, had moved to the island from another country were ordered to emigrate. To protect himself from deportation, Marcos persuaded a friendly bureaucrat to declare him a native of Santiago de Cuba. Spanish officials' handling of the Conspiracy of the Staircase alienated Creoles and emancipated men and women who saw it as one more example of Spain's repressive, arbitrary policies. Those who opposed slavery were forced to conclude that abolition would occur only after Cuba won its independence from Spain.

In early 1845, a pregnant Mariana left the farm in Majaguabo and traveled to Marcos's house on Providencia Street in Santiago to await the birth of her child. Antonio de la Caridad Maceo y Grajales was born on June 14. His baptism took place in late August and was followed by a party hosted by the baby's parents and his godparents, Don Ascencio de Asencio and his wife Salome. Don Ascencio was a wealthy Creole lawyer of some standing in the city, a dutiful godfather, and over the years a true friend of Marcos and Mariana's. On Antonio's baptismal certificate, not notable for its accuracy, the baby was described as the "legitimate son" of Marcos Maceo, "a native of this city."[2]

Mariana celebrated her thirty-seventh birthday shortly after Antonio was born. Eight more children followed—Baldomera, José, Rafael, Miguel, Julio, Dominga, Tomás, and Marcos, each separated from the next by a year or two. On July 6, 1851, Mariana and Marcos were married in San Luis, an act that merely reaffirmed the bond between them. Over a period of fifteen years, she bore Marcos's children with a strength that belied her advancing age. In 1857 two children were born—Dominga in the spring, Tomás scarcely eight months later—and in 1860, their last child appeared several months after Mariana's fifty-second birthday. Of Mariana's thirteen children, only one, Manuel Regüeyferos, died before reaching adulthood.

Throughout the 1850s and 1860s Mariana watched over her family from the ample, rough stone house at Las Delicias. Her kitchen garden boasted an abundance of herbs—mint and lemon balm for tea, thyme and coriander for soups, medicinal plants like bright orange and yellow calendula blossoms for salves and remedies. Plantain and banana trees grew so close to her kitchen that she picked the fruits only minutes before they were to be prepared, and orchards lay beyond the tobacco shed, stable, and other outbuildings. Over all of this towered the trees of Majaguabo, casting shade on the wide veranda of the house and the patio outside. When Mariana went to Santiago de Cuba, she carried large sacks woven of *majagua* twine and filled with provisions to restock the storeroom of the house on Providencia Street.

The family grew and prospered as though protected by some magic charm. Mariana and Marcos, through careful planning and frugality, bought a second farm in Majaguabo and called it La Esperanza—Hope. Even before they grew their first mustaches, the sons were a formidable workforce, helping with chores on the family farms and driving the mule team that Marcos hired out to carry produce and tobacco from farms in Majaguabo to market in Santiago. Mariana controlled her tribe by enforcing a few basic rules—respect for parents, a reasonable curfew, and above all strict attention to duty.

THE MACEOS AND THE MASONIC CONSPIRACY

All was not work, however, and in spite of the curfew, the younger Maceos became the central attraction of Majaguabo's social life. Broad-chested and handsome, the older boys enjoyed the attentions of young ladies and the approval of other young men who admired their skill with horse and machete. It was said that the Maceos never missed a dance, never lost a race. When they were old enough, the boys went to school in Santiago de Cuba. Spanish law prevented them from progressing beyond elementary studies, so after a few years they were back in Majaguabo to work full-time on the farm.

In 1862, Antonio joined his older half brother Justo Regüeyferos in managing their father's mule train, which pulled cargo into towns. Business often took them into Santiago, and they kept abreast of the news of the day. It was Antonio and Justo who brought word of the independence of Santo Domingo and stories about the war to end slavery in the United States. In that manner news of the wider world penetrated the backcountry of colonial Cuba.

Of all the regions of Cuba, resentment against colonialism was strongest in Oriente—or eastern—Province. During the mid-1860s, support for independence spread through a network of Masonic lodges in major towns of eastern Cuba. The Grand Lodge of Colón was founded in Santiago in 1859, and shortly thereafter Vicente Aguilera, Carlos Manuel de Céspedes, and others founded Redemption Lodge in Bayamo. In August 1867 Aguilera and other wealthy Creoles set in motion the mechanisms of revolt. Creoles in major cities and towns formed revolutionary juntas to search out potential leaders for the struggle against Spain. Communication between towns was set up, supporters identified, military supplies stockpiled, and plots hatched. Cuba thus geared up for rebellion four decades after the rest of Spanish America had seized its independence from the crumbling Spanish Empire.

Thanks to Don Ascencio, Antonio was part of that effort. Ascencio de Asencio had long recognized special qualities in the Maceos' firstborn, and although he feared Antonio's race would prove a handicap, he was an unflagging supporter of the young man. When Antonio married María Cabrales of Majaguabo in 1866, his godfather acted as his sponsor. Two years later, Ascencio de Asencio sponsored him again, this time when Antonio Maceo was initiated into Santiago's Masonic Grand Lodge.

Well into 1868 secrecy shrouded the Masonic conspiracy, for Creole revolutionaries feared Spanish retaliation should suspicions be aroused. As leaders emerged from the various lodges and as regional responsibilities were assigned, increasing numbers of Cubans, both Black and White, joined the plot. The Maceos were among them. Still, leaders disagreed on the proper moment to unleash the forces of revolution. The more cautious ones urged that they wait until the following spring after the sugar harvest, when food and cash would be most abundant. Others worried that the cover of secrecy might soon evaporate and that the juntas might be arrested before a shot had been fired.

By September 1868 word to prepare for revolution reached the countryside. During a trip to Santiago that month, Marcos agreed to organize Majaguabo for the approaching conflict. He knew without a doubt that the revolution was imminent, yet conflicting emotions assailed him as he returned to the farm. What would Mariana say? They were no longer young; what would happen to her once the revolution began? What if she didn't want him to fight? Silent and sad, Marcos entered the house early in the afternoon before any of his sons had returned from the day's work. As he slowly described to Mariana all that he, Ascencio, and the others had been planning for so many months, her happiness was apparent. At age sixty she saw at last the end of Cuba's enslavement by Spain, of Black enslavement by White people; and she had no reservations about sacrificing all they had to rid Cuba of the Spanish or, failing that, to die in the attempt.

In the month that followed, the Maceos fanned out through the Majaguabo district to enlist their friends and neighbors in the coming struggle. María Cabrales, who had been living with her husband Antonio at La Esperanza, was sent to join Mariana and the other women at Las Delicias, and the isolated farm was turned into a military depot and encampment. In early October, Mariana traveled to Santiago on family business. Ascencio contacted her there and told her that he needed to see Marcos as soon as possible. Understanding that the matter was urgent, she hurried back to Las Delicias with the message. When Marcos reached the home of his friend, Ascencio told him that the revolution would break out at any moment. The small army that the Maceos had raised over the past weeks would be contacted by an officer of the revolutionary command as soon as the time for action arrived.

A few days later, in a move that surprised even some of his fellow conspirators, Carlos Manuel de Céspedes, wealthy Creole, Mason, and revolutionary, declared Cuban independence at the village of Yara, near the town of Bayamo, in eastern Cuba. The Grito de Yara marked the beginning of the bloody Ten Years' War. Spanish Captain General Lersundi received news of the declaration of independence with some skepticism. Cuba was well garrisoned with loyalist soldiers and volunteer militiamen, many of them veterans of the wars in Santo Domingo. Doubting that Creole-led forces could even begin to challenge such an army, he nevertheless ordered a general alert and prepared to meet the rebels on the battlefield. Throughout eastern Cuba, Creole landowners, lawyers, and merchants sympathetic to the revolution transformed themselves into officers and soldiers.

News was slow to reach Majaguabo, and the Maceos grew increasingly uneasy as days passed with no word from the revolutionary command. To increase the population's uncertainty, the Spanish spread rumors that bands of outlaws were loose in Oriente and that no one in the countryside was safe. The women—Mariana, Dominga, Baldomera, and María Cabrales—worried that they might be attacked while their men sat waiting at La Esperanza. Finally, Marcos sent sixteen-year-old Miguel to a nearby country store to find out what was happening beyond the borders of Majaguabo. There he met Captain Juan Bautista Rondón, a friend of the Maceos who was in command of some four hundred rebel troops, their first contact with the revolutionary army. In a matter of hours Rondón joined Marcos, Antonio, and the others at La Esperanza. While the Majaguabo volunteers hurried off to say last farewells at home, the Maceos and Rondón's company left for Las Delicias.

Mariana and the other women were startled by the shout that called them to the door, but when they recognized the voice as Marcos's, they stepped outside to see him standing with a handful of men. "Do you know this gentleman?" boomed Marcos, pointing to Rondón. Mariana's only answer was a gasp, for at his signal Rondón's four hundred armed men moved out of the shadows and formed a great semicircle behind them. "These," laughed Marcos, "are the highwaymen you were so worried about! The revolution has begun!"

Recounting the scene nearly thirty years later, María Cabrales described "la vieja Mariana" as immensely pleased that there were so many men determined to fight for their country. "Overflowing with happiness," she went into the house, took the crucifix from her room, and returned to the veranda. "On your knees, fathers and sons," she cried, "before Christ who was the first Liberal to come into the world. Let us swear to free our country or to die for her!"[3] Antonio, José, Justo, Felipe, Julio, and Fermín, the oldest of Mariana's sons, rode off to war that night. With them went the Majaguabo recruits, who swelled Rondón's company to almost eight hundred men.

BLOOD, SWEAT, AND TEARS: REVOLUTION AND FAMILY

From the first, the conflict included civilians as well as soldiers. The Spanish command treated families of rebels as rebels themselves, and many elderly people, women, and children took refuge in the mountainous jungles—the *manigua*—of Oriente. For several days Marcos stayed with Mariana, their daughters, daughters-in-law, and the two youngest boys—Tomás, eleven, and Marcos, eight—while they packed and moved to El Piloto, a secluded farm not far from Majaguabo. They left none too soon, for a Spanish sympathizer denounced the Maceos to authorities in San Luis, and troops rode out to Las Delicias to arrest them. Eighteen-year-old Rafael Maceo had stayed behind to guard the farm when his family left for the mountains. He was seized by Spanish soldiers who burned every building to the ground, then carried him off to prison.

When Marcos heard of his son's capture, he rode to San Luis to offer himself in exchange for Rafael's freedom. Spanish officials jailed Marcos but did not free Rafael. Several days passed before two friends of Marcos, both Spaniards, secured his release; Rafael later escaped thanks to the inattentiveness of his guards. Both men, father and son, joined Antonio and the others. Of the older children, only Miguel remained in hiding with Mariana, but when she sent him to Antonio's encampment with a supply of clothing, he decided to stay there and fight. By early November nine Maceos were fighting for Cuban independence.

High spirits, excitement, and illusions of an early victory were fueled by early rebel successes. Revolutionary forces wrested control of Bayamo and Jiguaní from the Spanish. Many who had waited to see if the movement was viable now joined the patriot ranks. Veterans of Santo Domingo's war for independence—Luis Marcano, Máximo Gómez, Modesto Díaz—assumed command of the army and taught Cubans the basics of war in that most effective of classrooms, the battlefield.

Antonio's progress through the ranks was spectacular, a source of pride for his mother and his young wife. All the Maceos were exceptionally good fighters, but Antonio combined that quality with a seeming inability to lose a battle. He rose overnight from soldier to sergeant on the strength of his leadership of the Majaguabo volunteers. Other promotions followed quickly. When he visited Mariana in November, he was already a lieutenant. In December he was promoted to captain, in January to commander, and scarcely ten days later he earned the insignia of lieutenant colonel. To those who fought with him, he seemed most comfortable with a machete in hand, astride one of his magnificent horses, plunging after a platoon of Spanish soldiers.

After a few initial victories, the revolutionary forces found further success elusive. Spanish troops, well armed and experienced, poured onto the field, where they posed a striking contrast to the undersupplied rebels. Céspedes, president of Cuba's new republican government, had failed utterly in persuading the United States and Great Britain, seemingly natural allies of Free Cuba, to recognize the revolution in 1868. Arms, supplies, and ammunition, so desperately needed to bring the war to a speedy and successful close, were not forthcoming from either nation. Only small shipments of supplies managed to reach Free Cuba, and those were far from sufficient.

A few Cuban generals proved able to fight under such conditions, most notably Máximo Gómez, the wily guerrilla fighter from Santo Domingo; his best pupil in matters of war was Antonio Maceo. Suffering from constant shortages and threatened by far superior forces, Máximo Gómez divided his command into highly mobile guerrilla units that spread out through mountainous eastern Cuba. From their forest encampment, Gómez's commanders planned attacks on lowland sugar plantations, on Spanish garrisons, and occasionally on towns and villages held by the Spanish. Their most important weapons besides the machete were surprise and well-planned retreats into the wilderness of highland Oriente Province. Antonio Maceo excelled in guerrilla warfare, never leaving any detail of the attack to chance and ensuring that each fallen enemy soldier contributed his supplies to Maceo's men. So successful was he that as the months and years of war dragged on, his men were well clothed and reasonably well armed and fed at a time when many of Free Cuba's soldiers were half-naked and hungry.

During the first year of the war, the Maceo family suffered a series of painful losses. The revolution was scarcely a month old when Captain Justo Regüeyferos was captured and shot while visiting his wife near San Luis. In mid-May, Antonio, commanding a company that included his own father and brothers, attacked the Spanish garrison San Agustín. During the encounter, Marcos Maceo fell from his horse, mortally wounded. He died in Antonio's arms knowing that he had kept his promise to Mariana. Six days later Antonio was shot in the thigh, his first wound. His men carried him on a makeshift cot to the old *palenque*—the runaway slave settlement—where Mariana, María Cabrales, and the families of other rebels lived.

Deep in the *manigua*, in a crude jungle hospital, Antonio's wound healed rapidly. Mariana, grieving at the death of her faithful Marcos just days earlier, displayed a fortitude that would carry her through difficult days to come. Like a civilian general whose army was made up of elderly people, women, and children, she enforced certain rules that applied to all who nursed the wounded rebels, the mambi soldiers. They were to bear death, defeat, and the discomfort of life in the *manigua* without complaint. When Mariana approached her son's hammock, she chided him for letting so insignificant a scratch slow him down. "That'll heal in a minute," she said, "and then you can go get a real wound, something to worry about!"[4]

In June 1869, before Antonio was fully recovered, tragedy struck three times in quick succession. Antonio and Maria's first and only children, a boy and a girl, died within days of each other. Then word came from Santiago that sixteen citizens, Masons involved in the revolution, had been carried off to a remote farm and executed with machetes, their bodies robbed and mutilated. Among them was that of Antonio Maceo's godfather Ascencio de Acencio.

Mariana was in her sixties when the war cut her off from the past and thrust her into an uncertain future. The shady veranda and cool rooms of the house at Las Delicias had gone up in smoke; the house on Providencia Street was useless to her as long as the Spanish controlled Santiago. She put the familiar routines, expectations, and possessions of a lifetime behind her without regret. From the circle of huts in the *manigua* she watched over the families of soldiers, nursed the wounded, and grieved silently for the dead. If the heavy rains that seeped through flimsy roofs made her old bones ache, no one ever heard her complain. If at night she lay awake remembering her beloved dead or worrying about the seven sons whose lives were in constant danger, no one ever saw her serene face creased with anxiety. She stoically cared for her sons and family, and she spoke at all times of her uncompromising support for the war and an independent Cuba.

RESISTANCE TO THE DEATH: "EL SILENCIO" AND THE COST OF REVOLUTION

As Spanish reinforcements poured into Cuba, the Count of Valmaseda, commander of the counterinsurgency forces based in Bayamo, issued a proclamation that showed how far the Spanish were prepared to go in order to put down the uprising. "He who is not with me is against me," announced Valmaseda. He continued:

> And so that my soldiers may recognize the enemy, I issue the following general order: Every man, fifteen years or older, found outside his farm, and who cannot justify his motives, will be executed. All uninhabited dwellings will be burned. All dwellings not flying a white flag as a sign that its occupants desire peace will be reduced to ashes. All women who are not living in their own homes or with relatives will be concentrated in the towns of Jiguaní and Bayamo, where they will be maintained. Those who do not present themselves voluntarily will be taken by force.[5]

Soon after this declaration of war on civilians, the Spanish began methodically executing all rebel soldiers taken in battle. In response, the revolutionary forces formed a brotherhood called "El Silencio," complete with rites of initiation and secret ceremonies. Each soldier swore to risk his own life to keep his wounded fellows from falling into Spanish hands. So well did the system work that wounded rebels were dragged to safety even under the heaviest gunfire. Tales abounded of men whose arms were broken and whose mangled limbs were torn off as they were dragged over rough terrain. Brutal though such treatment seemed, many of the wounded lived to fight again, and the Spanish were deprived of whatever satisfaction the executions might have given them.

One reverse after another threatened the revolution with total collapse in the early 1870s. The coasts and cities of Oriente swarmed with Spanish troops and, as if that weren't enough, cholera afflicted the island as well. In Santiago de Cuba, gravediggers abandoned the congested cemeteries, and citizens piled their dead into long ditches that served as common graves. Out in the once-productive countryside, fertile farms lay idle and abandoned, the rural population severely reduced by the double onslaught of war and epidemic.

Cholera finally reached into revolutionary encampments and mambi settlements of the *manigua*, with even more disaster on its heels. With the plague came redoubled Spanish efforts to crush the rebels. Loyalist troops pursued the mambi fighters into the mountains and succeeded in cutting off the trickle of supplies that had reached Free Cuba. Whole platoons fell because the weakened rebels lacked ammunition with which to answer the attacks, and even Antonio Maceo's men, well provisioned compared to others in the Cuban army, fell back before Spanish advances. At one point Maceo's company withdrew to the settlement where Mariana and the other women maintained a field hospital. Spanish troops surprised them there, and for over an hour Mariana was trapped in a ditch as the battle raged around her.

Gradually and against all odds, the Cuban army overcame the setbacks of the early 1870s. The cholera epidemic subsided, and the opposing armies reached a kind of equilibrium. Patriot forces throughout Oriente Province adopted Maceo's method of ambushing enemy columns for supplies and taking food from abandoned farms. Each unit became self-sufficient, although none was so well supplied that it could mount frontal assaults on Spanish positions. The rebels carried out ambushes and skirmishes while the Spanish stayed close to fortified positions.

Máximo Gómez understood that failing decisive action, the revolution was at a stalemate. As long as rebel-held territory remained within the borders of Oriente and Camagüey, the Spanish military command was free to concentrate large numbers of troops in those regions. Sugarcane plantations in western Cuba continued operations as though the war did not exist, providing the Spanish with vital food supplies and revenue. Efforts to draw western Creoles into the war were met with obstinate opposition. Wealthy landowners supported many goals of the revolution, but they were not eager to see their slaves freed or their cane fields turned into a battleground. Efforts to carry the war into the west were further complicated by regionalism. When Máximo Gómez led his men into Camagüey, he found that revolutionary commanders there consistently placed personal ambitions and regional jealousies above the welfare of Free Cuba. In the case of Antonio Maceo, those jealousies took the form of racial prejudice. Creole officers of Las Villas who found themselves under Maceo's command refused to fight under a non-White man and complained bitterly to the government. In a few months Maceo returned to Oriente, frustrated by the prejudices and divisiveness he saw in the west.

By 1874, the midpoint of the war, Mariana had lost four more sons: Fermín and Felipe Regüeyferos, and Julio and Miguel Maceo. The death of Miguel after the Battle of Cascorro was especially tragic. Twenty years old when he was fatally wounded, Miguel had already shown an aptitude for battle challenging that of his famous brothers Antonio and José. When word arrived at camp that Miguel was dead, Mariana turned to fourteen-year-old Marcos, her youngest son, and commanded, "And you, stand up straight. It's time you fought for your country!"[6] Mariana believed that one son should replace another, so she sent them to battle one by one—until none were left to send.

After his brief excursion into Camagüey Province, Antonio returned home and continued his harassment of the Spanish. Still the specter of racism followed him, for on February 1, 1876, Modesto Díaz was named commander of Oriente after the previous commander's capture by the enemy. The post should have gone to Antonio Maceo, but the revolutionary government followed a policy of giving Creole officers preference over Black or mixed-race men. Old Mariana's hopes that the revolution would be color-blind were betrayed, and her son found himself on the defensive despite his devotion to Free Cuba.

Throughout 1876 and the first half of 1877, Maceo and his men ranged nearly at will over Oriente Province, destroying military posts, burning cane fields, and freeing slaves. Then, on August 7, 1877, Maceo rode his big mare Concha into a wooded glen called Mangos de Mejía where a Spanish company lay in wait. For once his luck abandoned him and enemy bullets knocked him from his horse. His brother Tomás threw him on a stretcher made of saplings and vines and carried him to Félix Figueredo, a medical doctor attached to their unit. Only the blood trickling from his mouth and nose gave Tomás Maceo hope that his brother still lived. When that limp and bloodied body reached the settlement at Los Indios where Mariana was camped, the women gathered weeping and wailing around her hut. Mariana shooed them away, shouting, "Out of here, skirts, out of here! There's no time for tears!" With water and rags, she washed the blood from Antonio's broad back and shattered right hand, then stepped back as Colonel Figueredo and Máximo Gómez arrived to inspect the wounds.[7]

No one who saw the extent of Antonio's injuries believed he could recover. Five bullets had pierced his back, two penetrating the chest cavity and a lung; three had struck his hand, and the palm was studded with bits of metal from his own revolver. From the first day he burned with fever as his body fought the wounds. Signs of gangrene began to appear in his hand. Figueredo had few medicines and could only pray that the two bullets in Antonio's chest, one very close to the spine, had not damaged a vital organ.

Some days later Máximo Gómez departed to take command of Antonio Maceo's troops, leaving José Maceo and twelve riflemen to protect their fallen commander. Spanish forces, some two hundred strong, pursued Antonio Maceo to finish the work begun at Mangos de Mejía. Meanwhile, José moved his brother from one hiding place to another to elude capture. Eventually Antonio was moved into the region controlled by mambi Lieutenant Colonel Antonio Rodríguez. By that time gravely wounded Antonio Maceo managed to travel on foot, stumbling rather than walking, led by Mariana and followed by María. Once during the ordeal, as the Spanish came within rifle range, he called for his horse and, incredibly, mounted and rode away to safety. In late September physician Félix Figueredo wrote these lines to Máximo Gómez:

> This General Maceo, like all good insurgents, heals better with water, iron, and fire than with balms and ointments; while his doctor takes notes so that, should the patient save himself from Death's clutches and survive, he can ask the wise men of the Academies and medical professors if it is possible that in this land of tetanus and malaria, a man prostrate on a rough bed of twigs . . . his lungs

pierced with the lead slugs of a Remington . . . can get up amid the seriousness of his wounds, walk miles on foot, eat nothing, sleep not a wink in three days, ford rivers, ride off on horseback, and say at the end of such violent fatigues, that he feels much better.[8]

After two weeks of unrelenting pursuit, the Spanish brigadier pursuing Antonio Maceo had only the wounded man's abandoned cot to show for his efforts.

Once he was fully healed, Antonio vowed to collect with interest the debt owed him by the Spanish. During the last months of 1877 and into the first weeks of February 1878, he attacked Spanish commander Martínez Campos's troops, wiping out entire columns and moving freely in the area north of Santiago.

One week after his remarkable string of victories, a small party of Cuban officers led by Máximo Gómez made its way to the mambi camp. Gómez had come to say goodbye to Mariana and to relay some bitter news to her son. Even as Maceo and his men were performing brilliantly in Oriente, revolutionary leaders had signed a pact destined to end the war. The Pact of Zanjón was the result of several factors, among them dissension within the Cuban ranks, the conciliatory policy initiated by Captain General Martínez Campos months before, and, most of all, a profound weariness on both sides of the conflict. But the pact did not free Cuba of either Spanish rule or slavery. Two weeks later, with his vow to free Cuba ringing in his ears, Antonio met Martínez Campos at a place near Santiago called Baragua and categorically rejected the Pact of Zanjón. Although hostilities broke out anew on March 23, Martínez Campos ordered the Spanish troops to respect the cease-fire at all costs. Even Antonio Maceo could not bring himself to fight against soldiers who answered his fire with white flags and shouts of "Viva Cuba!" The War of 1868 was at an end.

Under the Pact of Zanjón, Martínez Campos provided safe passage for members of the Maceo family who wished to go into exile. Mariana, María, the Maceo daughters and their families, Tomás, and Marcos left their beloved Cuba in April 1878 and went into exile in Kingston, Jamaica. Antonio, José, and Rafael stayed behind, hoping they could fight on. Both sides—loyalist and revolutionary—conspired to remove Antonio Maceo from Cuba so that the peace agreed to by a majority of the antagonists could settle over that exhausted island. In May, Antonio agreed to leave Cuba for Jamaica and New York in search of financial support for the war. Whether he truly believed that he could stop the drift toward peace is doubtful, although he later claimed that he had been "deceived" by both his friends and his enemies into accepting a voluntary exile. Only José and Rafael stayed in Cuba. They returned to the house on Providencia Street in Santiago for a short time but soon became embroiled in the hopeless "Little War." At the end of that conflict, they fell into Spanish hands and, with their families and friends, were sent to prison, first in North Africa and later in Spain, where Rafael died.

Mariana, depressed by a penurious exile in Kingston, began to feel the terrible weight of old age, hopelessness, and grief. A decade of bloody struggle and the sacrifice of her husband and six sons seemed to have accomplished nothing. What was worse, Rafael had died far from home, José languished in a Spanish prison, and Antonio wandered about the Caribbean in a fruitless attempt to find support for a second rebellion. In that state of discouragement Mariana received a letter from José, who described the sad state of his affairs and expressed the fear that he would not live to see her again. Never before had Mariana asked a Spaniard for a favor, but the mother who had proudly sent her sons to war could not bear to let another one die miserably in prison. She visited the Spanish consul in Kingston to beg for José's freedom. In his dispatch to Madrid dated September 3, 1878, Consul Francisco E. Gómez wrote with some astonishment that he had received the "mother of the terrible Cuban chieftains Antonio and José Maceo," and that she had assured him of her sons' desire to live in peace with Spain.[9]

Shortly after Mariana's visit to the Spanish consul, José Maceo escaped prison and made his way through North Africa to France and then to the United States, finally arriving in Kingston in January 1885. Soon thereafter the chagrined Spanish once again received word of plotting by the "terrible Maceos."

CONCLUSION

Mariana did not live to see Cuba become independent in 1902 or to see Antonio and José Martí renew the battle, fulfilling with their deaths in 1896 the vow they had made to her nearly thirty years before. But she had always known that Cuba would someday be free, whether by her sons' hands or by those of younger men like Jose Martí, who visited her in 1891, just prior to her death. "She caressed my face and looked on me like a son," wrote Martí, whose talk of liberating Cuba brought a sparkle to her dim eyes. He sat with the old woman and watched her wrinkled face grow animated as she reminisced about a particularly outstanding lance thrust by one of her sons, or about the time another, "bleeding from every part of his body, lifted himself and with ten men drove off two hundred of the enemy." Martí sensed the power that Mariana exercised over all who came into contact with her, and it was he who wrote the epitaph that catches the essence of her contribution to Cuban independence: "And if one trembled when he came face-to-face with the enemy of his country, he saw the mother of Maceo, white kerchief on her head, and he ceased trembling."[10]

NOTES

1. José Luciano Franco, *Antonio Maceo, apuntes para una historia de su vida*, vol. 1 (Havana: Instituto Cubano del Libro, 1951), 28.
2. Franco, *Antonio Maceo*, 15.
3. Antonio Maceo, *Papeles de Maceo*, vol. 2 (Havana: Academia de la Historia de Cuba, 1946), 46–47.
4. Maceo, *Papeles*, vol. 2, 190–91.
5. Murat Halstead, *The Story of Cuba, Her Struggle for Liberty: The Cause, Crisis, and Destiny of the Pearl of the Antilles* (Akron, OH: Werner, 1898), 297–98.
6. José Martí, *Obras completas*, vol. 2 (Havana: Editorial Lex, 1946), 200.
7. Luis F. Le Roy y Gálvez, "Las heridas de Maceo en la Guerra de 1868," *Revista de la Biblioteca Nacional José Martí* 10, no. 3 (September–December 1968): 63–77.
8. Le Roy y Gálvez, "Las heridas de Maceo," 63–77.
9. José Luciano Franco, *La ruta de Maceo en el caribe* (Gainesville: University of Florida Press, 1960), 12–13.
10. José Martí, *Obras*, vol. 1 (Havana: Academia de la Historia de Cuba, 1946), 617.

REFERENCES

Castellanos, José G. *La casa donde nació Antonio Maceo*. Santiago, Cuba: Talleres Poligráfica, 1957.
Escamilla, Luis. "Mariana Grajales Cuello." BlackPast.org. April 13, 2009. https://www.blackpast.org/global-african-history/grajales-cuello-mariana-1808-1893/.
Foner, Philip Shelton. *Antonio Maceo: The "Bronze Titan" of Cuba's Struggle for Independence*. New York: Monthly Review Press, 1978.
Franco, José Luciano. *Antonio Maceo, apuntes para una historia de su vida*. Vol. 1. Havana, 1951.
———. *La ruta de Maceo en el caribe*. Gainesville: University of Florida Press, 1960.
Halstead, Murat. *The Story of Cuba: Her Struggle for Liberty. The Cause, Crisis and Destiny of the Pearl of the Antilles*. Akron, OH: Werner, 1898.
Henderson, James D. "Mariana Grajales: Black Progenitress of Cuban Independence." *Journal of Negro History* 63, no. 2 (April 1978): 135–48.
Le Roy y Gálvez, Luis F. "Las heridas de Maceo en la Guerra de 1868." *Revista de la Biblioteca Nacional José Martí* 10, no. 3 (September–December 1968): 63–77.

Maceo, Antonio. *Papeles de Maceo*. 2 vols. Havana: Academia de la Historia de Cuba, 1948.
Martí, José. *Obras completas*. Vol. 1. Havana: Editorial Lex, 1946.
Torres Hernández, Lázaro. "Mariana Grajales: Una madre sublime." *Bohemia*, January 28, 1972, 100–104.

Chapter 3

Eliza Lynch, 1833–1886

INTRODUCTION

Paraguay's most notable feature might well be the indelible influence of its original inhabitants, the Guaraní Indians. Yet over the first three hundred years of the country's history, during the sixteenth through the nineteenth centuries, the Guaraní appeared astonishingly loyal to their leaders, all of whom were of European descent. This was true from the earliest times, when the Guaraní embraced their first colonial administrator, Spanish conquistador Domingo Martínez de Irala, who founded Asunción in 1537. Indigenous Paraguayans were likewise devoted to Jesuit fathers who presided over missions among them for more than two centuries during the colonial period. The Jesuits converted the Guaraní to Christianity, taught them European ways, and protected them from slave hunters from neighboring Brazil. To this day, Paraguayans are bilingual, as they are fluent in both Guaraní and Spanish. Nowhere else in the Americas is this the case.

Landlocked Paraguay was ruled by three authoritarian presidents after its independence in 1813. The first was José Gaspar Rodríguez de Francia (1766–1840), a theological scholar and a military leader. Doctor Francia, as he was universally known, in office from 1814 until his death in 1840 from natural causes, favored matriarchal Guaraní norms and set sociocultural precedent in Latin America. Francia was succeeded by businessman-politician Carlos Antonio López (1792–1862). Lopez's presidential term extended from 1844 until his death, also from natural causes, in 1862. Carlos Antonio López in turn was succeeded by his son, Francisco Solano López (1826–1870). The last of Paraguay's trio of authoritarian chief executives, Solano López led the nation to the brink of destruction; he ruled from 1862 until his death in 1870 at the hands of Brazilian soldiers.

Postindependence, Doctor Francia made Paraguay a hermit state in order to protect it from the designs of its large and powerful neighbors, Argentina and Brazil—and from European nations bent on exploiting its natural resources. Francia was likewise determined that the moneyed White, or Creole, elite of his country should not rise to dominance, as was the case elsewhere in Latin America. To achieve this goal, he decreed that Paraguayans were forbidden to marry within their own ethnic group. The extraordinary measure had the effect of intensifying *mestizaje*, the condition of being of mixed race, in Paraguay. The decree also caused many Paraguayans to live in free union until the time of Francia's death. That in turn had the effect of benefiting Paraguayan women. Unable to celebrate a traditional Catholic Church wedding, they avoided being bound by the complex of Christian norms and laws fostering patriarchy.

Doctor Francia's experiment in social engineering was odd, even bizarre, by Western Hemisphere standards. Yet El Supremo, as Francia was also known, knew his people. His race-mixing decree played to the Guaraní norm of matriarchy, which defined descent through the female line. Such societies regard women as coequal with men. Francia's anti-marriage measure also had relevance to the Guaraní custom of fostering peace with potential enemies by giving them their women in either marriage or concubinage. For example, when Domingo Martínez de Irala appeared among them in 1535, tribal leaders sent him six wives. The Spaniard happily accepted his indigenous spouses and fathered many children with them. His wives, in turn, schooled the Spaniard in the Guaraní language and customs.

Among the matriarchal Guaraní, women possessed property in such a way that they were not beholden to spouses or other male relatives. Thus, they wielded sociopolitical and economic influence not seen in other indigenous or European cultures. Over the centuries Guaraní matriarchal values were transferred to Paraguayan women of all races and classes, values that Francia's anti-Creole policies helped promote. Over time, Paraguayan women even came to be viewed as superior to their spouses in numerous areas of life. This led anthropologist Barbara Potthast-Jutkeit to characterize Paraguay as "a country of women."[1]

How is it, then, one might logically ask, that Paraguay's most notable female figure is not Paraguayan but rather the Irishwoman Eliza Lynch? The answer to this additional curious fact about Paraguay is bound up in the country's nineteenth-century history.

THE EARLY LIFE OF ELIZA LYNCH

Eliza Lynch was twelve years old in 1845 when Ireland's potato harvest failed. The result was a years-long famine known to the Irish as the Great Hunger. It ultimately killed a million Irish and forced another million to emigrate. But for the potato famine the life of Eliza Lynch would likely have been pleasant and uneventful. The daughter of John Lynch, a physician, and Jane Lloyd Lynch, of a family well known in British Admiralty circles, she and her family formed part of the upper middle class in the town of Charleville, in south-central Ireland. Charleville lay at the center of one of Ireland's richest agricultural districts. In 1846, the second year of the spreading famine, a cholera epidemic struck Charleville, claiming the life of John Lynch. Jane Lloyd Lynch and her four children fell into poverty and soon took refuge with relatives living in England. Not long after that Jane Lynch sent her eldest daughter, Eliza, to live with an aunt and uncle living in France, in the seaside village of Boulogne-sur-Mer, across the English Channel and just south of Calais. William Boyle Crooke was a retired British naval officer married to Eliza Lloyd Crooke. Eliza Lynch was in fact named after the wife of W. B. Crooke. The family enrolled Eliza Lynch in a local school, where she became fluent in French.

By age seventeen Eliza Lynch had matured into a graceful young woman, tall and curvaceous and possessed of a vivacious personality. She was also headstrong. Unfortunately, those qualities combined to spell trouble of a romantic nature. During the early months of 1850, schoolgirl Eliza Lynch met and fell in love with a thirty-four-year-old French army officer named Xavier Quatrefages. On June 3, 1850, she and Quatrefages eloped across the English Channel to the village of Folkstone, Kent, where they were married in a civil ceremony. Their witnesses were Eliza's mother and a civilian friend of the groom. Before many weeks had passed the young bride found herself posted with her husband to a dusty military base in Algeria. Not long thereafter, Eliza Lynch understood that her marriage to Quatrefages had been an awful mistake.

Little is known of the three years Eliza Lynch lived with her French husband in North Africa. Years later she wrote that her health suffered while living there. Beyond that, it is clear the couple's relationship had soured. To her dismay Eliza discovered that in the heat of their elopement Quatrefages had not requested permission to marry from his military superiors. Nor did he inform the French army about his marriage following the couple's return from England. Whether he did these things intentionally is not known. What is known is that he never introduced Eliza Lynch as his wife; hence under French law they were not married. That in turn meant that in the eyes of all who knew the couple Eliza Lynch was nothing more than the mistress of Xavier Quatrefages. After three stormy years of living in humiliation in rural Algeria, Eliza Lynch left him and returned to Europe to live with her mother, who by then lived in Paris with family friends.

Upon arriving in Paris, nineteen-year-old Eliza Lynch found herself living in a state of near poverty. And by then she was no longer marriageable. In terms of nineteenth-century Victorian social discourse, she was "damaged goods" in the marriage market. Still, things could have been worse. She was young, beautiful, unattached, and living in the world's most exciting city. While records are lacking on her activities during the latter half of 1853, it is known that Eliza Lynch briefly became part of Parisian salon culture. There was always a place for decorative young women at elegant social gatherings in the Paris of 1853, a city in full flower under Emperor Napoleon III. At the time when Eliza Lynch first lived there, Paris was modernizing at breakneck speed, becoming the place of sweeping boulevards and elegant buildings, of flowers and fountains that the world knows today. There was excitement in the air too, as allies France and Great Britain readied their armies to fight Russia in the Crimean War (1853–1856). Within that heady setting Eliza Lynch appeared to have made the acquaintance of Princess Mathilde Bonaparte, the daughter of Jérôme Bonaparte, brother of Napoleon Bonaparte. In her youth Princess Mathilde had been engaged to marry a second cousin named Louis-Napoleon, the French politician who later had himself proclaimed Napoleon III.

Mathilde Bonaparte was thirty-four years old when she befriended Eliza Lynch. She had much in common with the younger woman. Both had fled unhappy marriages, both were exceptionally attractive, and both loved the rarefied atmosphere of Parisian high culture and flourished in it. Salon culture of the day featured conversation with luminaries from the world of art, music, literature, and the theater. Men and women of the European aristocracy were always present at the most elevated salons, as were members of the international diplomatic community. Such were the social gatherings hosted by women like Mathilde Bonaparte. A photograph of Eliza Lynch, perhaps taken on her birthday, November 19, 1855, shows a happy, smiling young woman dressed as a peasant girl of Provence, her long hair braided and decorated with ribbons (see figure 3.1). It was likely the outfit she wore when she turned heads at a salon hosted by Princess Mathilde—or it might have been the costume she wore a few weeks later at a New Year's gala at the Tuileries Palace, hosted by Emperor Napoleon III and Empress Eugénie. That was the night Eliza Lynch met Francisco Solano López, son of the Paraguayan president and future leader of his nation.

Much had changed for Solano López and Paraguay since he first commanded troops as a teenager in early 1846. During the Platine War (1851–1852), Brazil and Argentina had vied for influence over Paraguay and Bolivia, resulting in the overthrow of Argentine dictator Juan Manuel de Rosas. The Argentine Confederation quickly recognized Paraguayan independence, as did Britain, France and the United States. Still, that did not mean Paraguay's future was secure. The country remained strategically important for both Argentina and Brazil. Paraguayan independence continued to be at risk. That was why in 1853 President Carlos Antonio López dispatched his eldest son to Europe on an important diplomatic mission.

Minister Plenipotentiary Francisco Solano López, then twenty-five, and an entourage of forty arrived in Southampton, England, on September 14, 1853. The party traveled with an unlimited line of credit provided by Solano López's father. Those considerable moneys were to be spent on advanced weaponry and anything else deemed useful in improving Paraguay's defense infrastructure. While in Britain, Solano López commissioned the construction of a state-of-the-art warship to be named the *Tacuarí*, and he hired dozens of military experts, engineers, and craftsmen who would travel to Paraguay to assist in military modernization. He and his group were so impressed with England's rail lines that he arranged to have a railroad built at home. The Paraguayan delegation was also enthusiastic about snow, which they experienced for the first time during their visit. While in England Solano López was granted an audience with Queen Victoria and Prince Albert. Then in late December he and his group traveled to Paris, where he was warmly received by Napoleon III. The French emperor invited López to be his guest at the city's New Year's Day parade and to attend a gala to be held three days later at his residence, Tuileries Palace. Between the parade and the gala, Francisco Solano López and his fellow Paraguayans went to the circus on two consecutive evenings and spent an entire day visiting the city's zoo.

Figure 3.1. Eliza Lynch, circa 1855

Eliza Lynch almost certainly met Solano López at the Tuileries Palace ball, where hundreds of revelers attended the glittering event hosted by the emperor and his wife. It is possible that Lynch and López were introduced by Paraguay's chargé d'affaires in France, Juan José Brizola. Their first encounter must have been electric. Eliza Lynch had every reason to be impressed with López. Though short in stature he was handsome and possessed a commanding presence. She learned that he was the chosen heir to the presidency of his country, as well as a general officer in the Paraguayan army. He spoke passable French, had winsome and friendly eyes, and was exceedingly charming. And most important for a cash-strapped young woman adrift in the world, Francisco Solano López was immensely wealthy.

When López met Eliza Lynch he could scarcely believe his eyes. Before him stood a beautiful, statuesque, and elegant woman of twenty who spoke perfect French and appeared to be on speaking terms with everyone at the ball. He likely had learned from Brizola that she was separated from her husband and therefore available. Solano López had met and slept with many women. But never had he encountered one like this.

Over their first few hours together Francisco Solano López and Eliza Lynch seemingly made unspoken decisions based on differing calculations but ending in the same place: they would cast their lots with each other. That meant she would have, if not marriage, a fascinating and powerful man of apparently unlimited wealth to protect her. Solano López would have not only the most ravishing female on the Paris social circuit but someone potentially useful in helping enlighten his backwater nation—and perhaps him as well. Thus began the fateful relationship between Francisco Solano López and Eliza Alicia Lynch.

Members of the Paraguayan delegation were aghast when their leader began his love affair with Eliza Lynch. When Francisco Solano López was not closeted with Madame Lynch she was at his side. López instructed members of his group not to mention the presence of Eliza Lynch in their official correspondence. Lieutenant Rómulo Yegros, who had been keeping a journal of the mission, was more than happy to comply. On January 14, 1854, Yegros suspended work on his diary noting that "an inflamed carbuncle on my wrist has forced me to stop writing."[2] An "inflamed carbuncle" would be one of the less scathing terms used by members of the Paraguayan establishment when alluding to Eliza Lynch. Yet despite her frosty reception by López's colleagues, Eliza Lynch soon brought her influence to bear on the Paraguayans. Operating with an unlimited budget provided by her lover, she had the delegation's gaudy military uniforms toned down. And she had stylish wool suits made for Solano López, which observers said compared favorably with those worn by England's Prince Albert. It was also apparent to all that the

Paraguayan chief of mission loved appearing in public with Eliza Lynch. Not only did she tower over him by at least five inches but she was always the most striking female present in any mixed group. He relished other men's envious looks when he strolled down Parisian boulevards with his lover on his arm.

The couple traveled to Rome in April 1854, and while there López successfully established diplomatic relations between Paraguay and the Vatican—to a point. The pope refused him an audience when he learned the South American was traveling with a woman who was not his wife. It was likely during their stay in Rome that Eliza became pregnant with the couple's first child. Upon their return to Paris, López installed her in the Paraguayan consulate. Mid-1854 found the two in negotiations with her erstwhile husband Xavier Quatrefages. Eliza desperately wanted a divorce from the Frenchman so she could marry Solano López. The Paraguayan seemingly had other ideas. After months of negotiations Quatrefages signed a document renouncing any claims to property owned by Eliza Lynch at that time or at any time in the future. Once the agreement was notarized, on October 19, 1854, the Paraguayan delegation returned home. Eliza Lynch was seven months pregnant when she boarded a Buenos Aires–bound passenger liner at Bordeaux. A day later, on November 11, López and his party followed her on the newly commissioned gunboat *Tacuarí*.

Francisco "Panchito" López was born to Eliza Lynch in Buenos Aires in January 1855. Those attending the birth were her English maid Susan, a Spanish servant named Vicente Montes, and her French hairdresser Henri Castaing. Eight weeks after the birth of his son, Solano López sent an army officer to escort Eliza and her party to Asunción. When their boat left the Plata estuary it made its way northward, up the Paraná River, stopping briefly at Rosario four days into the trip to board passengers and to take on fuel. Rosario stood at the edge of the Argentine Pampas . Then the riverboat continued northward for another two weeks, eventually reaching Corrientes, at the confluence of the Paraguay and Paraná Rivers. Along the way the vegetation became increasingly tropical. Vast marshlands teeming with wildlife extended into the distance and lay on either side of the river. Travelers were beset by plagues of mosquitoes and other stinging insects. At Corrientes the Paraná turned northeast, extending along the southern border of Paraguay, eventually turning northward into Brazil. From Corrientes the Paraguay River bore Eliza and her party another 180 miles farther north. At last Asunción came into view. A small group awaited the travelers at dockside.

AN IRISHWOMAN IN PARAGUAY

Francisco Solano López had likely not prepared Eliza Lynch for what awaited her. First there was Asunción, a sepia-colored town of twenty thousand at the edge of a mud flat on the eastern shore of the Paraguay River. Most of its houses were of a single story, with only the church steeple adding relief to the humdrum landscape. The reception given to Eliza and Panchito was disappointing as well. Solano López was there, anxious to receive his mistress and their infant son. Eliza's brother John Lynch was there also. Formerly a British naval officer, John Lynch had been named by Solano López second-in-command of the *Tacuarí*. A few army officers were also present. Notably absent, though, was any other member of the López family. Eliza Lynch would soon learn that her presence in Asunción was welcomed neither by Solano López's family nor by any other member of Paraguay's social and political elite. In fact, they detested her.

Members of Paraguay's European delegation had amply informed the country's leaders about Eliza Lynch. She was, by their account, a courtesan Solano López became infatuated with while in Paris. They said he gave her large sums of money that she spent with reckless abandon. Even worse, she was not only married to a Frenchman but pregnant with a child she insisted was fathered by Solano López. While López's parents had always turned a blind eye to their son's womanizing, this was simply too much. In the words of Solano López's mother, Juana Carrillo, the presence of Eliza Lynch "hostilized" the decent families of Paraguay's capital. "She has sold her body in every brothel in Europe," opined Spanish-born Purificación de Bermejo, a close friend of Paraguay's first lady. Benigno López, younger brother of Solano López, referred to Eliza Lynch as his brother's concubine. And straitlaced US minister to Paraguay Charles A. Washburn referred to her as "an imported Jezebel."[3]

Hostility toward Eliza Lynch reached its peak a year after her arrival in Asunción. Solano López had asked her to host the spouses of a French delegation in connection with the inauguration of a new town called New Burdeos, to be populated by French immigrants. The town site was on the Paraguay River a few miles north of Asunción. López and other dignitaries rode upriver on horseback while their ladies traveled there by riverboat. When Eliza Lynch, elegantly dressed in an apple-green silk dress, emerged on deck to join the women for lunch, one of them turned to another and said, "If I had known this evil woman was here, I would not have come." Madame Cochelet, the wife of the diplomat heading the French mission, said in a voice all could hear, "It is an experience for a memoir to be hosted by an Irish courtesan." Meanwhile the women arranged themselves so their hostess had no place to sit. At that Eliza Lynch called for the luncheon to be served. When the steward and his assistants arrived with the food, she ordered them to throw it over the side. Then, gazing at Cochelet, she said evenly, "And it shall be written in my memoir that I refused to serve cats at my table." Later, when Eliza described the event to Solano López, he laughed uproariously. According to foreigners living in Asunción, the riverboat incident "turned the social tide in favor of Eliza Lynch." The vignette was told and retold throughout Paraguay, always accompanied by laughter and a sense of admiration for the elegant companion of the president's eldest son.[4]

Eliza Lynch was actually far too busy building wealth to be fazed by the vicious gossip and personal affronts of Paraguay's upper class. Solano López had given her free rein to undertake projects beneficial to Paraguay—and to the two of them as well. Within days of her arrival in Asunción in May 1855 she deposited the immense sum of £5,000 in gold in the national treasury. Then, with a business partner named Captain Francisco Fernández, she applied the money to mortgage lending that yielded an annual profit of 12 to 15 percent. She found other business associates and with them began to trade in tobacco and cattle. President Carlos Antonio López granted her a monopoly over textiles and imported clothing. As Eliza earned money for herself and her family, she began investing it in real estate. Over ten years she bought twenty-three lots in downtown Asunción with an eye to eventually having "tall buildings with large shopping areas" constructed. Her goal was likely to build a shopping center modeled on Le Bon Marché, the world's first department store, which opened in Paris in 1852. If Paris had the first department store, she likely reasoned, why shouldn't Asunción have the second?

During her first year in Asunción, Eliza Lynch flung herself into two other notable projects. The first was the creation of a national theater, a task she seemingly accomplished at lightning speed. The theater was inaugurated on November 4, 1855, with a well-attended production of *El Valle de Andorra*, a zarzuela (operetta) directed by Spanish playwright and conductor Ildefonso Bermejo, who had been hired by Solano López while on his European tour. Her second project involved the decoration of her new house in the center of Asunción. Spacious and endowed with a large interior patio ideal for hosting social gatherings, the mansion on Fábrica de Balas Street would serve as both a home for Eliza and her family and a venue suitable for receptions and other such events for visiting dignitaries. No such place had been available in Paraguay prior to her arrival there. There at her elegantly furnished home, she hosted many foreign officials, the first of whom was Brazilian diplomat José María da Silva Paranhos (later Viscount of Rio Branco). So successful was the April 1856 formal gathering organized for Paranhos that Eliza Lynch quickly became an unofficial diplomat for Paraguay. The Brazilian was enchanted by the accomplished and elegant twenty-one-year-old who hosted him. His friendship would prove invaluable to Eliza Lynch and her children fourteen years later, at the end of the War of the Triple Alliance, known in Paraguay as the Great War.

By August 1856 Eliza Lynch was involved in two new projects. The first involved helping to upgrade furnishings in Paraguay's presidential residence. The second centered on establishing a place where foreigners living in the national capital could gather to socialize and relax. Known as the City Club, it became the venue where men making up the town's small international community could network, drink imported whiskey, smoke cigars, and read the only English-language newspaper permitted in Paraguay, the *Standard*, which was published in Buenos Aires.

Eliza Lynch's institution-building activities were interrupted on August 6, 1856, when she gave birth to a daughter named Corinne Adelaide, her second child with Solano López. Her recovery did not take long. By August 18 she was back at work, placing a large order with purchasing agents located in Buenos Aires, Paris, London, Edinburgh, and Dublin. Among the items ordered were electroplated knives and forks, two dinner services, one for eighteen place settings and the other for twenty-four place settings, five silver trays, two size 1 ball gowns (one pink and one white) embroidered with flowers and feathers, and two ladies' sidesaddles of French design and adorned with flowers. These items, along with numerous pieces of museum-quality furniture destined for the presidential residence, won the admiration of foreign visitors to Paraguay's capital. At the end of the War of the Triple Alliance, that furniture was looted by Argentine soldiers and placed in their country's presidential residence. It can be seen there today.

Perhaps the most important contribution that Eliza Lynch made to Paraguay during the decade she lived there prior to the country's Great War was at the level of popular culture. Because the country had been kept in isolation for so long during the Francia years, many refinements common in other Latin American nations had not been introduced there. Eliza Lynch brought the first piano, for example, to Paraguay. When she hosted a formal event at her home, ordinary Paraguayans passing by in the street were enchanted by the ethereal sounds produced by another musical instrument previously unknown to them: the modern European harp, which she also introduced to the country. Paraguayan musicians soon made the harp integral to their national music and became virtuoso players of the instrument.

Eliza Lynch also had a stylistic effect on Paraguayan women, rich and poor alike. Madame Lynch, as she had come to be addressed, always appeared in public dressed in the latest European fashions, and with her hair coiffed in the French manner by her hairdresser Henri. When she ventured out on horseback she usually did so riding astride, to the admiration of ordinary women and to the horror of elite women. And whereas women of the Paraguayan upper class usually let themselves go after childbirth, often becoming obese, Eliza Lynch regained her figure quickly after giving birth. Everything about her caught the attention of Paraguayan women. Like it or not they all began following her example. Women in the country started moving away from the traditional way of wearing their hair pulled back in a bun. By the early 1860s even women in the president's family had begun asking her advice on fashion. In short, Eliza Lynch was an object of study and contemplation, as well as of endless speculation among Paraguayan women. Men and women alike stopped and gazed at her when she ventured outside her mansion, dressed and made up to perfection, riding astride with regal bearing and towering above most of the men making their way on horseback through the muddy streets of Asunción.

Paraguay was flourishing at the midpoint of the nineteenth century. The nearly twenty-year program of opening the country to the outside world that had begun under Carlos Antonio López had at last started to bear fruit. Exports of cattle, tobacco, and cotton soared, along with those of the country's most lucrative product, yerba maté. The vitamin-rich tea brewed from the yerba maté tree, which was indigenous to Paraguay, was a dietary mainstay throughout the Southern Cone. Over 350 European craftsmen and professionals, most of them British, had been brought to the country to hasten its modernization. By 1860 the country's first railroad, inaugurated a year earlier, snaked southward along the east side of the Paraguay River, toward Corrientes in Argentina.

Solano López and Eliza Lynch also flourished during those years. Over their time in Asunción a routine developed between them by which they lived together with their children in the house on Fábrica de Balas Street. At the end of his workday López traveled there to have dinner with Eliza and their children. He relaxed afterward, played with the children, and then retired with his consort. López rose every morning at four, departing by a side door at five, riding to military headquarters where he met first with his security chief and then with his commanders. Eliza's day was spent dealing first with the children and then with her business ventures. The year 1860 witnessed her supervising construction of a lavish country retreat thirty miles south of Asunción at a spot called Patiño Cué. The mansion was close to the new rail line, at a scenic spot where steep hills rose above it to the east. Patiño Cué was also a place of pilgrimage, where Paraguayans visited a chapel built near a cave where Saint Thomas the Apostle was believed to have once dwelled. Farther east, beyond the hills, lay the village of Paraguarí, where a hundred years before Jesuit fathers had supervised a Guaraní *reducción*, or settlement, having extensive fields and orchards, and thirty thousand head of cattle. Eliza Lynch was content. As of 1860 she had borne Solano López two additional sons, Enrique and Federico Carlos. Their father had recognized all four of the couple's children at baptism. By mid-1860 she was pregnant again, with the couple's fifth child, Carlos Honorio, who was born on March 14, 1861.

Francisco Solano López achieved fame in 1859. That year his father designated him minister mediator tasked with helping end civil strife between Argentine caudillo Justo José Urquiza and president of the Argentine Federation Bartolomé Mitre. Theirs was a long-standing conflict that diplomats from France and Britain had been unable to help end. But Solano López, with what one historian described as "deftness, psychological insight, and perfect timing in the management of powerful personalities involved," brought Mitre and Urquiza together in signing the Pact of San Carlos in December 1859. A grateful Urquiza awarded his sword to López. Soon after that, admiring women of Buenos Aires showered Solano López with roses during a ceremony honoring his achievement.[5]

By early 1862 construction on a new presidential palace for Paraguay was well underway in Asunción. It was being built on choice riverfront property given to Solano López by his godfather, wealthy landowner Lázaro de Roxas y Andrada. The gift was at once magnanimous and full of meaning for the presidential family. Its members knew, as many outside the family suspected, that Lázaro de Roxas y Andrada was in fact the father of Francisco Solano López.

Carlos Antonio López had married Juana Carrillo on July 22, 1826, two days before the birth of Francisco Solano. Roxas y Andrada had apparently impregnated Juana Carrillo and then promised Carlos Antonio López his patronage if he would salvage the girl's honor by marrying her. That would have explained Roxas de Andrada's kindness to the López family over the years. It also would have explained the fact that Solano López did not resemble his four younger brothers and sisters. Benigno López, especially, was resentful when his father designated Francisco Solano as his successor to the presidency. The hostility between Solano López and his siblings explains, at least in part, his willingness to bring the exotic creature Eliza Lynch to live in their midst and to show them up as the narrow provincials they were. Finally, the suspect parentage of Francisco Solano López and the lifelong familial animosity it generated goes far toward explaining how a deranged Solano López could threaten the lives of his brothers and sisters, and even his mother, over the course of the War of the Triple Alliance.

Paraguayan president Carlos Antonio López became ill in early 1862, and by midyear it was clear that his death was near and that his eldest son would soon succeed him. For Eliza Lynch that meant her eight years of living away from the public eye was at an end. She might have hoped that once Solano López became president, he would find a way to have her previous marriage annulled and then marry her. In any event, the illness of the senior López permitted Eliza Lynch to adopt the public persona she had long been denied. April 1862 found her in Buenos Aires hosting a dinner for the British minister to Argentina. According to M. G. Mulhall, editor of the *Standard*, the fact that she was the only woman present made the dinner doubly interesting. Four months later Eliza Lynch and Solano López hosted a giant party for the people of Asunción. As members of the city's elite enjoyed themselves in the recently constructed and elegant Club Nacional, and in several homes owned by members of the López family, four thousand ordinary citizens, all in high spirits, partied at the new train station and in the city's central plaza, where a large tent had been erected to protect them from the rain. After midnight their hosts appeared at the train station, where they spent an hour dancing and mingling with the crowd.

Eliza Lynch loved parties. Two months after the death of Carlos Antonio López, on September 10, 1862, she organized a masked ball for which she prescribed the costumes to be worn by top government officials. At the time of the ball Francisco Solano López had been in the presidential office for two months, unanimously elected to the post by Congress just two days after his father's death. He was at Eliza's side at the ball, accompanied by the couple's three eldest sons. Eliza, who had a good sense of humor, was richly costumed as Elizabeth I, England's Virgin Queen. The masked ball was a kind of coming-out party for Eliza Lynch. According to one person who attended, "She provoked shock both of admiration and stupor, admiration for her elegance and beauty, her garb and gait, which were that of a woman from a wonderful and unknown universe."[6] Not all were so charitable. In early 1863 a Paraguayan wrote the following to a friend living abroad:

> Until a short time ago she did not appear in public, but now does so brazenly and even speaks at banquets. If you want to do well, these days you're forced to worship this great whore who accompanies the President.[7]

The most stupendous fiesta ever seen in Paraguay was organized by Eliza Lynch to honor Solano López on the occasion of his thirty-seventh birthday, July 24, 1863. It was a party given not so much for the elite as for the people of Paraguay. In that sense it was a populist celebration for Guaraní-speaking Paraguay, given as much for them as for their beloved leader. The celebration continued for fifty-six days. Horse races and rodeos were featured on weekends, with circuses and puppet shows given for the children. During weekends bands played until midnight in the central plaza. Copious amounts of food and drink were always present. Solano López and Eliza Lynch made frequent appearances among the revelers. Public drunkenness and acts of violence were rare. An English military engineer in Paraguay's army, George Thompson, was impressed by the pacific nature of Paraguay's ordinary citizens. In his experience crime was rare in the country. Every family owned its own farmland, which yielded abundant crops of every sort. Thompson doubtless mused on these things as he enjoyed festivities surrounding the seemingly endless birthday celebration honoring Paraguay's new president. At that moment, he wrote, "The mass of the people were perhaps the happiest in existence."[8]

Sadly, though, Paraguay's early "golden years" soon came to an end. Within two years the country would be engulfed in war. Five years after that, at war's end, nearly all the men and boys who celebrated the thirty-seventh birthday of Francisco Solano López would be dead. So too would a substantial number of the women and children who had attended the gala honoring him.

THE WAR OF THE TRIPLE ALLIANCE

Many historians have offered explanations as to how small Paraguay fell into a war claiming the lives of half its population and leading to the loss of something approaching half its territory. Some argue that the country's small size and strategic location, between large and predatory neighbors, made its staggering losses inevitable. Others venture that turbulent Rio Platine politics inevitably drew Paraguay into war. Still others hold that the war was solely the responsibility of Francisco Solano López. It was he, they point out, who had his national congress declare war on Brazil and Argentina, thereby inviting catastrophe. By another metric, however, the country's mixed-blood Guaraní-speaking majority can be faulted for their docile inclination toward authoritarian rule. Three centuries before Paraguay's Great War, and up to it, the Guaraní and their descendants had placed their faith in trusted leaders, the last of whom proved unworthy of such support.

The immediate cause of the War of the Triple Alliance was the occupation of northern Uruguay by Brazil in October 1864. Brazil had always aimed to possess the land lying east of the Uruguay River extending south to the Plata estuary, the *banda oriental*, or "east bank," of the Uruguay River. But Argentina and Uruguay, by then constitutional republics, could not tolerate the conquest of strategically positioned Uruguay by Portuguese-speaking, slave-owning, imperial Brazil. Francisco Solano López, whose country had shown solidarity with Uruguay since the time of Doctor Francia, rushed to the aid of turbulent Uruguay. When Uruguay's president, Anastasio Cruz Aguirre, sent López a frantic plea for help against the Brazilians in late 1864, Solano López responded, "I will help you reclaim your land." At that moment López possessed a well-trained and well-equipped fifty thousand-man army, the largest in the Southern Cone. In November 1864 he had Paraguay's Congress declare war on Brazil. López immediately closed the Paraguay River to Brazil and dispatched a three thousand-man force northward to occupy disputed territory in the Brazilian state of Mato Grosso. Shortly thereafter he sent another twenty thousand troops marching southward toward Uruguay. Because their route took them across the Argentine province of Misiones, and because Argentina denied him permission to cross its territory, López had his Congress declare war on Argentina as well, on March 18, 1865. The declaration of war shocked the Argentines. It was obvious to all that Paraguay had no chance of winning the war. All, that is, save Francisco Solano López.

War fever gripped Paraguay during 1864–1865. Eliza Lynch was caught up in the excitement. The night Paraguay's Congress declared war on Argentina, a crowd gathered at her house, where the president's consort gave a patriotic speech ending with a ringing declaration that she was a Paraguayan. At that moment she was nine months pregnant with her seventh child, a son, born that same night. The infant's parents named him Miguel Mariscal López, in recognition of the fact that Congress had just appointed Solano López mariscal, or supreme commander, of the Paraguayan military.

Paraguay's Great War was lost almost as soon as it started. In mid-1865 Solano López ordered his twenty thousand best-trained and best-equipped troops into Uruguay, on a route that eventually took them along the southwestern edge of Brazil's state of Rio Grande do Sul. As the Paraguayan force moved southeast toward Uruguay, representatives of Brazil, Argentina, and Uruguay met in Buenos Aires and on May 1, 1865, signed the Triple Alliance Treaty against Paraguay. Little more than a month later, on June 11, 1865, López lost the greater part of his naval fleet in a battle on the Paraná River below the Argentine town of Corrientes. Brazilian ironclads had little trouble sinking Paraguay's wooden-hulled warships in an engagement called the Battle of Riachuelo. Less than a month later, in mid-July 1865, a combined Brazilian-Argentine force surrounded and destroyed the Paraguayan expeditionary force, which was trapped in the Brazilian town of Uruguayana on the eastern bank of the Uruguay River and just north of the Brazilian-Uruguayan border. Paraguayan troops who were not killed in the battle were either forced to become part of the allied army or were sent to Brazil as slaves. Uruguayan troops did not fight in either the Battle of Riachuelo or the Battle of Uruguayana. The country's own turbulent politics kept Uruguay from participating in the War of the Triple Alliance.

The two Paraguayan losses, Riachuelo and Uruguayana, made it impossible for Solano López to mount any new offensive against the allies. Thus, from mid-1865 until the war's end nearly five years later, the War of the Triple Alliance was a defensive struggle with Paraguayan forces forever in retreat.

During 1866–1867 López and his army halted allied forces at the Paraguay River fortress of Humaitá, located 140 miles south of Asunción. Eliza Lynch and the couple's five sons (daughter Corrine Adele had died shortly after birth) spent much of 1866–1867 with López at Humaitá. Eliza's longtime companion Isadora Díaz, the wife of an army officer already slain in the war, accompanied the family and helped care for the children. Solano López had a sturdy house built for his family at Humaitá, safely removed from the constant bombardment of allied warships. At the end of most days the mariscal dined with his family, played with his children, and retired with his consort, as had been his custom in Asunción.

After the military reverses of mid-1865 Solano López grew increasingly suspicious of those around him. He fell into the habit of ordering the execution of anyone who angered him, including senior military officers who had served him loyally for years. Eliza Lynch became his only confidant. A function of the growing paranoia of Solano López was the fact that when he was with Eliza he spoke only in French, a language that no one around them understood. In 1866 Eliza Lynch became pregnant with the couple's eighth child, Leopoldo, who was born in February 1867. Two months after that, twenty-six-month-old Miguel Mariscal died in a cholera epidemic that swept both Humaitá and Asunción.

During this time, Paraguayans increasingly called for an end to the war. In May 1866, after many sons of the elite had died in the Battle of Tuyutí, López's mother traveled to Humaitá and begged López to sue for peace. Three months after that, during the interval between the Battles of Curuzú and Curupayty, in September 1866, López conferred with Bartolomé Mitre, commander of the Argentine forces and president of the Argentine Confederation. The Argentine asked López to enter into peace talks. López rejected his overtures. The year 1867 witnessed three peace initiatives. The first was undertaken by US minister to Paraguay Charles A. Washburn, the second by commander of the Brazilian forces Luiz de Alves de Lima e Silva (the Duke of Caxias), and the third and most intensive by the British minister in Buenos Aires, G. Z. Gould. Emperor Pedro II agreed to grant López the right to European exile in exchange for peace, this despite the fact that Pedro II detested the Paraguayan and wanted him dead. But in the end each peace initiative ended with Lopez's refrain, "We must go on and finish the war with honor . . . and I will never compromise."[9]

Paraguay's position deteriorated sharply in 1868. In February Brazilian ironclad ships passed Humaitá and shelled Asunción before retreating down past the river fortress. The shelling of Asunción had two important consequences. First, it accelerated talk in the capital of removing Solano López from military command. Second, it led to the evacuation of civilians from Humaitá. On March 3, under cover of darkness, López moved his family and some two thousand others, both soldiers and civilians, to the west side of the Paraguay River. It was a virtuoso feat carried out by Paraguayan troops severely weakened by three years of hard fighting, short supplies, and illness. At that moment the Paraguayan army had been reduced to fewer than twenty thousand, half of them elderly men and adolescent boys. Most of these troops were barefoot and clad in rags.

The retreat of Solano López to the swampy west side of the Paraguay River was a desperate measure. That was also true of the group's trek twenty miles northward through swamps and across numerous rivers and streams. On March 30, López and his party recrossed the Paraguay and traveled down its eastern shore to San Fernando, a swampy spot forty miles north of Humaitá. There, at what everyone soon called the "mud camp," López had a house built for his family on its only available patch of dry land. Everyone else set to work draining surrounding wetlands so barracks could be constructed.

Before long the mud camp passed from being an unpleasant home to a place of horror. In mid-1868 hundreds of shackled prisoners began arriving there as well. They were members of the Paraguayan government and of the country's elite, all charged with treason for having plotted against the mariscal. At that time Paraguay's legal code was based in part on a thirteenth-century Spanish code known as the Siete Partidas, according to which anyone charged with treason was questioned under torture and summarily executed following confession. From mid-1868 and well into 1869 police and security forces rounded up and jailed upward of a thousand people in and around Asunción, foreigners and native-born Paraguayans alike. All were charged with plotting to overthrow Francisco Solano López and sent to the mud camp, where they lived in utmost misery until being brought to trial. López created three tribunals, known as "councils of blood"—they were charged with trying and sentencing the prisoners, and having them executed. Two of the tribunals were headed by Paraguay's leading religious figures, Bishop Manuel Antonio Palacios and Father Fidel Maíz. Both priests extracted confessions by smashing fingers with wooden mallets and subjecting the accused to torture by the "Uruguayan pillory" (*cepo uruguayo*). Victims subjected to the *cepo uruguayo* were tied seated or in a kneeling position, with rifles placed under their knees and behind their arms. Then one or more rifles were laid across their necks and shoulders. They were left for hours in that position. Many of those charged were not accused of directly plotting against López, but seemingly had been arrested simply for opposing him. Many were arrested on the word of anonymous accusers, and a few simply at the whim of López. That was the case of Juliana Insfrán, the young wife of Colonel Francisco Martínez, the officer who surrendered Humaitá in July 1868. A furious Solano López had declared Martínez a traitor and had his wife arrested. During July 1868 Juliana Insfrán was tortured repeatedly and executed on August 4. The emaciated young soldier ordered to execute her by lance thrust was unable to kill the condemned woman cleanly, so he was forced to stab her repeatedly until she died. Among others executed at the mud camp were the husbands of Solano López's two sisters, shot by firing squad as their wives looked on. In early 1869 López authorized the torture and execution of his younger brother Benigno. He, along with his sisters and mother, had been arrested on treason charges. Some five hundred of those arrested were executed during the latter half of 1868. During that time Eliza Lynch protected her children from witnessing the nightmare unfolding around them.

In December 1868 López withdrew northward in the face of allied advances. He reestablished his headquarters at a spot called Lomas Valentinas, midway between Humaitá and Asunción. There he and a motley and poorly equipped force of five thousand were attacked by twenty-five thousand fresh and well-supplied Brazilian troops under the command of the Duke of Caxias, who had been ordered by Emperor Pedro II to risk his last man to end the war. When the Battle of Lomas Valentinas ended on December 21, Caxias learned that four thousand of his troops had died, including 78 percent of his officers. Sixty percent of the Paraguayan army died as well. That slaughter, coupled with the flight eastward of Solano López and two thousand survivors of the battle, apparently convinced Caxias that the war was over. Rather than pursuing and destroying López and his remaining forces, he occupied Asunción, declared the war ended, and asked to be relieved of his command. But the war was not over. As the Brazilians and their Argentine allies celebrated victory with a Te Deum in Asunción's cathedral, López reestablished his headquarters forty miles southeast of the national capital in the village of Piribebuy. There he rebuilt his army and awaited the enemy.

Foreign observers could scarcely believe the ferocity with which the Paraguayans fought. The new US minister to Paraguay, Martin T. McMahon, was present at Lomas Valentinas. McMahon was an Irish-born veteran of the US Civil War. No stranger to combat, he was one of the first recipients of the country's new award for military heroism under fire, the Congressional Medal of Honor. He later published an eyewitness account of the battle, writing that he had not seen more savage fighting in the US Civil War than that exhibited by Guaraní-speaking Paraguayan soldiers at the Battle of Lomas

Valentinas. He marveled at the way they hurled themselves on allied cavalry, armed with little more than lances and machetes. One such charge disoriented and turned back a far superior Brazilian force. McMahon watched as a group of Paraguayan women, led by Eliza Lynch, rescued a wounded officer who was at the point of being captured by the Brazilians. But it was Paraguayan child soldiers who impressed McMahon most: "They neither wept nor cried, nor asked for surgeons or attendants. At the end they would lie down and die as silently as they had suffered."[10]

Emperor Pedro II was furious when he learned the Duke of Caxias had permitted Solano López to escape, despite information reaching him that the Paraguayan force was virtually without weapons and made up mostly of elderly men and prepubescent boys. Pedro II ordered his new commander—his son-in-law, the Frenchman Comte d'Eau—to show no quarter to the enemy "until such time that injuries inflicted on allied forces by the Tyrant of Paraguay . . . are sufficiently avenged."[11] The Comte d'Eau complied with the order. When Brazilian troops overran the Paraguayans at the Battle of Piribebuy on August 12, 1869, Brazilian trumpets sounded the *degüello* (cut their throats). Seven hundred defenders died at Piribebuy, many of them young boys wearing false beards and painted-on mustaches. After the battle the Brazilian commander ordered his troops to cut the throats of two hundred prisoners and to burn alive several hundred wounded Paraguayan soldiers housed in a hospital. Solano López, his family, and a few hundred of his troops escaped Piribebuy. From there they fled northeast, into the Amambay Mountains. The pursuing Brazilian troops had no trouble following their route—it was littered with dead and dying men, women, and children.

The War of the Triple Alliance ended March 1, 1870, at a spot called Cerro Corá, in the Amambay Mountains of northeastern Paraguay. On that day López, his decimated army, and a handful of civilians calmly awaited the Brazilian attack. Francisco Solano López and his officers had taken a vow to die fighting, while Brazilian commander José Antônio Correia da Câmara had reserved for himself the honor of killing Francisco Solano López. Meanwhile Eliza Lynch focused on saving her children. She drilled them on how to say in Portuguese, "Don't kill me! My mother is a British citizen!" all the while huddled together with a Union Jack draped around their shoulders.

Francisco Solano López died not far from his family. Correia da Câmara trapped him at the bank of a small stream and lanced him in the abdomen. López was not killed outright and managed to pull himself into a sitting position. When Correia da Câmara ordered him to surrender his sword, López replied, "I die with my country!" At that a Brazilian soldier shot him dead. At about that same moment a Brazilian officer ordered fifteen-year-old Panchito López to surrender his sword. When the boy replied, "A Paraguayan colonel never surrenders," the officer laughed and shot him dead in front of his mother. When the fighting ended Eliza Lynch used a broken bayonet to dig the graves of Solano López and her eldest son.[12]

POSTWAR SPOILS: ELIZA LYNCH IN EXILE

Having survived Cerro Corá, Eliza Lynch turned to the struggle that filled the remainder of her life: finding the means of supporting herself, her four surviving sons, a foster daughter, and her companion Isadora Díaz. Her financial tribulations began even before departing Paraguay. The country was full of enemies who wanted to strip her of her possessions. Beyond that they were divided as to whether Eliza Lynch should be executed as a war criminal or merely expelled from the country.

After the Battle of Cerro Corá the family members of Francisco Solano López, escorted by Brazilian soldiers, made their way westward toward the Paraguay River. There a Brazilian gunboat awaited them at Concepción, a village 140 miles north of the capital. Two days after their arrival in Concepción a warship transported the bedraggled group downriver to Asunción. Eliza Lynch, her children, and her other dependents were accompanied by Solano López's mother and his two sisters. Solano López had ordered both shot just hours before the war ended but had been unable to carry out the executions of his sisters Inocencia and Rafaela, and his mother Juana Carrillo. On March 15, 1870, the ragged survivors of Paraguay's Great War reached the national capital.

As soon as Asunción learned that Eliza Lynch was present in the capital, women of the city's elite class presented an unsigned letter to the city's military governor. In it they demanded that Eliza Lynch "return the spoils stripped from so many victims." Luckily for her, the officer in charge of the Port of Asunción was her old friend and admirer, José María da Silva Paranhos. The Brazilian not only protected her from the angry elite women of Asunción but saw to it that she kept the personal funds that she had safeguarded throughout the war. Paranhos also ensured that she and her family reached Buenos Aires safely and from there were allowed to continue on to Europe. As soon as Eliza Lynch departed Paraguay, the country's new government passed a law confiscating property she had acquired there. The law contained a clause declaring Eliza Lynch to be "a monument of infamy and public scandal," and a warning that if she ever returned to Paraguay she would be tried as a war criminal.[13]

Four years later, in 1874, Eliza Lynch, then living in Paris, was surprised to receive a letter from Paraguay's president, Juan Bautista Gill, inviting her to return to Asunción. He promised that if she returned, his government would allow her to pursue her legal claims to her property there. Gill's plan was surely to seize Lynch upon arrival and force her to divulge the location of a treasure in gold rumored to be buried somewhere along the road leading to Cerro Corá. Despite warnings that Gill could not be trusted, Eliza Lynch accepted his offer and bravely if naively returned to Asunción, arriving there aboard the steamship *Cisne* on October 23, 1875. Unfortunately for President Bautista Gill, whatever plans he may have had for Eliza Lynch were spoiled when she arrived bearing a letter from the British consul in Buenos Aires, Lionel Sackville West, instructing the commander of a British gunboat anchored in port, the HMS *Cracker*, to protect her. In his letter Sackville West warned the ship's commander that Madame Lynch was in danger as long as she remained in the city. When the *Cisne* docked, Bautista Gill was further dismayed to see that as soon as Eliza Lynch made her appearance on the deck, she was greeted by hundreds of women gathered on the dock. They were friends and admirers who wanted to see and speak with her, or simply to touch her. The Paraguayan president spent four hours glumly watching the happy scene unfold, hidden from view in the harbormaster's watchtower. After hours of happy visits onboard the steamship, dozens of women surrounded and therefore protected Lynch as she walked through the streets of Asunción to a friend's house, where she spent the night. Many of the women flocking to see her were members of the non-elite, the "Little Gold Combs," or market women, who had revered the consort of Francisco Solano López and respected what she stood for. Late the next day, convinced that her life was in danger, she allowed her admirers to escort her back through town to the HMS *Cracker*, which departed immediately for Buenos Aires.

Reaching the Argentine capital in November 1875, Lynch paused long enough to write a long, angry, semi-autobiographical document titled *Exposition and Protest*. In it she denounced Bautista Gill as duplicitous and corrupt, going on to list the numerous properties she had purchased legally while living in Paraguay and for which she held notarized bills of sale. *Exposition and Protest* is a valuable document in that it contains many personal details about the life of Eliza Lynch. Perhaps its most telling sentence, though, in light of all that had gone before, was the sentence reading, "I had nothing to do with the politics or government of Francisco Solano López."[14]

Following her return to Europe, Eliza Lynch led a quiet life, most of it spent in Paris but punctuated by trips to England and Ireland. Then in her forties, she still turned heads when she passed in the street. In France she was usually addressed as "Madame la Mariscal." During one of her stays in England, Eliza Lynch renewed contact with members of her mother's family, the Lloyds—and, especially, with her young niece Maud Lloyd. Years later Maud Lloyd recalled spending long afternoons with her aunt, listening to stories about her life in Paraguay. From time to time during those visits Madame Lynch would pause to point out features of the country on a large map of Paraguay. At age seventeen Maud Lloyd became the daughter-in-law of Eliza Lynch, marrying her son of twenty-four, Enrique Solano López. Maud Lloyd remembered her aunt as a kind lady who never spoke ill of those who had wronged her:

> She rarely talked of the terrible things she had seen, or of the tragedies she had lived through. Nor did she give herself any importance because of her association with them. She never expressed any animosity against the people who had slandered her so bitterly.[15]

EPILOGUE

Eliza Lynch spent her last years living in a modest apartment on Boulevard Pereire in Paris. She died in her sleep there at age fifty-two, and was buried at the nearby Père Lachaise cemetery, near the spot where thirty-one years earlier she had first met Francisco Solano López. But Eliza Lynch did not rest in peace. Both before her death and afterward her critics and defenders published a steady stream of articles and books about her. First and perhaps most influential among the negative accounts was that of Argentine journalist Hector Varela. In 1870 Varela published a mildly pornographic best-selling biography of Lynch. Over a century later another of her unsympathetic biographers characterized Eliza Lynch as one of the world's wickedest women. Two widely read positive articles on Eliza Lynch appeared in the United States in 1870. They were written by US minister to Paraguay Martin T. McMahon. The US official depicted the companion of Francisco Solano López as a heroic survivor of the War of the Triple Alliance. In recent years Irish scholars Michael Lillis and Ronan Fanning published what stands as the definitive sympathetic biography of Eliza Lynch.

How should history judge Eliza Lynch? In Paraguay, at least, that question has been answered. A century after the War of the Triple Alliance, the dictator of Paraguay, General Alfredo Stroessner, rehabilitated Eliza Lynch. Stroessner had her designated his country's national heroine (*Heroína Nacional*). Her remains were exhumed and brought to Asunción, where they briefly reposed beside those of Solano López in the National Pantheon. However, when the Catholic Church objected that the couple had never married, her remains were reinterred on the eastern outskirts of Asunción in Recoleta Cemetery, not far from the grave of her second child, Corinne Adelaida, whom she and Francisco Solano López had buried there over a century earlier.

NOTES

1. Barbara Potthast-Jutkeit, ¿*"Paraíso de Mahoma" o "País de las Mujeres"?: El rol de la familia en la sociedad paraguaya* (Asunción, Paraguay: Instituto Cultural Paraguayo-Alemán, 1996), 17.
2. Michael Lillis and Ronan Fanning, *Calumnia: La historia de Eliza Lynch y la Guerra de la Triple Alianza*, trans. Gladys Croskey (Asunción, Paraguay: Santillana, 2009), 64.
3. Lillis and Fanning, *Calumnia*, 98ff.
4. Gilbert Phelps, *The Tragedy of Paraguay* (London: Charles Knight, 1975), 55–56; Lillis and Fanning, *Calumnia*, 103.
5. Phelps, *Tragedy of Paraguay*, 60; Michael Lillis and Renan Fanning, *The Lives of Eliza Lynch: Scandal and Courage* (Dublin: Gill & Macmillan, 2009), 88–89.
6. Lillis and Fanning, *Calumnia,* 116.
7. Phelps, *Tragedy of Paraguay*, 66.
8. Phelps, *Tragedy of Paraguay*, 185.
9. Lillis and Fanning, *Lives of Eliza Lynch*, 130.
10. Lillis and Fanning, *Lives of Eliza Lynch*, 135.
11. Lillis and Fanning, *Lives of Eliza Lynch*, 130–31.
12. Phelps, *Tragedy of Paraguay*, 257–58. According to Lillis and Fanning, *Lives of Eliza Lynch*, 156–57, the last words of López were, "I will not yield up my sword. I die with my sword and with my country."
13. Lillis and Fanning, *Lives of Eliza Lynch*, 263–66. Those governing Paraguay at the time accused Lynch of "the almost total annihilation of the Paraguayan people."
14. Lillis and Fanning, *Lives of Eliza Lynch*, 209.
15. Lillis and Fanning, *Lives of Eliza Lynch*, 202.

REFERENCES

Lillis, Michael and Ronan Fanning. *Calumnia. La historia de Eliza Lynch y la Guerra de la Triple Alianza*. Translated by Gladys Croskey. Asunción, Paraguay: Santillana, 2009.

———. *The Lives of Eliza Lynch: Scandal and Courage*. Dublin: Gill and Macmillan, 2009.

McMahon, Martin T. "Paraguay and Her Enemies." *Harpers New Monthly Magazine* 40, no. 237 (February 1870): 421–30.

———. "The War in Paraguay." *Harpers New Monthly Magazine* 40, no. 239 (April 1870): 633–47.

Nichols, Margaret. *The World's Wickedest Women*. London: Bounty Books, 1984.

Phelps, Gilbert. *The Tragedy of Paraguay*. London: Charles Knight & Company, 1975.

Potthast-Jutkeit, Barbara. *¿"Paraíso de Mahoma" o "País de las Mujeres"?: El rol de la familia en la sociedad paraguaya del siglo XIX*. Asunción, Paraguay: Instituto Cultural Paraguayo-Alemán, 1996.

Varela, Hector F. *Elisa Lynch*. Buenos Aires, 1934. First published 1870.

Wigham, Thomas L. *The Road to Armageddon: Paraguay Versus the Triple Alliance, 1866–1870*. Calgary: University of Calgary Press, 2017.

Chapter 4

Clorinda Matto de Turner, 1852–1909

INTRODUCTION

By the time her female-run printshop had been looted and burned down to the ground, Clorinda Matto de Turner knew that she would flee Peru. In 1895, the conservative leader Nicolás Piérola had seized power, a culmination of the Peruvian Civil War (1894–1895) that was sparked by the election as president of progressive Andrés Avelino Cáceres. Matto de Turner, long a Cáceres supporter, may have anticipated challenges ahead—but perhaps none so severe for her as her departure from Peru. A few days prior to the arson, soldiers had burst into her brother David's house in Lima, frightening his children and threatening David and Clorinda with imprisonment or worse. A doctor, David was no overt activist, but he and his sister had long supported the newly elected Cáceres. The soldiers dragged David away. Thanks to the intervention of a fellow doctor who recognized and vouched for him, he was released, and the soldiers were called off.

A power-hungry autocrat, Piérola had staged a bloody coup against President Cáceres and directed the elimination of all potential threats to his regime. Over one thousand Peruvians died in that contest for power, and more still were hounded for their allegiance to Cáceres. These included forward-thinking groups and people such as journalist, editor, novelist, and publisher Clorinda Matto de Turner. She was a longtime champion of justice, and her work highlighted the plight of women's and Indigenous people's education and rights. Given the bloody clashes for political control, Clorinda Matto de Turner was lucky to escape alive.

The ashes of La Equitativa, her short-lived feminist printing press, had hardly stopped smoldering when Matto de Turner went into voluntary exile—not that she had much choice. Once the toast of the nation, she would now work beyond Peruvian borders. How had it come to this? Not twenty years earlier, in 1877, in the thriving capital of Lima, Clorinda Matto de Turner was a writer on the rise. There, in the storied salon of feminist, novelist, and educator Juana Manuela Gorriti (1819–1892), and in the company of Lima's most innovative and progressive-minded literary talents, acclaimed authors celebrated the young writer for her clear-eyed views and burgeoning talent. They acknowledged Matto de Turner as one of their own—bent on nation building, justice, and reform—and ever ready to write such a vision into reality.

The writers gathered in her honor were each in their own way trying to both preserve and highlight a complex Latin American past and present. Ricardo Palma, for instance, deftly wove Peruvian history in his *Tradiciones*, a genre he developed that was "somewhere between history, legend and the short story—between fact and fiction."[1] The reality, however, was more stark. Nearly fifty years after Latin American independence from Spain and with it, the failure of Simón Bolívar's dream for Gran Colombia and a "United States" of Spanish South America, separate nations struggled into being and engaged in territorial disputes with each other. Conservatives and liberals vied for control, seizing power, each in turn pushing forward their agendas. By the 1880s, disputes played out around notions of order and progress, colored by liberal resistance to and conservative support of the Catholic Church. Such tensions both unearthed and glossed over severe challenges confronted by marginalized classes.

By the end of the nineteenth century, crisis and change marked the former colonies in dramatic fashion, at both the individual and state levels. Whether they were members of the European-descended elites, disenfranchised Indigenous laborers, or newly arrived immigrants seeking opportunity across the Atlantic, all former subjects of the Spanish Empire wrestled with their own status. Where did they fit in a modernizing world and state?

In print and in person, Clorinda Matto de Turner promoted the positivist argument that education for every Peruvian—including women and Indigenous people—not only was a moral good but also would speed national progress. Oppressive landholding and labor practices slowed Peruvian growth in the long run. She and her fellow progressives advocated for an educated populace that would build a thriving national economy and with it, a strong nation. Clorinda Matto de Turner highlighted corruption in the church and scandalous priestly behavior that preyed on Indigenous men and women already bowed by repression. She wove twin threads of justice and reform through most of her work. For her writings, and in particular her novels, she would pay dearly. Still, she rose to regional and transatlantic acclaim.

Clorinda Matto de Turner saw the destruction of her own press, but she rose from its ashes to continue her work beyond Peruvian borders. Like her mentor and fellow writer Juana Manuela Gorriti, she would be forced to endure exile until the end of her days. From her new home of Buenos Aires, and on her final voyage abroad—this time, a tour of Europe's educational institutions—Matto de Turner continued to write and offer a vision of and routes toward a more expansive, equitable world. She was never able to return home, but neither did she give up on promoting a progressive future. Hers was a truly modern vision of nationhood, with men and women across social classes joining forces to determine the destiny of their lives and of her beloved Peru.

TRACING SUPPRESSION IN PERU

In eighteenth-century Peru, Indigenous and mixed-descent men and women, including Tupac Amaru II and his wife Micaela Bastidas, helped spark early rebellion against unjust conditions and increasingly repressive practices. The Spanish had long extracted riches from South Americans, but with the implementation of the Bourbon reforms, taxes became even more burdensome to Indigenous Andeans. Tupac Amaru and Micaela Bastidas's bloody rebellion foreshadowed the end of the Spanish Empire in America. Captured, tortured, and finally executed, they did not live to see full-scale revolution catch on across the land, but their rallying cry resonated in the decades that followed.

Since the colonial heyday of the Potosí and Zacatecas silver booms that enriched and then bloated Spain's treasury, Indigenous peoples continued to work in the mines and elsewhere under repressive labor conditions. While the *mita*, or labor draft, ceased to exist formally in 1812, during and after Spanish rule many workers remained bound, by virtue of ethnicity and heritage, to mining and textile production well into the next decades. In late nineteenth-century Peru as elsewhere in Andean Spanish America, the plight of Indigenous workers, long bound to agricultural work, went largely ignored by an elite populace who profited from their labor.

During independence, Creoles—American-born White people like Simón Bolívar—drew from the support of marginalized peoples in pursuit of independence. But the high-flown ideals of the Liberator and other ruling elites who followed did not fully apply to them. Inequities and oppression abounded in newly independent Spanish America. Besides dangerous work in the mines, small workshops called *obrajes* persisted for years in the Andean economy. Worse than sweatshops, these factories employed Indigenous people to produce most of the textiles, especially woolen goods, in New Spain.

They endured long hours, horrific conditions, and minimal or withheld pay; none of that changed much after independence. *Obraje* workers were largely tethered to the economy as consumers: they could purchase necessary supplies, often at exorbitant prices, only from the company stores. During this time, a *pongo* system also reduced their circumstances: in exchange for use of a small plot for subsistence and cash crops, they owed their landlord several days' labor per week for its continued use.[2]

Traditional institutions and labor practices hindered reform. The Catholic Church continued to wield social influence even as the liberal-minded—including positivists—challenged spiritual authority and pushed for an expansion of education in the name of modernity. In another context, *gamonalismo*, the repression of Indigenous people by large landowners and merchants (known as *gamonales* in the Andean highlands) marked the political and economic disenfranchisement of Indigenous people. The *gamonales* employed a practice known as *enganche*—literally, to capture—to entice Indigenous laborers to leave their communities and work on haciendas. Once there, as they purchased supplies and living necessities from the landowners, they would find themselves increasingly indebted and unable to return home.[3] Nearly a century after independence, reform-minded writers finally called for a more equitable national vision for all Peruvians.

It was into this complex world, in the ancient Incan capital of Cusco, on November 11, 1852, that Grimanesa Martina Mato Usandivaras was born to parents of Spanish descent. Clorinda, as she came to be known, along with her mother Grimanesa Usandivaras, her father Ramón Mato, and her brothers, lived most of the time in the family hacienda in the town of Paullo Chico. There she played with Indigenous children and learned Quechua from them. She would later come to be known as Clorinda Matto, as she added an extra *t* to create the Quechua word "Matto." Her early years were untroubled as she roamed free to play, read, or boss around her two younger brothers.[4]

Clorinda experienced deep loss early in her life, and from a young age shouldered responsibility well beyond her years. When she was ten years old, her mother fell ill and died. Clorinda was then enrolled as a boarding student at what is known today as the Escuela Nacional de Educandas. There by the age of fourteen she began serving as school newspaper editor; she also wrote skits. Records indicate that as a student, she was exempt from paying fees, and that she took on a wide range of studies. This included classes in natural history, philosophy, and physics.[5] Despite the abrupt change in pace of learning, she quickly adapted to life at school and immersed herself in her studies. Encouraged by her female teachers, she proved to be a precocious student, successfully pursuing independent study.

When she was sixteen, Clorinda returned home to help her father care for her younger brothers. This must have been as much of a shock for her as it was to leave for school six years earlier. Yet she was privileged in this regard: in late nineteenth-century Peru, not all daughters of elite households enjoyed much education at all. Like most young women her age, she did not attend university. Tradition dictated that she either enter a convent or marry. Clorinda's inability to further her formal education, combined with her childhood experiences, likely sparked her desire to contribute to building a more just state with opportunities for all.

The economic boom and liberal reforms that Peru experienced under the government of President Ramón Castilla, in power for the better part of twenty years (1844–1863), meant improved social and economic conditions, but only for select sectors of society. By 1871, Clorinda had married a wealthy English doctor and entrepreneur, José Turner. She and her husband moved south to the small Andean town of Tinta in the same year as the formation of the progressive party, the Partido Civil. Though removed from liberal trends in Lima and caught up in the realities of running her own household, the young wife was keenly aware of the painful conditions—both present and past—of local Indigenous people.

On the one hand, Tinta was a lovely colonial town high in the Andes; on the other, the vestiges of its history included a struggling Inca people living in a world very different from her own. Far above the tree line at over eleven thousand feet in altitude and in the ecologically diverse Puna zone, Tinta drew naturalists, opportunists, and other fiercely independent thinkers.[6] This was, after all, the town from which Tupac Amaru II—also known as the *kuraka* José Gabriel Condorcanqui—and his wife Micaela Bastidas led an unsuccessful three-year uprising against *corregidores* and Spanish rule.

From her childhood experiences in Paullo Chico, Clorinda well knew that as a *criolla*—American born of Spanish descent—she belonged to a world wrought by conquistadores, while her Indigenous playmates struggled at the margins. Personal loss aside, she had received the privilege of an education, with which she would be able to support herself while sharing stories of injustice that played out in plain sight. For Clorinda, living in Tinta, the epicenter of the historic Tupac Amaru rebellion, the ghosts of the past were all around her, ready to be brought into the present, and to guide her in building a better future.

IDEAS INTO ACTION: POSITIVISM IN LATIN AMERICA

In postindependence Lima, intellectual activists drew on modern philosophy articulated across the Atlantic to agitate for national social, economic, and political reform. Auguste Comte's *Cours de philosophie positive* (*Course of Positive Philosophy*), published between 1830 and 1842, emphasized the application of the scientific process to understanding social phenomena. By challenging or at least de-emphasizing the metaphysical influence of the church and highlighting the use of scientific thinking, Comte envisioned a secular world of justice and progress through education.

The French scholar's writings on reform made an impression on Latin American elites who encouraged Comtean ideals—to a point—from the 1860s on. In the physical environment, positivist thinking led to the broadening of boulevards and creation of parks in Buenos Aires, Mexico City, and Rio de Janeiro. This was to encourage better circulation of air and keep disease at bay. To that same end, cemeteries were moved away from the churches to more scenic, fresh-air locales. Given social Darwinist notions of the day and with it, a racism markedly different from colonial caste systems, such urban restructuring meant that Indigenous and other marginalized peoples were pushed out of city centers, to be resettled once again in less desirable areas. This, it was argued, would make room for progress. José de San Martín may have claimed, back in 1821, that all "Indians" were now Peruvians, but decades later, urban reform placed them literally on the periphery of nation building and in some cases, quite literally out of sight—toiling away in elite households, in hated *obrajes*, or crowded into church.[7]

While *científico* Auguste Comte argued that educational advance would promote national progress, the Latin American reality was that opportunities in women's and Indigenous education also lagged behind potential for progressive reform. Even liberal leaders sidestepped discussion of universal human rights in Spanish America, fixing instead on notions of modernity in the form of economic growth. Positivism also countered traditional Catholic and Iberian values, offering instead that a strong nation was built not on spirituality but on advances gained from science and industry.

In Spanish America, which was still roiling from the aftershocks of independence, positivist thinking did, however, afford room for female participation in nation building—to an extent. Positivists argued that modernity could be achieved through education. It was in this context that elite women gained greater access, if not to formal education at the university level, then to scholarly discussions and the ability to share, deconstruct, and discuss their work and that of others. European notions of womanhood had long confined the "fairer sex" to the home or convent, but by the middle of the eighteenth century, women could and did earn their keep from educational endeavors and from writing.

Progressive thinking in nation building was not confined to Lima. From Tinta, Clorinda Matto de Turner shared such views, writing poetry and prose for various circulars and periodicals under pseudonyms including Lucrecia, Betsabé, and Rosario.[8] Far from the unaware little girl who played with Inca children, chattering with them in Quechua, she began addressing the social inequities that had come into view for her when she moved to Tinta. She wrote about the education of women and mistreatment of Indigenous people, and began promoting notions of reform. She also organized a literary group whose members shared written work and also refined and articulated ideas of change. By 1876, Clorinda's activism and writing merged when she founded the magazine *El Recreo de Cusco*, which covered the arts, literature, and science. Her work was well received. Soon the circulation of the magazine picked up and Matto de Turner made a name for herself beyond Tinta.

Thanks in no small part to the economic boom and a burgeoning press, the latter half of the eighteenth century bustled with Latin American women's literary activities; as a female writer, Clorinda Matto de Turner was not alone in her efforts and publication success. Journalists and writers went so far as to build their own printshops to publish and promote their own work and that of other women—she would do the same by 1892.[9] In this way, toward the end of the nineteenth century, female writers pushed the boundaries of the traditional Spanish and Spanish American concept of *ángel del hogar*, or "angel of the hearth," with women bound to the home. They did so in a radical new way: by publishing work for and by women that pushed for societal reform.

Juana Manuela Gorriti, one of Clorinda Matto de Turner's early mentors, was one such forward-thinking writer. Hailing originally from Argentina, she and her family fled the conservative Rosas regime and settled in Bolivia. Gorriti was then thirteen years old, but soon met and married Manuel Isodoro Belzú, a future president of Bolivia. She bore two daughters in rapid succession, but as he consolidated his political power, the marriage became strained; with mutual accusations of infidelity, she left him, moving with her daughters to Peru. Once in Lima, unable to obtain a divorce and under pressure to support herself and her daughters, Gorriti founded a primary school as well as a school for young ladies. A prolific writer, she also published extensively. General Belzú was assassinated in 1865; the following year, in a twist of fate, Gorriti finally received the long sought-after divorce papers. Yet she had managed to not only support her family but also carve out a social and intellectual niche thanks to a network of similarly minded women, whom she encouraged as well. By the early 1870s she had heard of and met her young protégé Clorinda Matto de Turner, another progressive writer who was bent on educational reform and determined to expand opportunities for the marginalized.[10]

Etiquette-laced *tertulias* of the previous century now gave way to *velada*s featuring free-flowing conversation about everything from social concerns to literary analysis. This was a new type of revolution—one that made way for a new type of "women's work" in the context of nation building and reform. From 1877 to 1878, Juana Manuela Gorriti held near-weekly *veladas*, which featured and celebrated music, poetry, and discussions on topics as wide-ranging as the creative spirit and national progress. Topics of the day often addressed justice and education. Esteemed scholars mingled with students and invited guests from other Latin America nations. Men, including the renowned Ricardo Palma, joined the *veladas*, but the scene was primarily dominated by women. Attendees generally left personal politics at the door, but all were conscious of shaping a vision of a bold new Peru.

Gorriti's *veladas literarias* were the literary toast of the town, so important they merited press coverage, their own journal, and even a book dedicated to the prolific output of these events. Journalists reported on the proceedings of the near-weekly programs which featured discussions of music and art and critiques of creative endeavors. The attendees also played charades and other such games, and on a more serious note, appreciated and analyzed lectures on select topics.[11] After Gorriti's death in 1879, her son compiled a book featuring complete coverage of the first ten *veladas*—including the list of attendees and featured artists, musical scores, and more.

For her literary efforts, drive, and clear promise, Clorinda Matto de Turner was featured and crowned as a new talent in one of Juana Manuela Gorriti's famous *veladas*. The two became fast and lifelong friends. Through her mentor, Matto de Turner not only had a role model of an independent woman able to support herself through writing but also learned how to form a strong social network from which she would draw in later years. The subjects of Gorriti's gatherings often turned to women's rights and education, topics near and dear to the progressive attendees. Clorinda Matto de Turner began her writing career promoting better conditions for Indigenous people, but she came to take up the banner of women's rights as well.

Following a war-prompted pause and the loss of her husband, Clorinda Matto de Turner embodied the activism and literary richness of her late mentor. She applied herself with renewed vigor to reform. Through her novels, essays, and talks—products of her childhood and reflecting the schooling received at Gorriti's *veladas*—Matto de Turner painted the stark Indigenous reality and pointed the way to real progress.

PROSE ON HOLD: THE WAR OF THE PACIFIC (1879–1883)

In the last decades of the nineteenth century, Peruvian literary creativity reflected the nation's rapid change and expansion, perhaps occurring most of all in the economic sphere. By the second half of the nineteenth century, newly independent Latin American nations were engaging independently with the world market. As in the colonial era, western European states sought raw material exports, but the advent of industrialization brought new demands. Beyond products for immediate consumption—for instance, sugar, foodstuffs, textiles—the industrializing Western Hemisphere sought products that would promote even more growth. In Peru, this included mining guano for fertilizer, to help sustain crops for expanding populations.

Guano, excrement from seabirds, contained valuable nitrate that was used in the manufacture of products in demand worldwide. This industrial resource, largely produced and mined off the Pacific coast on the Chincha Islands, was exported to boost agricultural output in Germany, Great Britain, and the United States. Guano contains nitrogen, phosphate, and potassium, all nutrients essential for plant growth. It was also mined for the production of gunpowder and other explosive materials.

The *encomienda* of colonial days had long since vanished, but horrific labor practices continued unabated on the guano-mining islands. With the marked decline of Indigenous labor, most of which was tied up in the *obrajes*, British ships now ferried Chinese workers to mine the natural nitrate. Many migrants had fled the Taiping Rebellion (1850–1864) for the promise of a more stable life in the Americas. For most, that proved pure fiction. Packed tightly in ship holds, some men died on the trans-Pacific voyage, and thousands more at work. But demand for guano and the labor to mine it fueled Peru's overall fast-paced economic growth.

By the last quarter of the nineteenth century, Peru would be pulled into a drawn-out international conflict that would rock the economy and shake Peruvian self-confidence. This struggle was over saltpeter, another sought-after global commodity, mined by Chile and Bolivia and sold on the world market. The Saltpeter War, which also came to be known as the War of the Pacific, had regional consequences for years to come. Saltpeter, or potassium nitrate, was a key ingredient in gunpowder, explosives, and fertilizers. Given the global demand for such commodities, control of saltpeter mines became a contentious issue. Though Chile and Bolivia had agreed to share in the mineral deposits under an 1866 treaty, this agreement broke down within the decade. Bolivia repudiated the terms and signed a mutual pact with Peru in 1873. Tensions boiled over, and the border dispute between Chile and Bolivia over nitrate-rich land in the Atacama Desert south of the Bolivian port of Antofagasta expanded to a full-fledged war. When war broke out Peru was drawn in, with disastrous consequences.

As *El Recreo* gained in prestige, Clorinda remained largely oblivious to the conflicts over nitrates, and her literary efforts continued until national events began to intrude on daily life. Yet as was the case with many Peruvians, her world changed dramatically when Chilean troops crossed Peru's southern border in 1879. It was at this time that she and her compatriots began to brace for greater challenges, including the uncertainty that came with the prospect of occupation by foreign soldiers.

Perhaps drawing inspiration from her mentor and friend Juana Manuela Gorriti, Clorinda Matto de Turner turned her house into a field hospital to assist those who were fighting the Chileans. Gorriti, after all, had risked her life during the Spanish invasion of Callao in 1866, determined to save the wounded; for her efforts she was awarded Peru's highest military honor.[12] For her part, Clorinda Matto de Turner actively supported Andrés Cáceres and his Indigenous army as they defended the Andean region of Peru. Cáceres had once fought for liberal leader Castillo and would one day be president of Peru. During the War of the Pacific, he and Clorinda Matto de Turner forged an enduring friendship.[13]

None of that mattered when the Chilean army invaded Peru. Following failed mediation talks by the United States in 1880, Chilean forces marched into Lima. This proved a traumatic event for all *limeños* and indeed the entire nation. Peruvian resistance continued for three more years, with continued encouragement from the United States, but the war ended only after the loss of precious Peruvian territory on the Pacific coast. In 1883, the Treaty of Ancón marked Chile's final victory, and with it, the seizure of land that remains within Chilean borders to the present day. This was the nitrate-rich Tarapacá Province to the south and along with it, miles of Pacific coastline. Once-proud Peru, the home of the "guano miracle," now suffered crippling economic setbacks due to loss of land and lives, and damage to property.

Before the war was over, Clorinda suffered her own devastating loss. In 1881, her husband, Dr. Turner, died, leaving her an estate in bankruptcy and debt in arrears. A young widow, Clorinda had to try to rescue the estate and find a way to make her own living. Ever logical and practical, she cut down on expenses and ran a few businesses, including a wheat grain venture. But this was not enough to cover her husband's debts; she had to do more.

So within the year she moved farther south to the town of Arequipa and struck out on her own. Alone in Arequipa, Clorinda needed to cover her expenses as well as pay down her husband's debt. She turned to what she knew best and used her literary and writing skills to climb out of financial distress by writing a local column titled "La Luna" in which she covered all manner of cultural events and topics.

INKING CHANGE, PUSHING REFORM

In 1884, Clorinda Matto de Turner gained national prominence as she became the first woman to serve as editor of a daily paper in the Americas. Already an established writer and editor from her days at the helm of *El Recreo*, she became editor in chief of the daily *La Bolsa*. This paper included articles on the war and its effects, local goings-on, and advertisements for a host of services and products, and served a wide-ranging public. The newspaper took on a nationalistic tone under her direction, but it also addressed issues such as business, agriculture, industry, and more.

The young writer immersed herself in work, driven by a vision of a better Peru—and her own determination to sustain herself financially. During her editorial tenure at *La Bolsa,* she turned out her own work, celebrating the culture of Cusco. This included *Tradiciones cuzqueñas* (1884), a portrayal of Cusco traditions fashioned after the work of Ricardo Palma. She had met the celebrated Palma at Juana Gorriti's *veladas*. The originator of the *tradiciones* genre, Palma styled his words in an era of postindependence uncertainty to create narratives that were part fiction, part fact. Unlike Palma, hers was no tongue-in-cheek endeavor: she aimed instead to illustrate the real plight of the Indigenous people as part of the creation of Peru. In her *Tradiciones cuzqueñas*, Matto de Turner honored her "maestro" Palma; indeed, she credited him for inspiring her to venture beyond journalistic bounds in the first place.[14] Palma wrote the prologue, naming her his "disciple."

It was perhaps fitting that Clorinda's work emerged in the crucible of conflict. Her *Tradiciones* were first published in the last year of the war, but a seven-month civil war ensued as the nation struggled economically through the 1880s and for decades thereafter. Peruvians had, after all, lost life and land for a war that was not their own. Her *Tradiciones* may have been a way to forge a new identity by looking at an uncomfortable past.

Encouraged first by her late husband, and then by her new friends, Clorinda agitated for change and reform by deploying the weapon she knew best—her pen. Determined to empower long-marginalized Indigenous Andeans and help her readers better understand their plight, Clorinda Matto de Turner also turned out her first play in 1884: *Hima-Sumac*, which emphasized the importance of Indigenous heritage in rebuilding war-torn Peru. Depicting the life and death of Hima-Sumac, a woman who spoke truth to power, her three-act musical drama highlighted the Inca roots of the nation and the struggle for freedom, whatever the cost: "Those who come will know, like us, that the happiness of this world is not gold, but a pure heart that breathes satisfied with the love of its lovers on the smiling beaches of free Peru!"[15]

Clorinda Matto de Turner knew well how to position her work for her intended audience. As editor in chief, she proved excellent at promotion, often highlighting her own work when it came out. By now, however, she had several works published in book form, including a literature text for girls. Her works were advertised and well reviewed in *La Bolsa*. The Saturday, July 16, 1887, edition, for instance, featured notices of her first and second volumes of *Tradiciones cuzqueñas*. These were embedded in the paper's advertisements and ran on a regular basis.[16]

By 1886, with her husband's debts now paid off, and having established herself as a writer and editor, Clorinda Matto de Turner moved yet again, this time to Lima. There in the reemerging city, she launched a new level of work for a national audience that would bring her even greater recognition and, with it, controversy. She became editor in chief of *El Perú ilustrado*—another editorial first as the first female editor of a major American newspaper. This proved an even more fertile writing period for Clorinda. She wrote short biographies of celebrated Latin Americans, including an Indigenous priest, the seventeenth-century Juan de Espinosa Medrano, and the statesman José Domingo Choquehuanca. These "sketches" were included in her 1890 *Bocetos al lápiz de americanos célebres*.[17]

Matto de Turner was invited to join and contribute to the most prominent *limeño* literary groups, the Círculo Literario and the Ateneo. In November 1887, she addressed a large gathering of intellectuals at the Ateneo—a privilege reserved for those who had reached the highest echelons of literary achievement—making the case and arguing for social reform. Soon she hosted gatherings in her own home that like her mentor Gorriti's *veladas*, included music, talk of the future, and discussions regarding social change.

BEYOND THE SALON

At the turn of the twentieth century, in Europe and across the Atlantic, the *querelle des femmes*—literally, the "dispute of women"—evolved well beyond early modern investigation on the nature of women. In the context of industrializing states, such discussions now turned to how women could harness their skills to promote broad ideals. Literary-minded women dedicated themselves to the twin causes of education for females and global justice. In 1889, the same year Clorinda Matto de Turner's groundbreaking Indigenous novel *Aves sin nido* (*Birds without a Nest*) was published, German author and Nobel Prize–winning novelist Bertha von Suttner's *Lay Down Your Arms!* saw the light of day. For both women, their game-changing texts offered a bit of financial security, but more importantly a measure of success that came with recognition.

As editor of *El Perú ilustrado*, Matto de Turner oversaw the tremendous growth of the periodical, contributing many pieces and shaping the thematic direction toward justice, social reform, and rights of the Indigenous population. She also turned to writing fiction to expose and decry Indigenous suffering by turns at the hands of the government and the Catholic Church. Her *Aves sin nido* (1889) was a near-immediate sensation, as it revealed what so many understood: the equity gap, the corruption of the church, and the abuses some priests inflicted on their marginalized followers. Clorinda deftly wove Quechua words into the narrative, elevating Indigenous phrases to a national audience.

Often compared to Harriet Beecher Stowe's *Uncle Tom's Cabin*, Clorinda Matto de Turner's *Aves sin nido* put the literary world on notice: it would become known as the first indigenist novel.[18] Here, she focused on the plight of the Indigenous people through the conflicts and actions of her characters, as well as corruption in the church and state. Her main characters suffered a host of abuses from unwanted advances by a priest to pressure them to increase their tithe. The intervention of a liberal-minded, educated couple brought about a better situation for all. Like Harriet Beecher Stowe's *Uncle Tom's Cabin*, the work addressed the ill treatment of an oppressed group—in this case the Indigenous peoples of Peru and specifically Lima.[19]

Intent on attacking injustice where she found it, Clorinda Matto de Turner attempted to root out what she believed to be the problem with Peru. As a positivist, she was inclined toward a secular outlook. She took to portraying priests as wayward and corrupt, morally crippled by their inability to marry. To her and other progressive intellectuals, the church represented the dark shadows of the Peruvian past, with wayward priests bent on ruining Indigenous lives and inviting scandal and shame. In the following excerpt from *Aves sin nido*, a main character, Father Pascual, is seen here as excessively familiar with an Indigenous woman. He engages in acts that are shocking for a priest. In the following scene, Marcela and her daughter Margarida pay a visit to the priest to pay him off and do service:

"Where did you find this young girl so pretty and plump?"

"She is my daughter, Father," replied Marcela.

"And how is it that I am not acquainted with her?" inquired Father Pascual, grabbing hold of the girl's left cheek with three fingers.

"It is because I seldom come, for I had not paid our debt; that is why you do not remember her, Father."

"And how old is she?"

"I have counted some fourteen years since her baptism, señor padre."

"Ah then it was not I who sprinkled her [with holy water]; it is hardly six years since I came. And, well, this year you will put her in service of the church, will you not? She can begin by washing dishes and attending to other little things."

"Father!"

"And you, lazy one, when do you begin the *mita*? Is it not already your turn?" said the priest, fixing his eyes on Marcela and getting familiar with her, patting her on the back.

"Yes, Father," said the woman trembling.

"Or, have you come to stay now?"

"Not yet, Father. I have come to pay the forty pesos for the burial of my mother-in-law, that our potato crop can be free."[20]

Aves sin nido was met by celebration and not a little controversy, and as such it elevated Clorinda Matto de Turner to yet another level in her literary career. This meant, however, that she was now a target for conservatives who would silence her. In 1890, *El Perú ilustrado* published the work of Brazilian writer Henrique Coelho Netto, to disastrous effects for the periodical but an even worse fate for Clorinda. His was a story about Jesus Christ being attracted to Mary Magdalene—intimating that Jesus Christ had sexual feelings for her.[21] This was contrary to the teachings of the Catholic Church and considered pure heresy. For its challenge to church tradition, the bishop of Lima called for a boycott of the paper. He also denounced Clorinda, the writer, and all involved in its production.

The church moved swiftly against Clorinda Matto de Turner and *El Perú ilustrado,* excommunicating the editor in chief and blaming her for the publication of such a scandalous work. She in turn claimed she was ill the day the work was printed. The church, already put on notice by her less-than-flattering portrait of priesthood and Catholic practices in *Aves sin nido*, now formally denounced the book. Those who read the journal or her novel now did so under penalty of mortal sin. She was burned in effigy in Cusco and Arequipa, and *Aves sin nido* was formally put on a list of prohibited books. On July 7, 1891, the owner of the paper promised more oversight over content, and the archbishop's ban was lifted. Clorinda Matto de Turner resigned shortly thereafter.

The archbishop's ire did little to dissuade Clorinda from her work or cause her to stay out of the public eye. Instead, she deepened her commitment to feminist and Indigenous causes. In 1892, she set up a printshop that furthered her efforts, and where she would have greater control. She staffed La Equitativa entirely with women and published books by and about women. This included her own *Leyendas y recortes* (1893), in which she wrote about notable Latin Americans, and a new weekly edition titled *Los Andes*. In 1892 she published *Índole,* another attack on corruption in the church. In this novel, the priest is a villain, corrupt and evil. Clorinda also took aim at the church, army, and government, select practices of which she criticized. By 1893, she would produce *Herencia*, yet another novel on this theme.

Clorinda Matto de Turner nearly single-handedly created a new genre of literature that was both Peruvian and, more broadly, Latin American. Indigenist novels, as they came to be known, highlighted social issues rather than leaving them to the reader's imagination. As a leader of the movement to reveal the abuse of Indigenous people and their uneasy existence in Spanish America, Clorinda Matto de Turner aimed to expose their plight.

Matto de Turner's work also featured liberal, enlightened *criollas* who used their education and influence to bring about reform. In this sense, she offered an unusual, perhaps "American," variation on the Victorian domesticity that was so well regarded across the Atlantic. By this view, elite women received an education and training for the purposes of raising their children and serving their husbands. The family was seen as the foundation of society—an extension, perhaps, of nineteenth-century nation- and empire-building. But Matto de Turner offered a more human take on women—far from the fragile, delicate, pedestal-bound *ángel del hogar*, here women were partners who could and should work side by side with their husbands united in purpose.[22]

In 1895, the liberal political party of Clorinda's friend President Andrés Cáceres was overthrown by conservatives led by Nicolás de Piérola. The coup leader's troops went after all Cáceres's friends, including Matto de Turner and her brother. Her own house was looted; she and her brother escaped with only their lives. La Equitativa was destroyed, the printing machines were smashed, and Clorinda lost several manuscripts in the fire. It was not surprising that, given her political leanings and the recent publication of *La Herencia* criticizing the moral degeneracy of *limeño* society, Piérola sent troops to destroy her home and business.[23] Nicolás de Piérola went on to be inaugurated president of Peru on September 8, 1895.

LIFE IN EXILE

Following the destruction of her offices and home, Clorinda left Peru for Argentina and established herself in Buenos Aires (see figure 4.1). Her reputation preceded her: in short order she was inducted into the prestigious Ateneo de Buenos Aires, becoming its first female member. On January 4, 1896, after giving a speech in the Ateneo of Buenos Aires, a large auditorium generally reserved for the literati, she was featured in an article about her lecture on the role of women in American society, titled "The [female] Workers of Thought of South America." In that speech, she spoke of

> the women who write, true heroines who, with the valor of Policarpa Salavarrieta, who accepted death rather than reveal the secrets of her country and with the martyrs' belief in the truth of their work, fight day after day, hour after hour, to produce the book, the pamphlet, the newspaper, embodying the ideal of feminine progress.[24]

Figure 4.1. Clorinda Matto de Turner

Newspapers noted that a party followed Matto de Turner's talk, at which she was praised for the talk.[25]

Clorinda Matto de Turner still had to support herself as a journalist, playwright, and novelist.[26] Once settled in Buenos Aires, she found no shortage of work. The American Bible Society solicited her teaching services, and she also translated the Bible into Quechua for the society. She published widely and wrote numerous pieces appearing in *La Nación* and *La Prensa*. In addition, her sketches of notable Latin Americans, *Bocetos al lápiz de americanos célebres (*1889), proved a literary success.

While in Buenos Aires, Clorinda Matto de Turner also dedicated herself to instruction and educational reform. She taught at three of the city's schools while continuing to publish prolifically. In 1896 she founded the *Búcaro americano*, a feminist journal that promoted the advancement, or "evolution," of women as equal partners of men.[27]

Despite her successes in exile, Matto de Turner documented her sorrow at being far from home in her *Boreales, miniaturas y porcelanas (Northerners, Miniatures, and Porcelain)*, which was published in 1900. Still she continued to contribute to the intellectual and civic culture of her new home. In 1906 Matto de Turner departed Buenos Aires on a European tour paid for by a local organization dedicated to educational reform. While on the tour she visited schools, museums, and monuments, gave talks, and presented at conferences. Over her six months abroad she met with writers, educators, and famous people including the pope. Much to Clorinda's surprise, she found she was drawn to and favored the directness of German and English manners. Despite France's long cultural and philosophical influence in Latin America—and in particular, Auguste Comte's influence on Peruvian nation building—she found that she had less affinity for the French, whom she saw as snobbish and complicated. She visited six European nations in total, recording her impressions in her last book, *Viaje de recreo: España, Francia, Inglaterra, Italia, Suiza y Alemania* (*Travel for Pleasure*), published the year after her death. Clorinda Matto de Turner passed away shortly after returning to Buenos Aires, where she had lived in exile for thirteen years,[28] in October 1909.

EPILOGUE

Renowned as a writer, editor, and publisher, Clorinda Matto de Turner came of age during the tenure of liberal Peruvian president and reformer Andrés A. Cáceres. At that time, in the 1880s, feminist ideas had begun to take hold in the Americas. This required women to receive an education. But even then, in Peru, entrance to the highest levels of schooling was barred. Women began to challenge tradition, demanding entrance into universities and participation in the society they sought to reform.

The prolific Matto de Turner gave her life to writing, wielding her pen on behalf of women and Indigenous peoples. She incorporated her own early experiences playing among Indigenous children in Cusco and learning Quechua, as well as her own challenges as a young impecunious widow. Clorinda's deep friendships with other notable female positivists and writers helped nurture her talent and shaped the trajectory of her writing career. She was politically engaged beyond local and state borders too, backing activists and supporting Peru in the War of the Pacific. But it was in her writings, particularly her essays and novels, that she highlighted the plight of the Indigenous population and the dark side of the Catholic Church. Her most renowned work, *Aves sin nido* (*Birds without a Nest*), was hailed as a groundbreaking exposé of the Indigenous plight and, at the same time, vilified for casting the church in a harsh light.

Clorinda Matto de Turner collided with the inertia of tradition. Her political activism and prose challenged Peru's sociopolitical status quo, ultimately forcing her to flee her country. Yet she remained a staunch feminist. In Buenos Aires she continued to write and support women's and Indigenous rights. Clorinda Matto de Turner left behind a literary legacy that continues to resonate in Latin America and beyond.

NOTES

1. Margaret V. Campbell, "The 'Tradiciones cuzqueñas' of Clorinda Matto de Turner," *Hispania* 42, no. 4 (1959): 493.

2. See, for instance, David McCreery, *The Sweat of Their Brow: A History of Work in Latin America* (Armonk, NY: M.E. Sharpe, 2000).

3. John Crabtree, *Fractured Politics: Peruvian Democracy Past and Present* (London: Institute for the Study of the Americas, University of London, 2011), 31.

4. Campbell, "Tradiciones cuzqueñas," 492–97.

5. Campbell, "Tradiciones cuzqueñas," 492–97.

6. See, for instance, the work of naturalist Frank Chapman, "The Distribution of Bird Life in the Urubamba Valley of Peru," *Smithsonian Institute U.S. National Museum Bulletin*, no. 117 (Washington, DC: Government Printing Office, 1921).

7. Fiona Wilson, "Indian Citizenship and the Discourse of Hygiene/Disease in Nineteenth-Century Peru," *Bulletin of Latin American Research* 23, no. 2 (2004): 167.

8. Mary G. Berg, "Clorinda Matto de Turner," in *Spanish-American Women Writers: A Bio-Bibliographical Sourcebook*, ed. Diane E. Marting (New York: Greenwood Press, 1990), 303–4.

9. Sarah Moody, "Latin American Women Writers and the Periodical Press, 1890–1910," *Letras Femininas* (Winter 2010):145–46.

10. Leona S. Martin, "Nation Building, International Travel, and the Construction of the Nineteenth-Century Pan-Hispanic Women's Network." *Hispania* 87, no. 3 (2004): 440–42; Mary Berg, "Juana Manuela Gorriti," in *Spanish-American Women Writers: A Bio-Bibliographical Sourcebook*, ed. Diane E. Marting (New York: Greenwood Press, 1990), 227–28.

11. Berg, "Juana Manuela Gorriti," 228.

12. This was the "Estrella de 2 Mayo." Berg, "Juana Manuela Gorriti," 228.

13. Berg, "Clorinda Matto de Turner," 304.

14. Roy L. Tanner, "La presencia de Ricardo Palma en *Aves sin nido*," *Hispanic Journal* 8, no. 1 (1986): 97.

15. Mary Berg, "Passion and Nation in 'Hima-Sumac' by Clorinda Matto de Turner," Miguel de Cervantes Virtual Library, https://www.cervantesvirtual.com/obra-visor/pasion-y-nacion-en-hima-sumac-de-clorinda-matto-de-turner/html/ac20184c-48c2-11e0-b1fb-00163ebf5e63_2.html.

16. For example, see the Farfan y Casali advertisements in *La Bolsa* (Arequipa, Peru: Francisco Ibáñez, 1887), digitized by the Center for Research Library, Global Resources Network, General Collections, Latin American Materials Project, http://catalog.crl.edu/record=b2911279.

17. For an online version of this book, see Clorinda Matto de Turner, *Bocetos al lápiz de americanos célebres*, vol. 1 (Lima: Imprenta Bacigalupi, 1890), https://archive.org/details/bocetosallpizde00turngoog/page/n10/mode/2up.

18. Mary G. Berg, "Writing for Her Life: The Essays of Clorinda Matto de Turner," in *Reinterpreting the Spanish American Essay: Women Writers of the 19th and 20th Centuries*, ed. Doris Meyer (Austin: University of Texas Press, 2021), 80.

19. For a more detailed discussion of *Aves sin nido*, see Carlos Alberto Contreras, "Exploring Gender, Class and Ethnicity in Nineteenth-Century Latin America: Clorinda Matto de Turner's *Torn from the Nest*," *World History Connected* 4, no. 3 (2007), https://worldhistoryconnected.press.uillinois.edu/cgi-bin/cite.cgi.

20. Clorinda Matto de Turner, *Birds without a Nest: A Story of Indian Life and Priestly Oppression in Peru*, trans. J.G.H. (Austin: University of Texas Pres, 1996), 33.

21. Berg, "Clorinda Matto de Turner," 305.

22. Joan Torres-Pou, "Clorinda Matto de Turner y el ángel del hogar," *Revista Hispánica Moderna* 43, no. 1 (1990): 4–5.

23. Berg, "Clorinda Matto de Turner," 305.

24. Clorinda Matto de Turner, "Las obreras del pensamiento en la América del Sur," reading by the author at the Ateneo de Buenos Aires, December 14, 1895, *Asparkía: Investigació Feminista* 29 (December 29, 2016), 172. http://www.e-revistes.uji.es/index.php/asparkia/article/view/2342.

25. Clorinda Matto de Turner, "Conferencia," *La Bolsa* (Arequipa), January 4, 1896, http://ddsnext.crl.edu/titles/30952?terms=Clorinda%20%20&item_id=214731#?h=Clorinda&c=1&m=2965&s=0&cv=9&r=0&xywh=762%2C-191%2C3251%2C1785.

26. Moody, "Latin American Women Writers," 146.

27. Moody, "Latin American Women Writers," 146.

28. Vanessa Miseres, *Mujeres en tránsito: Viaje, identidad y escritura en Sudamérica (1830–1910)* (Chapel Hill: University of North Carolina Press, 2017), 112.

REFERENCES

Arnig, Ursula. "El análisis de los artículos de Clorinda Matto de Turner en *La Bolsa.*" "Clorinda Matto de Turner: las contradicciones de una identidad en un universo acotado." 4:3. Miguel de Cervantes Virtual Library. https://www.cervantesvirtual.com/obra-visor/clorinda-matto-de-turner-las-contradicciones-de-una-identidad-en-un-universo-acotado/html/e7024b99-e5f4-470c-a985-7ab89d518afb_52.html#I_0_

Berg, Mary G. "Clorinda Matto de Turner." In *Spanish-American Women Writers: A Bio-Bibliographical Sourcebook*, edited by Diane E. Marting, 303–15. New York: Greenwood Press, 1990.

———. "Juana Manuela Gorriti." In *Spanish-American Women Writers: A Bio-Bibliographical Sourcebook*, edited by Diane E. Marting, 226–40. New York: Greenwood Press, 1990.

———. "Passion and Nation in 'Hima-Sumac' by Clorinda Matto de Turner." Miguel de Cervantes Virtual Library. https://www.cervantesvirtual.com/obra-visor/pasion-y-nacion-en-hima-sumac-de-clorinda-matto-de-turner/html/ac20184c-48c2-11e0-b1fb-00163ebf5e63_2.html.

———. "Writing for Her Life: The Essays of Clorinda Matto de Turner." In *Reinterpreting the Spanish American Essay: Women Writers of the 19th and 20th Centuries*, edited by Doris Meyer, 80–89. Austin: University of Texas Press, 1994.

Campbell, Margaret V. "The 'Tradiciones cuzqueñas' of Clorinda Matto de Turner." *Hispania* 42, no. 4 (1959): 492–97.

Chapman, Frank. "The Distribution of Bird Life in the Urubamba Valley of Peru." *Smithsonian Institute U.S. National Museum Bulletin*, no. 117. Washington, DC: Government Printing Office, 1921.

Crabtree, John. *Fractured Politics: Peruvian Democracy Past and Present*. London: Institute for the Study of the Americas, University of London: 2011.

Contreras, Carlos Alberto. "Exploring Gender, Class and Ethnicity in Nineteenth-Century Latin America: Clorinda Matto de Turner's *Torn from the Nest*." *World History Connected*, June 2007. https://worldhistoryconnected.press.uillinois.edu/4.3/contreras.html.

Denegri Álvarez Calderón, Francesca. "Semblanza de la Imprenta La Equitativa (1892–1895)." Biblioteca Virtual Miguel de Cervantes—Portal Editores y Editoriales Iberoamericanos (siglos XIX–XXI)—EDI-RED, 2018. https://www.cervantesvirtual.com/obra/imprenta-la-equitativa-1892-1895-semblanza-888909/.

Forment, Carlos A. *Democracy in Latin America, 1760–1900*. Chicago: University of Chicago Press, 2003.

Hintze, Gloria. "Mujeres, feminismo y escritura pública." In *Escritura femenina: Diversidad y género en América Latina*, 97–119. Mendoza, Argentina: Facultad de Filosofía y Letras, 2004.

Mallon, Florencia E. "Indian Communities, Political Cultures, and the State in Latin America, 1780–1990." *Journal of Latin American Studies* 24 (1992): 35–53.

Martin, Leona S. "Nation Building, International Travel, and the Construction of the Nineteenth-Century Pan-Hispanic Women's Network." *Hispania* 87, no. 3 (2004): 439–46.

Matto de Turner, Clorinda. *Birds without a Nest: A Story of Indian Life and Priestly Oppression in Peru.* Translated by J.G.H. and emended by Naomi Lindstrom. Austin: University of Texas Press, 1996.

———. *Bocetos al lápiz de americanos célebres*. Vol. 1. Lima: Imprenta Bacigalupi, 1890. https://archive.org/details/bocetosallpizde00turngoog/page/n10/mode/2up.

———. "Las obreras del pensamiento en la América del Sur," reading by the author at the Ateneo de Buenos Aires, December 14, 1895. *Asparkía: Investigació Feminista* 29 (December 29, 2016): 169–79. http://www.e-revistes.uji.es/index.php/asparkia/article/view/2342

———. "Conferencia." *La Bolsa* (Arequipa). January 4, 1896. http://ddsnext.crl.edu/titles/30952?terms=Clorinda%20%20&item_id=214731#?h=Clorinda&c=1&m=2965&s=0&cv=9=&r=0&xywh=762%2C-191%2C3251%2C1785.

McCreery, David. *The Sweat of Their Brow: A History of Work in Latin America*. Armonk, NY: M.E. Sharpe, 2000.

Miseres, Vanessa. *Mujeres en tránsito: Viaje, identidad y escritura en Sudamérica (1830–1910)*. Chapel Hill: University of North Carolina Press, 2017.

Moody, Sarah. "Latin American Women Writers and the Periodical Press, 1890–1910." *Letras femeninas* (Winter 2010): 141–57.

Salvucci, Richard. *Textiles and Capitalism in Mexico: An Economic History of the Obrajes, 1539–1840*. Princeton, NJ: Princeton University Press, 2014.

Schlau, Stacy, ed. *Spanish American Women's Use of the Word: Colonial through Contemporary Narratives*. Tucson: University of Arizona Press, 2001.

Tanner, Roy L. "La presencia de Ricardo Palma en *Aves sin nido*." *Hispanic Journal* 8, no. 1 (1986): 97–107.

Torres-Pou, Joan. "Clorinda Matto de Turner y el ángel del hogar." *Revista Hispánica Moderna* 43, no. 1 (1990): 3–15. http://www.jstor.org/stable/30203235.

Wilson, Fiona. "Indian Citizenship and the Discourse of Hygiene/Disease in Nineteenth-Century Peru." *Bulletin of Latin American Research* 23, no. 2 (2004): 165–80. http://www.jstor.org/stable/27733635.

Chapter 5

Gabriela Mistral, 1889–1957

INTRODUCTION

Latin America's contribution to world literature is characterized by its richness and diversity. From the colorfully illustrated codices of anonymous Mayan and Aztec masters to the jewel-like fantasies crafted by Jorge Luis Borges and the magical realism of Gabriel García Márquez, countless memorable works have been produced by Latin American writers of prose and poetry. Some of the brightest lights among these writers appear in the field of poetry. Across the Atlantic, Sor Juana Inés de la Cruz, the seventeenth-century savant, was heralded as the "Tenth Muse" and the "Phoenix of the Americas." Later centuries saw Rubén Darío, founder of the modernist school, and Nobel Prize winners Miguel Ángel Asturias and Pablo Neruda, who continued the tradition of notable Latin American poetry.

Such writing has never been the sole property of a literary elite, but rather a part of the public domain. The people of Latin America have had an enduring love affair with the written word. Their Romance languages and temperament lend themselves to poetic endeavor. What lovesick adolescent has not poured out his or her emotions in verse, and what visitor spending any time in a Latin country has not been awakened in the night by verse set to the music of the serenade?

This widespread appreciation for the written word and for individuals skilled in the use of written language has had its practical applications. Many gifted writers and poets have achieved prominence solely on the strength of their mastery of the idiom. One of the most outstanding of these is Marco Fidel Suárez. The illegitimate, mixed-descent son of a washerwoman, Suárez became an accepted and honored member of the hidebound elite of early

Figure 5.1. Gabriela Mistral. By Marcos Chamúdez, 1946. Wikimedia Commons

twentieth-century Colombia. Suárez was ultimately elected president, having won renown in his twenties and thirties as a grammarian and essayist. Latin Americans prominent in nonliterary fields have also excelled in the writing of poetry and prose. The names of Bartolomé Mitre, Domingo F. Sarmiento,

Jorge Amado, João Cabral de Melo Neto, Andrés Bello, and José Martí are but a few of the many who can be cited.

The story of Gabriela Mistral highlights the prestigious place of gifted writers in Latin American culture. Mistral began her career as a schoolteacher in rural Chile—a station befitting an impoverished, rather homely country girl. But the provincial teacher felt a need to express her innermost feelings through the poetry that over a period of years earned her international fame. She would be lionized in her own country, and she is now as much a national resource as the forests, mountains, and rivers about which she wrote (see figure 5.1).

Gabriela Mistral was both an introspective person and one of the vocal and unselfish humanists of her day. Her first calling was teaching, and a great deal of her poetry was written to be read and enjoyed by children. She was also acutely attuned to the needs of women and children, especially those who were innocent victims of the European conflagration of the 1930s and 1940s. The imagery she employed was so powerful, yet so unique, that she has had no imitators. Neither did she follow any preexisting school of poetry.

Although she had a charismatic personality, an open face, and flashing smile that impressed all who met her, Gabriela Mistral was at heart an introvert—at the end of her life perhaps even a misanthrope. Like many gifted persons, she led an uneasy existence. Late in life she sought consolation in Franciscan Catholicism, but her constant travels and an innate pessimism deprived her of any real peace. Gabriela Mistral was much like the poetry she wrote—simple and unadorned yet hiding an intensity and meaning disturbing in their implications.

EARLY LIFE AND SCHOOLING

Gabriela Mistral claimed, almost sixty years later, that her only sweet memories were of the years before her tenth birthday. In the village of Montegrande on the banks of Chile's Elqui River, she—then little Lucila Godoy Alcayaga—breathed the country air and gazed at the Andean cordillera that opened like gigantic jaws around the river valley. Her education during those years was left to nature. She learned to distinguish one place from another using only her sense of smell, to tell one season from the next not by the calendar but by the fields and sky, to decipher the alphabet of country sounds before that of written language. "I was happy until I left Montegrande; and after that I was never happy again," she wrote, remarkably forgiving of the small disasters and poverty of those years.[1] Her father Jerónimo Godoy was as fond of Chilean wine as he was of his freedom, and he drifted away from home when Lucila was three. Petronila, his wife, welcomed him back without comment when, every few years, chance brought him to the Elqui valley. He never stayed long, however, and Petronila and Emelina, Petrolina's daughter by a previous marriage, had to manage the family without him. Lucila never resented her footloose father; neither did she forget the hardships suffered by the little family, brought on by his failings.

Yet pleasure far outweighed pain during her years in Montegrande. The stern Andes Mountains printed their image on her mind's eye, and the fertile earth of the valley scented her waking hours. Those shapes and smells never deserted her, even when she left for Vicuña, her birthplace, to begin her formal education at age nine. She attended school for only three years, hardly enough to qualify her as an educated person. In fact, in later years she included herself among the company of the self-taught. Emelina, her elder half sister, was a warm and devoted teacher who directed Lucila's education for several years after her formal schooling ceased.

Brief though it was, Lucila's educational career was important. She came into contact with popular poets and wrote her own first poems, dedicating them to her best friend and copying them carefully into a school notebook. To lighten the financial burden of her education, Lucila acted as a guide to the school's director, Doña Adelaida Olivares, who was blind and needed help getting to and from work. On more than one occasion she performed other duties as well. In 1902 Doña Adelaida entrusted thirteen-year-old Lucila with a quantity of notebooks to be distributed among her classmates as needed over a month's time. Somehow, she ran out of them too soon, and Doña Adelaida accused her of stealing them. Lucila, acutely shy in the best of circumstances, was unable to speak a word in her own defense even when the director denounced her publicly before the student body. Overwhelmed by the accusation, Lucila sank to the floor unconscious. Hours later, as she crept home from school, a small band of girls met her in the plaza and chased after her with taunts of *ladrona*—thief. Though her innocence was later proven, Lucila Godoy never did return to school, nor, characteristically, did she ever forget the incident.

The rankling memory of her unjustified disgrace was less damaging to Lucila than was the more subtle injustice of racial prejudice. During her first days in Vicuña, and perhaps before, she became aware that she was perceived with subtle disapproval as a country girl of undistinguished lineage, whose green eyes, dark heavy brow, and downturned mouth testified to the mingling of Chile's two major races in her ancestry. Lucila soon came to believe the racist notions popular in Chile (and in the rest of the Western world at that time), even as she absorbed the more positive love of sunlight, trees, and rural quiet from her Montegrande home. "I belong to the group of unlucky people who were born without a patriarchal age and without a Middle Ages," she wrote many years after she had achieved worldwide fame. "I am one of those whose insides, face, and expression are uneasy and irregular, because of the graft; I consider myself to be among the children of that twisted thing that is called a racial experience, or better, a racial *violence*."[2] On the one hand she was her own most acid critic, referring to herself at times as *mestizo de vasca*—an Indigenous and Basque half-breed—and attributing her failings to racial mixture. However, she bridled at any personal affront, attributing it to that same prejudice with which she was herself afflicted.

Economic necessity intruded early and forced Lucila to choose a profession. Her sister and father were teachers, and it was decided that she too would teach. Her education proceeded at home under Emelina's direction, and both mother and sister saved and borrowed enough to pay her way through the teacher training school in La Serena. In 1904 she passed the examinations required for entrance and prepared to begin her course of study. Unexpectedly, and at the last moment, she was turned away. No official explanation was ever given, but Lucila's impassioned, somewhat socialistic poems that had begun to appear in the local press undoubtedly prejudiced school authorities against her. Lacking the protection of a powerful or wealthy sponsor, Lucila Godoy had no choice but to continue her education privately under Emelina's gentle tutoring and to enter teaching through an alternate route. The following year, at age sixteen, she was named assistant to the primary schoolteacher in a small town a few miles from La Serena, and in 1906 she moved to La Cantera, where she occupied a similar position.

A young railroad employee, not yet twenty-five years old, first noticed Lucila when she visited the Cantera train station to pick up her mail. Soon he began to visit her boardinghouse, and the two established a bond of affectionate regard. Romelio Ureta was an intense young man given to wearing peculiar patent leather shoes with elongated toes and to waxing the ends of his rather sparse mustache. They shared an interest in poetry and read aloud the florid, grandiloquent verses of the Colombian José María Vargas Vila and other popular poets of the day. After a time, Romelio began to visit her less regularly. Lucila saw him in the company of another girl, suffered from the rejection, and poured her distress into verse.

FIRST PUBLICATIONS AND THE GLARE OF FAME

Several years passed, and no one came to take Romelio's place in Lucila's affections. She became involved in Santiago's theosophical society and studied Oriental philosophy, especially the writings of Rabindranath Tagore. She mused on reincarnation, pantheism, and other beliefs foreign to her Catholic background but congenial to her Franciscan temperament. Her poems and prose writings continued to appear in local newspapers—the *Voice of Elqui, El Coquimbo*, and *Reforma*—and she discovered a passion for letter writing that would last a lifetime. Slowly her name spread beyond the immediate borders of the region. In spite of the adolescent tone of some of those early works, Lucila Godoy already showed signs of remarkable power and sensitivity.

Then in November 1909 Romelio Ureta committed suicide. Only one item was found on his body: a postcard he had received some time before from Lucila Godoy. Although his death had nothing to do with Lucila, she was nonetheless deeply moved by it and by the inexplicable fact that he had remembered her shortly before taking his life. In the weeks following she wrote six, perhaps more, sonnets of such intense importance to her that she put them away and kept them from public scrutiny for several years.

The "Sonnets of Death," as they were called when Lucila Godoy entered them in a national contest five years later, were far different from her earliest poems. Those immature works, written when she was fourteen and fifteen years old and under the baneful influence of Vargas Vila, caused her some embarrassment later, and she wrote that she would "never forgive those who published my first babblings with great fanfare, misspellings and horrible taste."[3]

By 1909, however, the breadth of her experience was greatly increased. Rubén Darío, the great modernist poet, and Amado Nervo, a popular Mexican poet, as well as the Nobel Prize–winning poet Rabindranath Tagore, had earned her admiration and studious attention; the years of contact with the Bible—a thousand poems in itself—strengthened her style so that it could more easily carry the weight of her stringent, passionate honesty. The "Sonnets of Death" revealed for the first time that Lucila was a gifted poet. The impetus that drove her to express her deepest feelings in words and to send those pieces of herself off to be published set her apart from the mass of humanity who seek expression in unheeded tears, complaints, or confidences. Yet she sought an audience for her work hesitatingly, torn by her shyness on the one hand and the conviction, on the other, that the poet is a pathfinder, a seer whose words direct men and women toward greatness of spirit. Only the profound belief in her own poetic vocation could in the end persuade her to reveal the innermost thoughts and feelings of Lucila Godoy.

A year after the "Sonnets of Death" were composed, after four years as a teacher's aide and school clerk, Lucila went to a Santiago normal school to take examinations in a broad range of subjects, hoping to earn a teacher's equivalency diploma. Her work was brilliant, the product of many hours of study, and she was thereafter permitted to teach in secondary school. During the next two years she taught at high schools in Traiguén and Antofagasta. Then in 1912 she was assigned to the secondary school in Los Andes, not far from Santiago. There Lucila found an environment well suited to her needs and tastes. Accustomed to being criticized for her verses, she found herself the object of sympathetic interest in Los Andes. Her work in poetry and prose was now published in an increasingly broad selection of periodicals in Chile as well as in Rubén Darío's journal *Elegancia* in Paris. She had extensive contacts, among them Pedro Aguirre Cerda, a politician who occupied a score of important positions in Chile—including the presidency—and who was instrumental in helping her throughout her career. Through her letters and frequent trips into Santiago she established more and more connections with Santiago's literary elite.

Early in her stay in Los Andes, Lucila Godoy chose a pseudonym, not the juvenile kind she had used earlier, like "Soul," "Solitude," or "Someone," but a well-modeled one inspired in part by a French Provençal poet whose work she admired. From the archangel of good news and comfort she chose her first name; and from Frédéric Mistral—or perhaps from the Mediterranean wind that blows across southern France—she took a new last name. "Gabriela Mistral" fitted her new self far better than the old, fitted the persona she had created as carefully as her poems. As she wrote to Amado Nervo, "This soul of mine today is far different from the one I had at birth."[4] Indeed, by the time she reached her twenties, Gabriela Mistral scarcely resembled little Lucila Godoy, who was paralyzed by shyness, hardly able to speak in the presence of adults. In her new incarnation, that timidity was transformed into a stately reserve, a serenity that belied her relative youth. Convinced of her homeliness, she dressed plainly, in dull colors, wore flat-heeled shoes (perhaps to compensate for her height), and strode about Los Andes bareheaded in outright defiance of the fashion of the day. Any effort at self-adornment would have seemed ridiculous to her, rather like gilding a mud pie. But to those who sought her out, she was by no means unattractive. Rather, she seemed imposing and distant until suddenly she broke into a grin that showed her pure white teeth, a smile that changed her face so completely that she seemed like a different, much younger person. Gabriela Mistral continually charmed her admirers by these sudden contradictions: the green eyes and open smile in that dark face; the streak of whimsy hidden in a mantle of prim intensity; and her voice, measured and deep, that retained the rough country cadences of her native valley. Those who met her rarely forgot her.

In 1914 a panel of three judges named her the winner of a national poetry contest, the Juegos Florales. She had submitted three "Sonnets of Death" to the competition and won by a vote of two to one. The award ceremony took place at the Santiago Theater on December 22, 1914. It was an elaborate program of speeches, recitations, music, and even the selection of a queen in honor of the event. The only element missing was the award-winning poet herself. Claiming to be unable to attend, Gabriela came in disguise and watched from the balcony as her verses were read by another poet. One account of that peculiar occasion noted that she could not afford to buy a new dress, but it is far more likely that her own reticence made it impossible for her to appear.

In the aftermath of the Juegos Florales, Gabriela Mistral began to feel the effects of her growing fame. Her poems were in demand for anthologies and literature texts throughout Latin America. Yet disillusionment followed on the heels of her success. In a letter probably written in 1915, she complained vigorously about "undesirable people, by which I mean *literary* ones" in Santiago. She was repelled by the two-faced characters she met through the Juegos Florales: "That's why I told you that the J.F. was the most hateful thing in the world," she wrote. "I came to know firsthand several *luminous* cerebral types whose hearts are rotten and who don't know what loyalty is; I was placed among them and every time I'm with them, I wish I had never been anything more than Lucila Godoy." Her first experience with that common human tendency to praise and flatter, then criticize out of earshot, disgusted Gabriela. "I don't know if I have already told you this," she added in the same letter, "but nothing in the world is worth as much to me as a good man, a person whose heart is fresh and fragrant and doesn't spout green juice of ill-will."[5] Gabriela demanded absolute loyalty from her friends and was prepared to return it; but rumors, infighting, and criticism, endemic in Santiago's literary circles, revolted her and she became less tolerant of it as the years passed.

NURTURING TALENT

In that throng of false friends, Gabriela did find a few true and faithful ones. Doña Fidelia Valdés Pereira, director of the Los Andes secondary school, consistently gave Gabriela support and encouragement. As would be characteristic of her through life, Gabriela had a handful of intimate female friends. Perhaps her most influential supporter was Pedro Aguirre Cerda. Years later, at the height of her fame, she wrote of Aguirre that she owed everything to him and that he was the only Chilean who had faith in her—a comment that demonstrates, among other things, how demanding she was of her friends. It was he, as Chile's minister of justice and education, who named her director of the Punta Arenas secondary school for girls in 1918. With no formal education, the former clerk of a rural primary school now found herself in sole charge of a high school far away from her native Elqui valley. Punta Arenas was, in fact, far from almost everything. Located in Chile's extreme south, the small city was a port on the Straits of Magellan, a provincial capital where windblown clouds brought rain squalls, almost without warning, to torment sailors and city folk alike. That harsh region, where in summer the sun sets only reluctantly and winter nights last too long, affected Gabriela strongly, and she wrote a series of poems, "Patagonian Landscapes," about the austere south of Chile.

On her first night in Punta Arenas, she wrote the poem she considered to be her best, "Poem of the Son," and dedicated it to Alfonsina Storni, the Argentine poet. The poem recounted the powerful longing she had felt for a child and then, with the passing years, her bitter satisfaction that such a child had never been born:

A son, a son, a son! I wanted a son of yours
and mine, back in the days of the burning ecstasy,
when even my bones trembled at your murmur
and a broad glow spread over my brow.

I said: a son! as the tree touched
by spring sends its shoots toward the sky,
a son with the eyes of Christ made large,
forehead of astonishment and lips of longing!

....

While the flame of the pine tree burns, becalmed,
looking within myself I think what would have been
a son of mine, an infant with my tired mouth,
my embittered heart and my voice of defeat.

And with your heart, the fruit of poison,
and your lips that once again would have denied.
Forty moons he would not sleep on my breast,
that simply because he was yours he would have abandoned me.

....

I did not plant seed for my granary, I did not teach to make for myself
a loving arm for my last hour,
when my broken neck cannot hold me
and my hand touches the light sheet.

I gazed on others' children, I filled up the barn
with divine wheat, and only on You I wait,
Our Father who art in heaven! come for
my beggar's head, if tonight I die.[6]

Gabriela Mistral believed that she was never to have the most fundamental and most natural human experience: love that culminates in the birth of a child. By 1918, however, her sense of loss seemed on its way to a kind of healing. With no children of her own to care for, she would love and care for any and all children. While still in Los Andes, she wrote in a letter to a friend, "I'm not going to Santiago this month, I'm very tired and need to regain strength for my work, my only reason for living. I have given myself to the children and only for them do I guard my health and spirits. I'm an old maid in love with other people's children."[7] Teaching, already her profession, became, with poetry, her vocation.

For a number of years Gabriela Mistral had searched for a way to merge her two vocations: poetry and teaching. Aware of the scarcity of literature for children, she had often written verses for school occasions, many of which had found their way into print, but she continued to lament the dearth of good children's poetry suitable for school. As early as 1915 she hoped to publish a book of her school verses. "I have wanted to write a new kind of school poetry," she wrote that year, "because the poetry now in vogue doesn't satisfy me; school poetry shouldn't stop being poetry because it's for school use, it should be more so, more delicate than any other, deeper, full of things of the heart: quivering with the breath of the soul."[8] That was the spirit she gave to her poem "Hymn to the Tree," written in the 1920s and dedicated to Mexican educator and philosopher José Vasconcelos:

Brother tree, who affixed
by dull brown hooks in the soil,
your clear brow you have raised
in an intense thirst for the sky:

Make me kindhearted toward the muck
from whose muddy hands I maintain myself,
without allowing the memory to sleep
of the blue country from which I come.

Tree who announces to the passerby
the gentleness of your presence
with your broad refreshing shade
and the nimbus of your essence:

Make my presence known,
in the meadow of life,
my soft and warm influence
felt on the blessed child.[9]

With the passing of time the gentle sermons of "Hymn to the Tree," "Guardian Angel," and "Prayer for the Nest" were joined by a series of genres on similar themes: cradle songs, *rondas* (rounds, or choruses in verse), and prose poems, among others. Her ideal, the model she followed and wished to equal, was the body of Spanish popular verse, whose supple simplicity came from constant use over many years. In "The Luminous Circle" she pursued her theme with simplicity and in the language of the people:

Circle of little girls
circle of a thousand girls
around me:
Oh God, I am the owner
of this splendor!

In the barren land,
on that desert
bitten by the sun,
my circle of little girls
like an immense flower!

On the verdant plain,
at the foot of the mountains
that the voice wounds,
the circle was a single
divine tremor!

On the immense steppe,
on the steppe rigid
with desolation
my circle of little girls
burning with love!

In vain did they wish
to drown my song
with tribulation:
the circle sings it
under God![10]

Mestizo America had had little time to create its own popular poetry, and Gabriela confessed that her own efforts to write children's poetry had, with a few exceptions, failed. Years later she described her children's poems as a "stiff plaster mold, beside the elastic flesh of popular [verse]." Speaking of her "Cradle Songs" in particular, she continued, "They were born, poor things, showing their crippled feet, to induce some musician to set them walking, and I wrote them half out of love for the 'lullabies' of my infancy and half to serve other women's emotions—the poet is an un-tier of knots, and love without words is a knot, and it drowns."[11]

In 1919 Gabriela Mistral received word that she was to be transferred from Punta Arenas to Temuco. A photograph survives of the farewell ceremony—the *despedida*—given by the students of her school. It shows the entire student body assembled in the school's auditorium, the youngest girls carefully arranged on tiers in front and the older ones spilling onto the stage in a crowded jumble. In the center stands Gabriela Mistral, thick and tall in a long, dark, shapeless dress, hands clasped soberly in front of her, her face expressionless.

Gabriela was director of the Temuco girls' secondary school for only a short time, but she lived there long enough to meet a teenage boy, at the time called Neftalí Reyes, who approached her timidly, hoping to be allowed to use her library. She was happy to share her books. Thus began the friendship between Gabriela Mistral and Pablo Neruda, Chile's two greatest poets. Another encounter, less direct, took place in Temuco as well. As she later described it, she was walking through a poor neighborhood when she saw a pregnant woman resting uncomfortably in a doorway, obviously close to giving birth. While Gabriela watched, a man passed and made a crude remark, causing the woman to blush with embarrassment. Out of a sense of empathy inspired by the belief that maternity is the most sacred of all conditions, Gabriela wrote a series of prose "Poems for Mothers" expressing the powerful hopes and fears of women.

At the same time that Gabriela Mistral was writing with profound sympathy about women and children, she was becoming less and less like them. Virtually without family, in a literal sense she had no home. From time to time she did visit her aging mother and sister in the Elqui valley, but the frequent moves from one school to the next kept her from putting down roots anywhere. In 1915 she hinted at her bizarre lifestyle while answering a friend who had invited her to stay in his home. "I always stay in boardinghouses," she explained, thanking him for the invitation. "I am such an odious guest. I don't eat meat and I spend all day in the street. . . . Only in boardinghouses do they tolerate all of that."[12] Her only permanent dwelling was her school, where, surrounded by students, she worked, taught, and slept or, since sleep was an increasingly elusive luxury, wrote the letters, essays, and poems that kept her connected to the greater literary world of Chile and, increasingly, beyond. But this relative homelessness, the constant transfers, and the brevity of each stay bothered her very little. From her father she had inherited a love of travel; she was like him, *patiloca*, footloose: "I'm a vagabond and I don't deny it. The world is beautiful to see and perhaps when I'm dead I won't be able to roam about as much as I like."[13]

Gabriela Mistral's plans for publication of her school verses were never carried out, and although her work was well known outside Chile, no book bearing her name had yet been published. That initiative was reserved for Federico de Onís, a Spanish literary critic living in the United States. In February 1921 Onís delivered a lecture on Gabriela to students and teachers of Spanish at Columbia University. When he explained that no volume of her verses was available, that her poems were scattered far and wide throughout the Spanish-speaking world, they volunteered to help underwrite the costs of publication. On behalf of the North American Spanish teachers, Onís wrote to Gabriela requesting her consent in the undertaking. After some hesitation she agreed and forwarded to him a collection of poems that were published in 1922 under the title *Desolación*. The volume was an immediate success. A second edition was published in Santiago the following year, and an anthology of selected poems appeared soon thereafter in Spain.

In May 1921 Gabriela became the first director of the newly inaugurated Sixth School (*Liceo*) for Girls in Santiago, a large, impressive building with a faculty of thirty teachers. Some months after moving to Santiago she met the Mexican José Vasconcelos—philosopher, poet, writer of short stories and memoirs—who was at that time his country's minister of public education. Impressed by his interview with Gabriela, he returned to Mexico determined to secure her help in reforming Mexico's educational system. In the name of his government, he invited her and her friend, the painter and sculptor Laura Rodig, to spend six months in Mexico at that nation's expense. Gabriela accepted the invitation and arranged with the Chilean government to carry out a study of Mexico's extensive reforms during her stay.

The invitation, a gesture of friendship between the two nations, did not bring unqualified happiness. The failure of a Senate measure that would have provided her with some financial support from home, and the suspicion that Chile did not perhaps share Mexico's high opinion of her, were disappointing. Still, the excitement of leaving on her first international voyage buoyed her. Accompanied by Laura Rodig and another friend, Gabriela boarded the ship *Aconcagua*. They passed through the Panama Canal and traveled first to Cuba, then to Mexico, where Gabriela was received with warmth and enthusiasm.

"EMBRACED BY LIGHT": MISTRAL IN MEXICO—AND BEYOND

The six months stretched into almost two years. Everything possible was done to make her stay fruitful. Gabriela was given a comfortable house, and Palma Guillén, a bright young female university teacher, became her secretary, lifelong friend, and for a time, her romantic partner. Gabriela Mistral received an ample salary that was paid even after she left Mexico for several months' travel in Europe and the United States. During her stay, Mistral worked to establish a series of practical schools for women, the Escuelas-Hogar bearing her name. She traveled about the country helping organize educational programs in rural areas and overseeing new mobile libraries. Convinced that even the humblest citizen could and should appreciate first-class literature, she edited an anthology of poetry and prose that included many of her own pieces. Titled *Readings for Women*, the volume was published by the Mexican government in 1923.

Gabriela Mistral fell in love with Mexico as did Mexico with her. As she described it, the most powerful impression she felt during the first days in Mexico was that of peace: "I arrived at the house they have for me in the country. I went up to the roof. The horizon is immense and I felt embraced by light from the sky and by the silence of the fields all around me. For the first time in eighteen years, I know I can work in peace, without the sound of the hourly school bell, without money worries that perennially trouble my life."[14]

Laura Rodig described an incident that shows the depth of Gabriela's attachment to Mexico. A congress of campesinos (peasants and farmers) was to be held in the great auditorium of the University of Mexico. Gabriela decided to attend after being assured that she could go unofficially. But someone among the thousand persons in attendance recognized her, and she reluctantly agreed to appear on the stage with the other dignitaries. During the enthusiastic applause from the audience, a campesino in the balcony shouted above the noise, "I'd like to give that pretty lady a hug." It was almost by accident that he was heard at all, but Gabriela acknowledged him and with a gesture invited him to the speakers' platform. The audience responded to the novel event with shouts of encouragement and great hilarity. Sombreros sailed into the air as the young man made his way to the front. The trip seemed to take forever, and Gabriela and the directors of the congress felt increasingly uncomfortable. Finally he arrived, but upon coming face-to-face with Gabriela, his courage suddenly deserted him and he stood transfixed with fright. A tense, expectant hush fell over the audience. Sympathetic to his plight, Gabriela moved closer to him and, taking his hands—hands brown and hardened from manual labor—in hers, in a symbolic gesture that escaped no one present, gently kissed them.[15]

While Gabriela was still in Mexico, her friend José Vasconcelos had occasion to travel to Chile on official business. At one point he sent her a cablegram, its meaning quite mysterious at the time, saying, "More than ever convinced that the best of Chile is in Mexico."[16] Only after his return did Vasconcelos explain: during his visit a Chilean dignitary had asked him why the Mexicans had invited "la Mistral" when there were so many more interesting women than she in Chile. Vasconcelos's response was in the cable.[17]

Gabriela Mistral, the *patiloca*, found travel so much to her liking that after 1924 she never returned home for more than an occasional visit. Leaving behind at least one statue of herself and numerous schools, avenues, and libraries bearing her name, she departed Mexico for the United States and Europe. During that first trip abroad, *Ternura* (Tenderness), a collection of poems for children, many of them drawn from *Desolación*, was published in Madrid.

In barely three years she had published five books, establishing herself as one of the brightest stars in the world's literary firmament. If in 1912 she changed from Lucila Godoy into her own literary creation, the teacher-poet Gabriela Mistral, in 1924 she changed once again from persona to personage. Her every move was watched by admirers and critics, her comments dutifully recorded and reported, her travels punctuated by meetings with other well-known literary figures, by public appearances, by speeches and fanfare. Her fame made it impossible for her to fit back into the niche she had left behind in Santiago, so in 1925 at age thirty-six she retired on a small teacher's pension and began a kind of odyssey through the Americas and Europe as Chile's representative to one international organization after another: the League of Nations, the Institute of Intellectual Cooperation, the Congress of Educators in Switzerland, the International Federation of Universities in Madrid, the Institute of Educational Cinema in Rome, and so on. As she grew from simple teacher and poet to internationally recognized literary figure, she answered demands on her time by simplifying daily routines and depending on a circle of women friends and assistants for day-to-day existence. She was not interested in cooking or housekeeping, and she relied on others to track her finances and keep track of her speaking engagements. Her assistants were often highly qualified young women in their own right—writers, artists, professors—who were drawn to Gabriela and in many cases became her friends.[18]

During the late 1920s a military government came to power in Chile. Appreciating Gabriela's renown throughout Latin America, it offered her an ambassadorship to all Central America, a post she brusquely refused by speaking out against the government of Carlos Ibáñez. In retaliation her pension was suspended, leaving her virtually nothing to live on. Once word of her dilemma was made public, Eduardo Santos, editor of the Bogotá daily *El Tiempo* and future president of Colombia, offered her a sum equal to her pension in exchange for a monthly newspaper article. Similar arrangements were made with newspapers in Buenos Aires, Mexico, Costa Rica, and Madrid, so by dint of hard work Gabriela was able to support herself, her mother, and her sister.

Until 1930 Gabriela lived in France in rented houses near Paris, and later in southern France where she could enjoy both the sun and a less expensive way of life. During the late 1920s, possibly in 1928, she and her friend Paula Guillén adopted a nephew named Juan Miguel Godoy, reportedly the child of a half brother on Gabriela's father's side. The little boy was just an infant when she brought him to Europe, and she gave him a nickname—"Yin Yin"—in tribute to the light and joy he brought into her life. He later baptized her "Buddha" and inspired her to write for children with naturalness and spontaneity, free from didactic ends as she sought only to amuse her little Yin, as with her poem "The Little One-Armed Girl":

Well, a crab caught my little finger,
and the crab fell in the sand,
and the sea swallowed the sand.
And a whale hunter fished it from the sea
and the whaler got to Gibraltar;
and on Gibraltar the fishermen sing:
"We caught something new from the sea,
a little girl's finger:
Let the girl who lost it come for it!"

Well, give me a boat to go get it,
and give me a captain for the boat,
give me pay for the captain,
and for the pay I ask for the city:
Marseille with towers and plazas and ships,
in all the world the best city,
that won't be beautiful with a little girl
whose finger was stolen by the sea,
and the bands of whalers sing
and await on Gibraltar.[19]

Gabriela roamed the Western Hemisphere in the early 1930s. She taught courses at Barnard College, Middlebury College, and the University of Puerto Rico, and visited Central America and the West Indies. When the government of Chile returned to civilian rule, her pension was restored, and she was named honorary consul to Madrid in 1933. The post brought her no salary but carried with it certain social benefits. All was well until 1935, when a letter she had written to an old friend in Chile found its way into print. In the letter she criticized the Spanish character and ended by exclaiming, "I don't know what I'm doing in Spain!" It took a week or so for the bomb to explode. When it did, Gabriela left for Portugal, where she tried to discover who was to blame for her disgrace. She believed that someone wishing to cause her harm had brought that Santiago newspaper article to the attention of the Spanish public, with predictable results. Gabriela's estrangement from Spain never healed. She distrusted the Spanish, feeling herself—a *mestiza*, a *campesina*—at a disadvantage among them.[20]

In 1935 a group of outstanding European writers who admired Gabriela's work petitioned Chilean president Arturo Alessandri to find a place for her as a paid consul. On September 17, with the president's encouragement, the Chilean Senate named Gabriela Mistral a consul for life. From then on she would be free to live anywhere in the Americas or Europe on a salary sufficient to her needs, and only by an act of Congress could her position be suspended or modified.

Gabriela did not take the honor lightly. During her lifetime abroad she represented her nation and the Americas well, trying to dispel misconceptions about Latin America and speaking out for humble people—women, children, Indigenous peoples, mestizos, and campesinos. She pleaded their case in poetry, prose poems, and articles that appeared in periodicals throughout the Spanish-speaking world. The plight of women was especially important to her. She knew the trials of women whose men were destroyed by alcoholism, and she knew the subtle as well as overt discrimination suffered by women who leave traditional ways of life for careers in education and the arts. From the very start she had been aware of the discouraging treatment given women writers. Either they were not criticized sternly enough—implying that no woman could be judged by the same criteria that men apply to each other—or their work was dismissed as hopelessly feminine.

After several years in Lisbon and Oporto, Gabriela went to Guatemala as general consul and chargé d'affaires. From there, in 1938, she traveled down the Atlantic coast of South America, first to Rio de Janeiro, then to Montevideo, where she took part in a historic public meeting with Alfonsina Storni of Argentina and the Uruguayan Juana de Ibarbourou. The three poets read autobiographies in verse to an enthralled audience, not suspecting that in a few months the tormented Alfonsina would commit suicide. Later, in Buenos Aires, Gabriela met with Victoria Ocampo, who for many years was the director of the Argentine literary magazine *Sur* and the publishing house of the same name.

Out of that meeting came the decision to publish a volume of Gabriela's poems written since the appearance of *Desolación* and *Ternura*. Ocampo offered to underwrite the costs of publication herself, and Gabriela responded by giving the proceeds of its sale to Basque children who were victims of Spain's civil war. *Tala*, variously translated as *Havoc* or *Felling*, was Gabriela's personal favorite among the books of verse published under her name even though it was not greeted with the enthusiasm her earlier works had enjoyed. Collected in that volume, and dedicated to Palma Guillén, were the poems written after her mother's death in 1929, a series of verses about the American landscape, the disillusionment of middle age, and her feelings of rootlessness, of being forever in a foreign land.

Her already eventful journey was crowned by her reception in Chile. After an absence of thirteen years, however, she found herself a foreigner in her own country. Everywhere she went in Santiago during that visit, she was treated with glorious warmth by Chileans—and the smile that shines from photographs taken during the visit are proof of the pleasure she felt. But Chile was no longer home. She was more in touch with the Chile of her multicolored memories than with the nation that welcomed her in 1938.

A MOTHER'S GRIEF: LOSING JUAN MIGUEL

Gabriela returned to Europe and established a Chilean consulate in Nice on France's Mediterranean coast. When war broke out the following year, she moved to Brazil, settling first in Niterói and, in 1941, in Petrópolis. But the tentacles of war stretched across the Atlantic and followed her to her haven. To the south, the Argentine leader Juan Domingo Perón was at odds with the United States and, as a result, appeared to favor the Nazis and Italian Fascists in the coming conflict.

To the north, the United States entered the war on the Allied side, and in cities and towns throughout the Americas people took sides with varying degrees of vehemence. Gabriela was anti-fascist by temperament and philosophy and had opposed Franco's regime in Spain as she had Chile's military government of the late 1920s. In Petrópolis she and her son Juan Miguel favored the Allies, the French in particular.

Years of residence in France had given her adopted son, now in his teens, a decidedly French manner, and his schoolmates ridiculed him for being different. Gabriela worried about him, but when she counseled him to leave school, he refused. In 1943, at age seventeen, Juan Miguel became enamored of a young girl who was German by descent, and he was subjected even more to the taunts and teasing of other young men who laughed at his slight hunchback and tried to convince him that the girl mocked him in his absence.

"Yin" was visibly upset by such treatment but seemed able to put the attachment behind him. With Gabriela he made plans to continue his studies, paid annual dues to various organizations, and even rearranged his room. Then suddenly he was dead of arsenic poisoning. Gabriela sat at his bedside through the endless hours preceding his death, suffering an agony of the spirit that equaled his physical pain. In the days following his death she was unable to walk, unable to think, only aware of the devastating loss. Her son, her "Yin," was dead. It was impossible for her to believe that he had committed suicide. Someone must have driven him to it, or drugged him, or perhaps he was actually murdered by a band of evil youths. The rest of the world might believe that he took his own life, but she could not. Even so, it was difficult for her to understand the catastrophe: "Ah, but I have to return to my old heresy and believe in Karma from past lives in order to understand what phenomenal, what terribly high crime of mine was punished by my Juan Miguel's night of agony in a hospital, so frightening in spite of the incredible stoicism with which he bore the hot coals of arsenic in his poor, beloved body."[21] In her dreams she saw him alive again; she felt him nearby during hours of sleeplessness. Dangerously suspended between reality and her grief, she reached out to the dead youth, the companion of her years of travel, the arm she had leaned on in the strange streets of Europe. Juan Miguel had been her only blood tie to the future, and now she was alone, trapped in her own mortality. Among all the people who had known her, who had sought her out, she counted only six as friends. When Palma Guillén, one of that number, arrived in Petrópolis shortly after the tragedy, she found Gabriela alone, locked in her big house, in a dreadful state of isolation. Her bitterness spread out in waves, threatening to drown her in its venom.

For two years she languished in Brazil, her heart already weak, now doubly burdened by diabetes. Then on November 15, 1945, she received word that she had been awarded the Nobel Prize in Literature, the first Latin American poet and one of very few women so honored. Her comment on hearing the news: "Perhaps it was because I represent the women and children." Three days later she boarded a ship and sailed for Stockholm. The Nobel Prize enthroned Gabriela Mistral, crowned her queen of Latin America's literary kingdom. At the award ceremony Sweden's King Gustav, elderly and white haired, presented the award. Tall and straight, draped in a black velvet gown, the former schoolteacher and *campesina* faced the king and in the serene dignity of her manner rivaled him in majesty. In a short address of thanks, Gabriela accepted the prize humbly, not for herself, but for Latin America and for the "poets of my race."[22]

Like all "coronations," this one was preceded by years of political maneuvering. An Ecuadorian writer, Adela de Velasco, first suggested that Chile place her name in nomination while Gabriela's friend of many years, Pedro Aguirre Cerda, occupied the Chilean presidency. He wholeheartedly supported the idea and instructed Chile's diplomatic corps in Europe to promote her candidacy, a task that fell to another friend, Chile's ambassador to France, who was from Gabriela's native province. Excellent French and Swedish translations of her verses were prepared. Rumors swirled about her before the awards in 1944; they came to nothing. In 1945, similar rumors spread through Latin America, this time with glorious success, and Gabriela Mistral underwent the final transformation into queen of her aesthetic kingdom.

Not all queens are happy, however. Gabriela, honored by the world yet consumed by grief and her inborn melancholy, left Stockholm, toured Europe briefly, embarked for the United States, and finally came to rest in California, where she bought a house with her prize money. She who had brought unequaled honor to Chile rejected the warmth that her country could have offered in return and chose to live in a foreign country. Far from her own people, trusting only a handful of friends, Gabriela withdrew from the world and in solitude mourned her dead. She wrote a series of poems on grief and loss during those bleak years and later, in 1954, saw them published in her last volume of verse, titled *Lagar* (*Wine Press*). Among its poems was "Mourning," also known as "Luto":

In a single night it burst from my chest,
pushed aside the bones, opened my flesh,
its shoots reached my head.

Over shoulders, over backs,
it sent out great leaves and branches
and in three days I was covered,
rich with it as with my blood.
Where will they touch me now?
What arm will I give that isn't mourning?

Like the clouds of smoke
I'm no longer flame nor embers.
I am this spiral and this vine
and this ring of dense smoke.

....

In the length of one night
my sun set, my day went away,
and my flesh became a cloud of smoke
that a child cuts with his hand.

Color leached out of my clothes,
the whites, the blues, fled
and in the morning I found myself
turned into a pine of sparks.[23]

Now alone with her fame, her poetry, and memories of things too painful to tell, Gabriela Mistral continued to work on her poetry and her correspondence with other notables and the many people who contacted her. Among the latter was Doris Dana, a young academic from New York who first wrote to her in 1946 and soon became Gabriela's friend, traveling companion, and romantic partner, although it was not until fifty years after Doris Dana's death that Gabriela's letters were published by Doris Dana's estate. The publication laid to rest any questions about her love life. By mid-1949, Gabriela felt able to write, "I have only you in this world. I haven't told you this directly. I only have you, and I love only you."[24] Together the two women traveled to Gabriela's consular postings.

By that time, Gabriela's health was very poor. Upon arriving in Mexico, she suffered a collapse, and only the constant care of a physician saved her life. For a time, as Chile's consul in Veracruz, she remained in the land of so many warm memories, where schoolchildren by the thousands recited her *rondas*. Because she was forbidden by her doctors to travel to the capital city, Mexico's literary elite traveled to her and paid homage to the queen of poetry. In 1950 she began her travels once again: first to Washington, D.C., then to Naples and the little Italian town of Rapallo, where she established her consulate.

Age and fame did not bring Gabriela tranquility; if she felt pleasure over the honors and tributes paid her, it did not show. Even her most fervent supporters knew of *su memoria enemiga*, her hostile memory that seemed to cherish the bad and forget the good things of her life. Now a misanthrope, she expected the worst, saw the worst, and recounted with barely controlled passion the injuries and tragedies she had accumulated over many years. She fought with Federico de Onís, the original publisher of *Desolación*, and complained that she never earned more than a hundred dollars from that popular book. She was never reconciled with the Spanish people and until her last day, she spoke of the hatred she imagined Spain harbored toward her. The Chilean literary critic Raúl Silva Castro became her archenemy in 1935 when he published a study of *Desolación* and *Ternura*. Silva Castro wrote that her work was overvalued, that her poetry suffered from imperfections in rhyme and meter, and that her poetic vocabulary was often coarse and masculine. No matter that dozens of other critics praised her verses, recognizing that Gabriela's primeval spirit could never be contained in perfect poetic forms, that the words of mestiza America were as valid artistically as the vocabulary of Spain. Gabriela felt the wounds of criticism far more sharply than the balm of praise.

Most incomprehensible was her distrust of Chile. In the last decade of her life, she chose to believe that a minister of education had forced her to leave Chile in the 1920s by naming her delegate to an international institute in Paris—as though she were not happy to receive the post. She continued to believe that her short visit to Chile in 1938 had been marred by hostile glances cast toward her in the streets. She believed against all evidence that she could never return to Chile to live peacefully among her own people. Friends wrote constantly about the ceremonies in her honor throughout the country, about invitations from one organization after another. Gabriela remained skeptical. Even when a group of friends persuaded the Chilean government to award her an extraordinary prize of a half million pesos, Gabriela continued to doubt Chile's love for her.

Finally, after years of hesitation and excuses, she was persuaded to return home in 1954. Palma Guillén, by then a member of Mexico's diplomatic corps in Rome, helped her embark at Genoa. Accompanied first by Margaret Bates, then by Doris Dana, she wound her way through the Americas, from New York to Havana and finally to Chile. Wrapped as securely in her incredible fame as she was in the smoke from her ever-present cigarettes, the stately, melancholy queen moved from one mass reception to the next. Her stay in Chile was a triumph. Dressed in her long, shapeless coat, her face creased by fatigue and illness, she was decorated, applauded, and honored by the Chilean nation. Then, in the care of Doris Dana, she left home once again.

EPILOGUE

Gabriela Mistral's life ebbed and finally slipped away under an onslaught of physical ills on January 10, 1957. When she died of pancreatic cancer in a hospital on Long Island, New York, she weighed scarcely ninety pounds. Gabriela Mistral's final journey took her from New York to Santiago, and finally to a small hilltop in Montegrande. Her gift to the world, an inheritance in poetry and prose, remains in collections of verse, two of them published after her death, and a multitude of prose pieces, some gathered into anthologies and many still buried in newspapers and magazines. Original and unique, Gabriela Mistral left behind no crowd of young poets to follow in her footsteps, founded no new school of poetry. Her intense verse, chiseled by pain and empathy, belongs not to the literary elite but to the children who sing her *rondas*, to the mothers who nurse their babies in poor huts of the Andean cordillera, and to Latin Americans who look not to Europe but to their own land for sustenance. Gabriela was a teacher, poet, and a queen—an enigma wreathed in smoke who touched the deepest strains of human feeling as few have ever done.

NOTES

1. Santiago Daydí-Tolson, "Gabriela Mistral," Poetry Foundation, https://poetryfoundation.org/gabrielamistral.
2. Gabriela Mistral, "Colofón con cara de excusa," in *Ternura* (Madrid: Espasa-Calpe, 1979), 169.
3. Gabriela Mistral, "Cuaderno de los Andes (1914–1917)," in *Bendita mi lengua sea. Diario íntimo*, ed. Jaime Quezada (Santiago, Chile: Editorial Catalonia, 2019), 9.
4. Juan Loveluck, ed., "Documentos: Cartas de Gabriela Mistral a Amado Nervo," *Revista Iberoamericana* (September 1970): 499, fn. 2.
5. Gabriela Mistral, *Epistolario: Cartas a Eugenio Labarca (1915–1916)* (Santiago: Ediciones de los Anales de la Universidad de Chile, no. 13, 1957), 39.
6. Gabriela Mistral, "Poema del hijo," in *Poesías completas*, 4th ed., ed. Margaret Bates (Madrid: Aguilar, 1968), 102–6. See also *Desolación*.
7. Mistral, *Epistolario*, 36.
8. Mistral, *Epistolario*, 21.
9. Mistral, "Himno al árbol," in *Poesías completas*, 347–52. See also *Desolación*.
10. Mistral, "El corro luminoso," in *Poesías completas*, 241–42. See also *Desolación*.
11. Mistral, "Colofón con cara de excusa," 3.
12. Mistral, *Epistolario*, 36.
13. Marie-Lise Gazarian-Gautier, "La prosa de Gabriela Mistral, o una verdadera joya desconocida," *Revista chilena de literatura*, no. 36 (November 1990): 19; Cecilia García-Huidobro, *Tics de los chilenos: Vicios y virtudes nacionales* (Santiago, Chile: Editorial Catalonia, 2018), 7.
14. Esther Andradi, "Gabriela de México," *Jornada de Baja California*, May 6, 2016.
15. Pedro Pablo Zegers B., *Gabriela y México* (Santiago, Chile: R/L Editores, 2007), 32–33.
16. Zegers B., *Gabriela y México*, 33.
17. Zegers B., *Gabriela y México*, 33.
18. Velma García-Gorena, "Gabriela Mistral's Letters to Doris Dana," *Massachusetts Review* 56, no. 49 (Winter 2015): 596.
19. Mistral, "La manca," in *Poesías completas*, 280. See also *Ternura*.
20. Hernán Soto, "Gabriela y España," *Cultura*, no. 832 (July 24, 2015): 21.
21. Germán Gautier, "La llama dulce de mi vida," *Reportajes: Gabriela Mistral y Yin Yin*, Fundación La Fuente, November 27, 2015.
22. Hjalmar Gullberg, "Award Ceremony Speech, December 10, 1945," Nobel Prize in Literature 1945, https//www.nobelprize.org.
23. Gabriela Mistral, "Luto," in *Poesías completas*, 711–13. See also *Lagar*.
24. García-Gorena, "Gabriela Mistral's Letters to Doris Dana," 608.

REFERENCES

Andradi, Esther. "Gabriela de México." *Jornada de Baja California*, May 6, 2018.
Bates, Margaret. "Gabriela Mistral's Poema de Chile." *Americas* 17, no. 3 (1961).
Comité de Homenaje a Gabriela Mistral. *Antología general de Gabriela Mistral.* Santiago, Chile: Editorial Roble de Chile, 1970.
Daydí-Tolson, Santiago. "Gabriela Mistral." Poetry Foundation. https://www.poetryfoundation.org/gabrielamistral.
Fiol-Matta, Licia. *A Queer Mother for the Nation.* Minneapolis: University of Minnesota Press, 2002.
García-Gorena, Velma. "Gabriela Mistral's Letters to Doris Dana." *Massachusetts Review* 56, no. 4 (Winter 2015).
García-Huidobro, Cecilia. *Tics de los chilenos: Vicios y virtudes nacionales*. Santiago, Chile: Editorial Catalonia, 2018.
Gautier, Germán. "La llama dulce de mi vida." *Reportajes: Gabriela Mistral y Yin Yin.* Fundación La Fuente, November 27, 2015. https://www.fundacionlafuente.cl/reportajes/gabriela-mistral-y-yin-yin-la-llama-dulce-de-mi-vida/.
Gazarian-Gautier, Marie-Lise. *Gabriela Mistral: The Teacher from the Valley of Elqui.* Chicago: Franciscan Herald Press, 1975.
———. "La prosa de Gabriela Mistral, o una verdadera joya desconocida." *Revista chilena de literatura* 36 (November 1990).
Gullberg, Hjalmar. "Award Ceremony Speech, December 10, 1945." Nobel Prize in Literature 1945. https://www.nobelprize.org.
Iglesias, Augusto. *Gabriela Mistral y el modernismo en Chile*. Santiago: Editorial Universidad de Chile, 1949
Ladrón de Guevara, Matilde. *Gabriela Mistral, rebelde magnífica*. Buenos Aires: Editorial Losada, 1962.
Loveluck, Juan, ed. "Documentos: Cartas de Gabriela Mistral a Amado Nervo." *Revista Iberoamericana* (September 1970): 495–508.
Mistral, Gabriela. "Colofón con cara de excusa." In *Ternura*. Madrid: Espasa-Calpe, 1979.
———. "Cuaderno de los Andes (1914–1917)." In *Bendita mi lengua sea. Diario íntimo*, edited by Jaime Quezada. Santiago, Chile: Editorial Catalonia, 2019.
———. *Epistolario: Cartas a Eugenio Labarca (1915–1916)*. Santiago: Ediciones de los Anales de la Universidad de Chile, no. 13, 1957.
———. *Poesías completas*, 4th ed. Edited by Margaret Bates. Madrid: Aguilar, 1968.
———. *Selected Poems of Gabriela Mistral.* Translated and edited by Doris Dana. Baltimore: Johns Hopkins University Press, 1971.
Soto, Hernán. "Gabriela y España." *Cultura* 832 (July 24, 2015).
Valenzuela Fuenzalida, Álvaro. "Gabriela Mistral y la reforma educacional de José Vasconcelos." *Reencuentro*, no. 34 (September 2002): 9–26.
Zegers B., Pedro Pablo. *Gabriela y México.* Santiago, Chile: R/L Editores, 2007.

Chapter 6

Frida Kahlo, 1907–1954

INTRODUCTION

The early twentieth century brought profound change to everyday urban life in select cities of the world. Those years found automobiles starting to fill city streets and electricity coming to illuminate homes and offices. Theoretical physicist Albert Einstein published papers explaining his special theory of relativity, thus pointing the way to the approaching atomic age. Many members of the upper classes and those of the rapidly growing middle class prospered during this time of change. Not so the poor and uneducated of the world, a considerable majority of the global population. Not only were such people marginalized from fast-moving change but, rather, many of them were thrust ever deeper into poverty. Over the last years of the nineteenth century and the early years of the twentieth, cycles of economic boom and bust intensified the misery of the poor. This deepening of inequality across the world led to ever more strident demands for social reform. Reformers of the extreme Left embraced the violent ideology of German philosopher Karl Marx and Russian revolutionary Vladimir Ilyich Lenin. According to this political philosophy of communism, workers of the world would inevitably rise up against the exploitation they suffered and destroy capitalism and the economic elites who profited from it. The early twentieth-century world was at once a place of extraordinary technological change and a powder keg of social discontent.

Perhaps curiously, it was Mexico that became the setting of the new century's first popular revolt against the system of global capitalism that intensified the misery of the humble while lifting up the well-to-do. The Mexican Revolution of 1910–1920 was not Communist in nature. Rather, it was a populist uprising whose foremost leaders were not Marxist-Leninist ideologues.

This included Emiliano Zapata, a landless, charismatic peasant from central Mexico who led a ragtag army of people like him—men and women alike—to victory against the savage capitalism that dominated the world of his time.

Mexico's long and bloody revolution achieved many of its goals. Rising from it was the Constitution of 1917, the most progressive national charter in force anywhere in the world at that time. It had the effect of thrusting Mexico into the twentieth century at the level of social reform, and through it the country became more egalitarian than ever before. The 1917 Mexican Constitution empowered peasants and workers, and even members of the middle class, while liberating women to a remarkable extent. No one exemplified this new freedom more than the daughter of a Mexico City photographer named Frida Kahlo.

RAISING FRIDA: THE EARLY YEARS

The daughter of an adventurous German immigrant father and a Mexican mother, Frida Kahlo was born into a large family that included two half sisters. Her father, Wilhelm Kahlo, had departed Europe with two friends in 1891 to seek his fortune in the Americas. The trio chose Mexico City as their destination both because they had contacts within the city's German community and because they knew that Mexico valued the skills brought to the country by European immigrants. Once Kahlo and his companions reached the city, they found work in a German-owned jewelry store named the Pearl. Nineteen-year-old Wilhelm changed his first name to Guillermo and within three years married a Mexican woman his own age. She died in 1898 giving birth to the couple's second daughter. A distraught Kahlo, finding himself caring for two infant children, sought the help of an older female acquaintance, Isabel González de Calderón, the mother of one of his coworkers. Isabel González took matters in hand. She removed Kahlo's daughters from his life by packing them off to a convent to be raised by nuns and made daughters of the church. At the same time, Isabel González served as matchmaker between Kahlo and her daughter Matilde, the eldest of her twelve children. Unmarried at the age of twenty-four, Matilde was in danger of becoming an old maid—at least in her mother's opinion. In this way it came to be that in 1898 Guillermo Kahlo married Matilde Calderón. Over the next ten years the couple produced four children, all daughters. The third among them, born in 1907, was baptized Magdalena Carmen Frida Kahlo Calderón.

As he dusted off creative skills picked up in Germany, Guillermo Kahlo and his family flourished during the early years of the twentieth century.

Kahlo knew something of photography, having sold photographic equipment at his father's jewelry shop in Baden-Baden, Germany. Kahlo's father-in-law, a photographer, lent him a camera, and with it he established his own career. It helped that his wife's family was from Oaxaca, the hometown of the country's longtime president, Porfirio Díaz. Thanks to this connection, Guillermo Kahlo found himself called on to photograph the president and his family members. For this reason, he is remembered as Mexico's first official photographer. Kahlo's good fortune peaked in 1904, when Mexico's treasury secretary, José Limantour, awarded him a contract to create a photographic record of the country's greatest architectural treasures. They were to become part of a coffee-table book set for publication in 1910, during Mexico's centennial celebration of national independence. With the money earned from that commission the now-renowned photographer Guillermo Kahlo and his wife built a substantial house in the village of Coyoacán, five miles southwest of Mexico City. Faithful to the Oaxaca tradition of colorfully painted homes, Kahlo agreed with his wife's suggestion that the house be painted a vivid blue. To this day it is known as the Blue House.

In 1913, revolutionary factions waged a frightening artillery duel in the center of Mexico City. The incident of February 9–19, known as "The Tragic Ten Days," killed dozens of people. The Mexican Revolution also nearly destroyed the career of Guillermo Kahlo. When president Porfirio Díaz fell from power, the photographer lost access to government contracts, forcing his family to adopt a far more frugal lifestyle. Still, the Kahlos owned their own home and were blessed with four children, the liveliest of whom was Frida. Her father doted on her—especially after she contracted polio in 1913 at age six. Frida recovered quickly from the disease, but it left her with a slightly deformed right leg. When her father advised her to exercise to strengthen the leg, she took his advice. As revolution swept Mexico, residents of Coyoacán soon became used to seeing the child careening around the village on her bicycle and playing games with boys and girls alike.

In late 1921, fourteen-year-old Frida Kahlo prepared to begin her secondary education at Mexico City's German school, where students wore uniforms, attended gender-segregated classes, and were taught by Catholic nuns. But as the new school year approached, Minister of Education José Vasconcelos decreed that as of 1922 all public schools would enroll both male and female students who would attend class together. Secular-minded Guillermo Kahlo jumped at the chance to transfer his favorite daughter from the conservative and religious German school to Mexico's premier public high school, the National Preparatory School, known as the Preparatoria. Frida became a member of the institution's first freshman class, one of thirty-five females in a student body totaling more than two thousand.

Frida Kahlo flourished at the elite institution. Her sparkling personality, intelligence, and rebellious streak—not to mention her good looks—quickly earned her acceptance as a member of its dominant clique, *las cachuchas*, so named for the wool caps worn by its members. Soon Frida became the girlfriend of Alejandro Gómez Arias, the leader of *las cachuchas*. *Las cachuchas* divided their time between attending class and devising ways to torment their teachers, some of whom were Mexico's foremost intellectuals. One of their most memorable pranks was at the expense of orator and scholar Antonio Caso. One day just as class began, a member of *las cachuchas* placed a substantial firecracker outside a window high above the podium where Caso lectured. When it exploded, showering Caso with glass, the elderly scholar impressed his students by casually brushing the debris from his hair and shoulders and continuing his lecture. A year later Frida Kahlo carried out a less spectacular prank that resulted in her expulsion from the school. Upon learning of her punishment, a furious Frida walked down the street and stormed into the office of Education Minister José Vasconcelos. There she demanded readmittance to the Preparatoria. Whatever she said convinced Vasconcelos to readmit her to school. Vasconcelos telephoned the school's director, Vicente Lombardo Toledano, ordering him to readmit Kahlo: "If you can't manage a little girl like that," said Vasconcelos, "you're not fit to be director of such an institution."[1]

Artist Diego Rivera and his colleagues figured among the victims of *las cachuchas*. In the early 1920s Rivera, José Clemente Orozco, and David Alfaro Siqueiros were hired by José Vasconcelos to memorialize Mexico's revolution by painting murals on the walls of public buildings in and around the national capital. Two such buildings were the Preparatoria and the Ministry of Education headquarters, located a few blocks from each other in the heart of Mexico City. *Las cachuchas* liked to sneak under the scaffolds where the muralists worked and set fire to piles of wood shavings that had collected there. The pranks stopped abruptly when the muralists began wearing sidearms as they worked. That was about the time Frida Kahlo would hide in the shadows beneath the scaffold where Diego Rivera worked on murals on the Ministry of Education building. One evening Rivera's wife Lupe Marín was keeping him company. "Hey, Diego," Frida shouted, "here comes Nahui!" She was referring to Nahui Olín, a model of Rivera's who was his mistress at the time. Some months later, as Rivera continued working on his ambitious murals at the ministry building, Frida developed the habit of stopping by after school to watch him work. Soon she came to admire and like Rivera. Once Kahlo scandalized her classmates by announcing that she intended to marry Rivera and bear him a son. When one of her friends pointed out that the muralist was fat, ugly, twice her age, and not particularly fond of bathing, she defended him as a gentle and wise man, adding that when they married, she would "bathe and clean him."[2] She was only joking. The person she really intended to marry was Alejandro Gómez Arias, leader of *las cachuchas* and the most popular student at the Preparatoria.

Frida attached herself to Gómez Arias the moment she laid eyes on him. A compulsive letter writer, she bombarded him with letters from her earliest days at the Preparatoria. Soon she was closing them "All my love," and not long after that referring to herself as "your woman." By early 1925 Frida, now eighteen, promised that soon "we are going to love each other a lot," and she was making plans for both of them to live in the United States following their marriage.[3] She started taking part-time jobs to pay for two plane tickets to New York City. Unfortunately, problems of a sexual nature soon ruined Frida's relationship with Gómez. A few months into 1925 she was seduced by an older woman at the Ministry of Education library, where she worked part-time. When her parents found out, a scandal erupted. Afterward Frida wrote Gómez Arias that "not everything is as one would want it to be, and what's the point of talking about it." At the bottom of the letter she drew a crying face. Soon thereafter Frida was seduced a second time, this time by a friend of her father's named Fernando Fernández, a commercial printer. The same night Frida slept with Fernández she had her first sexual encounter with her boyfriend Gómez Arias. Many years later Gómez Arias told Frida Kahlo's biographer Hayden Herrera, "Frida was sexually precocious. To her sex was a form of enjoying life, a kind of vital impulse." In 1925, however, Gómez Arias was furious that the woman he had contemplated marrying had an entirely too open attitude toward sex.[4] He decided to break up with her. His only question was how to go about it. Within three weeks he had the answer.

On September 17, 1925, Frida Kahlo and Alejandro Gómez Arias were sitting together on a bus traveling from downtown Mexico City to Coyoacán. Suddenly the bus stalled on the tracks as a streetcar approached. The streetcar driver hit his brakes but could not stop before he slowly broadsided the bus. The bus bowed under the impact and exploded in a deadly cloud of glass, wood splinters, and metal. Three passengers were killed outright. Gómez Arias found himself under the bus unhurt. He climbed up through the wreckage looking for Frida and found her covered with blood, her clothing torn off by the force of the blast. He picked her up, carried her into a billiard hall, laid her on a table, and covered her with his coat. A bystander noticed a steel rod protruding from her side and slowly withdrew it. Frida's screams drowned out the siren of an approaching ambulance.

Chapter 6

FRIDA KAHLO, ARTIST

Doctors at the nearby Red Cross hospital believed Frida Kahlo would not survive the accident. In addition to being speared by the steel rod, her pelvis was broken in three places, her right leg fractured in eleven places, and her right foot crushed. Her collarbone and two ribs were broken, and her spine was fractured in three places. Yet Frida did not die. In fact, she appeared to recover quickly. Within two weeks of the accident, she was receiving a stream of visitors—family members, classmates, and friends from Coyoacán. But Alejandro Gómez Arias was not among them. As the weeks passed and Frida lay in bed covered in casts and bandages from her neck to her right foot, it became clear that something was wrong. Between October and November 1925, she sent Gómez Arias a stream of letters, always signing them "Your darling Friducha." Gómez never responded. At last, in early December, three months after the accident, Frida left the hospital and went in search of him. When she at last located Gómez at his parents' house, an argument ensued over his refusal to have a promiscuous girlfriend. Frida understood at last. On December 19, 1925, she wrote to Gómez Arias accusing him of telling her friends that she had slept with someone else "on the same day that I did it for the first time in my life [with you]." She defended her actions, writing, "I like myself just the way I am." She ended up justifying her liberal attitude toward sex: "It's what EVERYONE does, do you understand?"[5]

Frida Kahlo's recovery from her near death experience was as miraculous as her flowering as an artist. Describing herself as "bored as hell" during her months immobile in bed, she began painting with brushes and a palette lent by her father. She discovered that she liked to paint. By early 1926 she was at work on her first self-portrait, a gift to Alejandro Gómez Arias that she hoped would bring him back to her. When the painting was complete in September 1926, she wrote Gómez that her portrait was being delivered to his house and that he was to "put it in a low place where you can see it as if you were looking at me."[6] It was a striking portrait of a beautiful young woman whose golden skin was visible through the V-neck of a low-cut yet modest dress. She gazes out at the viewer with penetrating eyes, placid but full of promise. Her painting had the desired effect. The couple reconciled not long before Gómez Arias was dispatched to Europe by his parents, who were anxious to put distance between their son and Frida Kahlo.

In September 1926 Frida suffered a relapse. Doctors put her in a plaster corset to correct the displacement of three spinal vertebrae and put a cast on her right foot as well. Incredibly, no X-rays had been taken following her accident because her family could not afford them. Frida's relapse kept her confined to bed for the following nine months. While in bed she continued to paint portraits of friends and family, and of her old high school *cuates* (pals). *Las Cachuchas* (1927) was in the cubist style, popular at the time in Europe and the Americas. By year's end Frida was back on her feet—and Alejandro Gómez Arias was home from Europe. But as his parents hoped, his relationship with Kahlo had cooled. Within a few months he was engaged to marry one of his classmates from the Preparatoria. While Frida remained on good terms with Gómez Arias for the rest of her life, she at last accepted the fact that they would never marry.

In late January 1928 Frida met a young Cuban law student named Julio Antonio Mella, who was a leader of his country's newly formed Communist Party. He had been driven from the island under threat of death by the government of President Gerardo Machado. Once in Mexico, Mella met and became the lover of Tina Modotti, a fellow Communist and founder of Mexico City's radical salon, a social group made up of members of the artistic community and leaders of the nation's tiny Communist Party. Most of the artists were devout Marxist-Leninists. Modotti was an Italian-born photographer who had arrived in the city five years before and instantly became an important figure in the artistic community. She was also an ardent Stalinist. A beautiful young woman, she became a model for and then lover of Diego Rivera, figuring into the breakup of Rivera's marriage to Lupe Marín in early 1928. When Frida Kahlo met Tina Modotti, Diego Rivera was in Russia helping the Soviets celebrate the tenth anniversary of the Bolshevik Revolution. As general secretary of Mexico's Anti-Imperialist League and a member of the Mexican Communist Party (PCM), and his country's best-known artist, Rivera was the only member of his group invited to attend the Bolshevik celebration.

Rivera returned to Mexico City in May 1928. By then Frida Kahlo had joined the Young Communist League and taken to wearing khaki skirts and khaki shirts with a red star on the pocket, and a red scarf emblazoned with a hammer and sickle. She fit in politically with Modotti's salon. And she also knew how to party with the bohemian group. Frida Kahlo chain-smoked cigarettes and drank tequila like a mariachi—and swore like one too. In July 1928 she encountered Diego Rivera at one of Tina Modotti's parties and was thrilled when the muralist got drunk and shot a hole through the hostess's record player. Not long afterward Kahlo showed Rivera several of her paintings and was delighted when he praised her talent. Rivera, now single, accepted Frida Kahlo's invitation to see all her works. Their relationship deepened quickly. In December Frida appeared front and center in Rivera's mural *The Distribution of Arms* at the Ministry of Education. In it she is shown dressed in her Young Communist League uniform, distributing rifles to Mexican peasants. Tina Modotti is depicted in a less heroic pose and at the

Figure 6.1. Portrait of Frida Kahlo and Diego Rivera. By Carl Van Vechten, March 13, 1932. Library of Congress

extreme right side of the mural. When one of Rivera's friends saw the completed work, he remarked, "It looks like Diego has a new girlfriend." Indeed, he did. During 1929 Rivera and Kahlo were increasingly seen together, as in figure 6.1. In Mexico City's 1929 May Day parade, they marched side by side. By that time Rivera was visiting the Blue House in Coyoacán on a regular basis. In August he asked Guillermo Kahlo for permission to marry his daughter. Kahlo consented but warned, "She's a devil, you know."[7]

Why, one asks, did Frida Kahlo, a beautiful young woman of twenty-two, want to marry a fat and homely man of forty-three, twice married and known to be a womanizer? Similarly, why did Rivera, famous in his country and internationally, choose to marry a petite young self-taught artist from Coyoacán? The answers are fairly straightforward. Diego Rivera liked being married. He liked Frida's politics and was convinced that she promised to become an important artist. Finally, he liked her family, he liked Coyoacán, and he liked the Blue House. Frida's reasons for marrying Rivera included her admiration of alpha males—and no male was more alpha than Diego Rivera. She also accepted his proposal because he was Mexico's most famous artist, because he was kind, and because he told her he loved her. And who cared that he was fat and ugly and dwarfed her physically? She had considered those things years earlier when she told friends she wanted to marry Rivera, bear him a son, and bathe him on a regular basis. The two married on August 21, 1929. Rivera got drunk at the reception and shot one of the guests in the finger. Frida burst into tears and went home to the Blue House. Tina Modotti had the last word about the unlikely match: "Let's see how this turns out!"[8]

Two pivotal events followed hard on the heels of the Kahlo-Rivera wedding. First, Rivera resigned from the Mexican Communist Party (PCM), a decision he would regret for the rest of his life. Second, he accepted a commission that helped raise his visibility outside Mexico, especially in the United States. For months Rivera had been under attack by the PCM for taking lucrative commissions from the Mexican government and from wealthy members of the bourgeoisie. His fellow party members were especially angry over Rivera's refusal to accept the demand of Joseph Stalin that Communists slavishly follow his orders. At the moment of his break with the Communists, Rivera was in fact being handed the princely sum of $12,000 from Wall Street financier and US ambassador to Mexico Dwight Morrow. The ambassador hired Rivera to paint murals on the walls of his mansion in Cuernavaca, known as the Palace of Cortés, once the retreat of the conqueror of the Aztecs.

It was in the idyllic setting of Ambassador Dwight Morrow's vacation home that Frida Kahlo adopted the colorful dress of Tehuana Indians. Both Frida and her husband had come to love the Indigenous culture of far southwestern Mexico, on the Pacific Ocean side of the Isthmus of Tehuantepec. José Vasconcelos had taken Rivera to visit Tehuantepec in late 1923, and the muralist was electrified by what he saw. The lush jungles of Tehuantepec, its colorful wildlife, and handsome people became recurrent themes in his art after that time. Frida Kahlo also loved Tehuana culture. One of her earliest paintings, *Two Women* (1929), reveals striking Tehuanas against a lush jungle backdrop. The long indigenous skirts that became part of her costume had the added advantage of concealing her deformed and injured right leg. In explaining her new mode of dress and her embrace of indigenous themes in her art, Frida Kahlo wrote, "Rivera showed me the revolutionary sense of life and the true sense of color."[9]

By seizing on Mexico's Indigenous past to aid them in glorifying the country's 1910 revolution, Rivera, Kahlo, and others in Mexico's artistic community provided a vital service to all of Indigenous America. For half a millennium the people of Spanish- and Portuguese-speaking America had disparaged Indigenous peoples and their cultures and marginalized them from greater society. Suddenly, in the 1920s, the muralists Rivera, Orozco, Siqueiros, and their colleagues not only featured their country's native peoples in their work but glorified them. That invigorated what became known as Indianism (*indigenismo*), or idealization of the American Indian.

The artistic revolution brought by Rivera and his colleagues attracted the attention of North Americans put off by the crassness and excesses of the Jazz Age and then appalled by the Great Depression that followed. In Mexico they found the beauty and simplicity they felt their own country had lost. At the level of art, many of these Americans had grown tired of expressionism and cubism and were ready to be charmed by the romantic primitivism of postrevolutionary Mexican art. Consequently, and as historian Helen Delpar puts it, during the 1920s and 1930s there was an "enormous vogue of things Mexican" in the United States.[10]

During those years no Americans were more in love with Mexico than wealthy US ambassador Dwight Morrow and his wife. And at that time no Mexicans benefited more from Morrow's infatuation with their country than Diego Rivera and Frida Kahlo. While Rivera painted murals at the Palace of Cortés, Morrow organized a traveling exhibition of Mexican art in the United States that featured several of Rivera's paintings. Nearly five hundred thousand Americans viewed the exhibit. In late 1930, after Rivera completed his commission in Cuernavaca, Morrow used his influence to help the artist and his wife travel to the United States. Many more commissions and ever greater fame awaited Rivera there. Diego Rivera and Frida Kahlo departed for San Francisco in early November 1930. It was a visit that stretched to over three years.

Diego Rivera's American experience was an extended tour de force. He and his exotic and colorfully dressed wife were lionized wherever they went. They remained in San Francisco through most of 1931, save for Diego's two-month absence insisted on by Mexican president Pascual Ortiz Rubio, who demanded that he complete a mural at the National Palace. While in Mexico City Rivera supervised construction of what came to be known as the "double house," a residence on the outskirts of the city. While inspecting the new house, which featured an ample studio for Frida on its left side and an even larger studio for Rivera on its right, Rivera received Russian film director Sergei Eisenstein, the first of many notable foreign visitors who would seek him out over succeeding years. Returning to San Francisco, Rivera presided over a retrospective of 129 of his works, all the while painting murals at the San Francisco Stock Exchange and the San Francisco Art Institute. From California the couple traveled on to New York City, where in December 1931 Rivera presided over a major exhibition of his work at the Museum of Modern Art. It was a smashing success, leading one of the city's art critics to refer to the Mexican as "the most talked-about man on this side of the Atlantic."[11] From New York it was on to Detroit, where Edsel Ford commissioned Rivera to create an ambitious mural celebrating the triumph of the machine age. Finally, in March 1933, and near the end of the couple's stay, Rivera was commissioned to create a mural at New York City's Rockefeller Center, which was under construction at the time.

Frida did not much enjoy her stay in the United States. She hated its opulence amid the poverty and suffering that she observed throughout the Depression-straitened country. She was also repulsed by industrial America and its pollution. Still, her US experience had a profound impact on her art. A miscarriage she suffered while in Detroit set her on the path toward becoming the world's most forthright artist depicting the tribulations of childbirth. Her surreal painting *Henry Ford Hospital* (1932) depicts a weeping Frida lying in a pool of blood on a hospital bed that is floating in the air. Surrounding her and also floating, connected to her womb by blood-red tubes, are her badly deformed male fetus, her shattered pelvis, and other sobering objects. The most shocking of her birth-related paintings also dates from her year in Detroit. It was inspired by her husband's suggestion that she create a painting depicting each year of her life. Titled *My Birth* (1932), it shows Frida's mother, a sheet thrown over her upper body, giving birth to her. Frida's head has emerged from the birth canal, and she is obviously stillborn. However, the woman giving birth is not her mother. It is Frida. Kahlo has thus depicted herself giving birth to herself. The painting stands as the most terrible known vision of a human birth. It also stands as an anguished testimonial of Frida Kahlo's inability to bear a living child.

A second theme that emerged from Frida Kahlo's US residency is her reverence for nature and her belief in the organic interconnectedness of all life. Her *Self-Portrait on the Borderline between Mexico and the United States* (1932) shows Frida holding a Mexican flag, her right foot in a Mexico crowded with pre-Columbian artifacts and tropical plants. The roots of the plants extend deep into the soil. Her left foot rests on the US side of the border.

It is a country full of smoke-belching factories and electrical devices of the modern age. Her *My Dress Hangs There* (1933) is even more anti-American. In it her favorite Tehuana dress hangs over an ugly New York City crowded with breadlines, marching soldiers, and striking workers being brutalized by police. Diego Rivera also became critical of the United States, especially after the Rockefeller family refused to let him complete his Rockefeller Center mural *Man at the Crossroads* (1933). Without asking their permission, Rivera included the face of Vladimir Lenin in the mural. Angry anti-communists soon gathered at Rivera's scaffold, threatening both the artist and his work. On May 9 Nelson Rockefeller appeared at the worksite, paid Rivera off in full, and fired him on the spot. A few days later Rockefeller had the mural destroyed under cover of darkness. Frida and Diego became despondent. They lingered in New York for a few more months while Rivera completed murals at the Trotskyite New Workers School. By December 1933 both were anxious to return home. Out of money (Rivera was not a good money manager), the couple had to rely on a group of friends, led by composer Aaron Copeland, to hold a dinner on their behalf. It raised enough money to pay for their steamship tickets back to Mexico. The Riveras departed New York on December 20, 1933.

FRIDA AND DIEGO: ON AGAIN, OFF AGAIN

The couple arrived home during the Christmas season, happy to be reunited with family and friends. But both soon grew depressed. During the first half of 1934 Frida had her appendix removed and suffered additional surgery on her right foot. She also had a therapeutic abortion, her third. She was instructed by her physician to refrain from sexual intercourse. Meanwhile, Rivera, who had gone on a crash diet while in the United States and lost a hundred pounds—one-third of his body mass—suffered from the diet's impact. The diet left him ill and looking like a deflated elephant, his flesh hanging loosely on his body. Not even a fan letter from Albert Einstein cheered him up. In it the physicist expressed "profound admiration" for Rivera's work. It took a short trip to Tehuantepec to lift his spirits. But what truly made Diego Rivera happy was a new love affair—with Frida's younger sister Cristina. It was a willful act that had a profound impact on his relationship with his wife.

Frida was devastated when she learned of the affair. At first, she tried to come to terms with what had happened. In October 1934 she wrote her San Francisco physician Dr. Leo Eloesser that "it is not his fault; I am the one to compromise if I want him to be happy."[12] Reminding herself that she and Rivera had an open marriage, she promised not to be carried away by "idiotic prejudices." However, over the nine months that followed she remained in despair. In mid-1935 and on the spur of the moment, she flew to New York City with her friends Anita Brenner and Mary Schapiro, whom she had run into the prior evening at a dinner party hosted by her husband. On July 23, 1935, she sent Rivera a letter from New York that read in part, "[I now know that] all these letters, liaisons with petticoats, lady 'teachers of English,' gypsy models . . . only represent flirtations. . . . At bottom *you and I* love each other dearly [and] we will always love each other."[13] Still she could not shake her feeling of betrayal. She virtually stopped painting during the two years that the affair lasted. Her artistic production during those years was precisely three paintings.

Despite her apparent willingness to tolerate Rivera's callous disregard for her feelings, his affair with her sister changed Frida Kahlo and her paintings in two ways. First, her works revealed a Frida full of anger and psychological torment. Her painting *Memory* (1937) depicts her with cropped hair and tears streaming down her face. She is suspended in the air, has no hands, and a wooden stake pierces her body through a hole where her heart once was. Her hugely oversized heart lies on the ground beneath her gushing out its blood.

The second way Frida Kahlo responded to her husband's constant womanizing was to embrace her own sexuality. Whereas Frida had several affairs while living in the United States, one of them with artist Georgia O'Keeffe, she had at least a dozen others between 1934 and 1940, ten of them with men and two with women. Her lesbian affairs were so discreet that the women were known only through her allusions to them in paintings such as *Two Nudes in a Forest* (1939), showing Frida and an indigenous woman reclining in a jungle setting in a state of postcoital repose. Some of her affairs of the 1930s had the aspect of bedroom farce. During 1935 she had an intense eight-month liaison with New York photographer Isamu Noguchi. Early in the affair she would meet Noguchi in the Blue House—up to the day Rivera barged in, pistol in hand and bellowing, "I refuse to share my toothbrush with your lovers." He chased the half-dressed Noguchi over the back patio wall. Frida and Noguchi next rented an apartment in Mexico City. That worked out well until the bill for furnishing it was mistakenly delivered to Rivera. Again, he confronted Noguchi, pistol in hand, and threatened to kill the photographer the next time he saw him.[14]

Mexico City enjoyed following the escapades of Diego and Frida, as they were universally known. Nevertheless, there was a conventional side to the artists' relationship. Frida Kahlo and Diego Rivera in fact loved each other, albeit not in a conventional way. They lived together over most of their married lives in the double house, and occasionally in the Blue House in Coyoacán. They had the same friends and entertained them together, and they attended cultural events and parties together. Frida and Diego also admired each other's art and shared each other's communist political views. That became especially important in the late 1930s when the division between Stalinists and Trotskyites intensified. Frida was in the audience on August 26, 1935, when Diego, wearing a cape and a sword, debated Stalinist David Alfaro Siqueiros on the role of revolution in art and culture. At one point Rivera shouted that Siqueiros was a "son-of-a-bitch Stalinist" and waved his pistol in the air. When a US Communist in the audience broke into a grin, Frida leaped up and slapped him, cursing the "gringo bastards who come down from that f***ing country [to] make fun of us here!"[15] Two days later two *pistoleros* approached the couple in a Mexico City café, guns in hand. When Frida stood and confronted them, they fled in confusion.

Beginning in late 1936 the Riveras' relationship grew even more complex. On November 21, fellow Trotskyite Anita Brenner cabled Rivera from New York informing him that Leon Trotsky was in danger of assassination by agents of Joseph Stalin. She begged the muralist to find shelter for the communist luminary in Mexico. Rivera spoke with President Lázaro Cárdenas, who agreed to offer Trotsky asylum. On January 9, 1937, Frida, beautifully attired in full Tehuana garb, received Trotsky and his wife Natalia in Tampico. She escorted them to the Blue House in Coyoacán, where they were given around-the-clock protection. Rivera, who had been ill with a kidney infection, soon joined them and set to work turning his wife's home into an assassin-proof fortress. Trotsky and his wife lived there for the next two years.

Early in his stay at the Blue House, Leon Trotsky committed an egregious and ultimately fatal mistake: he had an affair with his host's wife. Frida had little trouble seducing Trotsky, whom she referred to as "el Viejo" (the old man). He was fifty-six and she twenty-nine. It was the perfect payback to a husband who plunged her into grief three years earlier. Frida's revenge was all the more satisfying because it took a year for her husband to discover the affair between Frida and his political mentor. Rivera was long unaware of the affair in part because once the Trotskys moved into the Blue House the muralist spent most of his time at the double house. Rivera may also have been distracted by the fact that during 1937–1938 Frida flung herself into her period of greatest artistic activity, producing eighteen paintings in fewer than twenty-four months. One was a stunning self-portrait titled *The Frame* (1938). Another was an elegant full-length portrait of herself gifted to Trotsky on the occasion of his fifty-seventh birthday. Also figuring among her works of that period is her angriest and most forthright work, *Remembrance of an Open Wound* (1938). In it she glares defiantly at the viewer. Her Tehuana skirt is hiked up to reveal blood dripping from her injured leg and her right hand hidden under her skirt. She told friends that the painting depicted her masturbating.

The year 1938 was when Frida the artist caught the public eye. In January she exhibited several paintings at a gallery in Mexico City. A month later she was contacted by Julien Levy, the owner of a small gallery in New York City specializing in surrealist art. Levy invited her to exhibit her works there in a one-person show. Shortly thereafter the leading theorist of surrealism, André Breton, arrived at the double house. Breton was a Trotskyite and eager to meet both Leon Trotsky and Diego Rivera, whom he had met years before in Paris. Yet it was Mexico, and Frida Kahlo's art, that made Breton's trip particularly memorable. Breton loved Frida's work, judging it to be "pure surreality"—surrealism being defined as the bringing together of fantastical images in an unnatural and often disturbing way. Breton particularly liked Frida's work *What the Water Gave Me* (1938). In it the artist's legs extend down her bathtub. The water is full of Brueghelesque figures including a skeleton and a strangled and naked Frida Kahlo half-submerged in water; Frida and a lesbian lover occupy a bed that bobs precariously on the bathwater. Meanwhile, a phallic skyscraper erupts from a volcano. That painting, along with her self-portrait dedicated to Trotsky, moved Breton to characterize the works as "a ribbon around a bomb." He pronounced Mexico "a surreal country" and Frida Kahlo's paintings as "pure Surrealism," containing "that drop of cruelty and humor uniquely capable of blending the rare powers that come together to form the potion that is Mexico's secret."[16]

Frida's New York exhibit was a great success. Prior to her departure Rivera helped her draw up a list of important people to invite to its opening, most of them friends and acquaintances from their earlier residency in America. Among them were Alfred Stieglitz, Lewis Mumford, Van Wyck Brooks, Nelson A. Rockefeller and his wife, John D. Rockefeller and his wife, and Clare Boothe Luce. Georgia O'Keeffe and many other members of the city's artistic community figured among the guests. André Breton wrote a glowing piece on Frida for the exhibit program, whose cover featured a photo of the artist standing next to her painting *What the Water Brought Me*. *Time* magazine reported that the exhibit created "the flutter of the week in Manhattan," and *New York Times* reviewer Howard DeVree praised the artist but grumbled that a few of her paintings were "more obstetrical than aesthetic." Frida was at once giddy and modest about her success. On the day the exhibition opened she wrote Alejandro Gómez Arias, "I really have terrific luck. The crowd here treats me with affection. . . . Did you see *Vogue*? There are three reproductions, one in color—the one that seemed the best."[17]

For the first time in her life Frida had money. Not long before flying to New York she sold four paintings to the actor Edgar G. Robinson for $200 each. She sold several others at the exhibition. All of this gave her a newfound sense of freedom. When she arrived in New York she led her friends to believe that her marriage to Rivera was in trouble. But she was deliberately vague on that point. One moment she would proclaim herself "fed up with Rivera," referring to him as "that old fat pig." Next she would say, "I'm so lonely for him. In a funny way I just adore him." Such mixed signals encouraged her suitors and permitted her to continue her affair with portrait photographer Nickolas Muray, a relationship that had begun a year earlier in Mexico City. She also found time for a fling with gallery owner Julien Levy. Back in Mexico City Diego Rivera was philosophical about his wife's affairs, saying, "I don't blame them for liking Frida. I like her too."[18]

In January 1939 Frida Kahlo departed New York City for Paris, where André Breton and Marcel Duchamp had organized an exhibition for her at the city's leading surrealist art gallery. At first gallery owner Pierre Colle rejected most of her pieces, declaring them "too shocking to show." For Colle, who was Salvador Dalí's dealer, the Mexican artist's frank and disturbing works were revealing in a way that surrealist art was not. Nor was the French artistic community comfortable with a female artist, least of all a swarthy and gaudily dressed one from tropical America. Colle at last agreed that fifteen of Frida's paintings could be exhibited. The result was another success. All the city's avant-garde artists were at the opening and they greeted Frida warmly. Rivera's old friend Pablo Picasso sang her praises, and Wassily Kandinsky was so moved by Frida's paintings that, by Rivera's account, "he lifted her in his arms and kissed her cheeks and brow while tears of emotion ran down his face." Joan Miró, by Frida's own account, gave her "a big hug."[19]

Frida Kahlo's relationship with the surrealists was paradoxical. She owed her newfound fame to them but did not consider herself a surrealist. She wrote, "I use Surrealism as a means of poking fun at others without their realizing it and making friends with those who do perceive it."[20] Nor was she drawn to the guru of surrealism, André Breton, whose endless theorizing she found boring. Finally, she loathed surrealist artists themselves, especially their boorishness and slovenliness. In a letter to Nickolas Muray she wrote the following: "You have no idea the kind of bitches these people are. They make me vomit. They are so damned intellectual and rotten that I can't stand them. . . . Shit and only shit is what they are." Nor was she especially impressed by Paris. While she admired the beauty of its architecture, she found the city irritating, referring to it as *"este pinchísimo París"* (this annoying Paris).[21]

Despite Frida's dislike of surrealism and surrealists, her Paris exhibition served her well. The surrealists embraced her as one of their own, and the Louvre purchased her painting *The Frame*. That made her the first Mexican painter to place a work in the museum's prestigious collection. All of this gave her pleasure and satisfaction as she departed France for New York City on March 25, 1939. Unfortunately, upon arrival there her happiness evaporated and a new time of troubles began.

Shortly after arriving in Manhattan, Frida learned that Nickolas Muray had jilted her for another woman. She was crushed because she loved Muray and had entertained thoughts of divorcing Rivera and marrying him. Upon reaching Mexico City in June 1939, Frida was shocked yet again when she learned Rivera was divorcing her. The muralist never spelled out his reasons for the divorce, though foremost among them was doubtless her affair with Leon Trotsky. Rivera may have been hurt over her love for the handsome Nickolas Muray. He may have also been jealous of her successes in Paris and New York. Frida did not contest the divorce, which was finalized in October 1939. She vacated the double house and returned to the Blue House in Coyoacán.

The immediate effect of Frida's divorce was to impoverish her. Luckily, surrealism again came to her aid. André Breton had selected Mexico City to host the Latin American iteration of the International Exhibition of Surrealism set for early 1940. Frida and Diego were invited to exhibit at what became Mexico's premier cultural event of the year. Late 1939 found Frida "working like hell" to complete two works for the show. One of them was *The Two Fridas* (1939), destined to become her most famous work. In it two nearly identical Frida Kahlos sit side by side on a bench holding hands. On the right is "the Frida that Diego loves," dressed in her favorite Tehuana dress. On the left is "the Frida that Diego does not love." Both Fridas' hearts are linked by a blood-red surgical tube. But the tube running to the heart of the unloved Frida is severed. Although the tube drips blood, Frida holds the flow in check with a pair of forceps. The heart of the Frida on the right is healthy. That of the Frida on the left is badly damaged. Blood has splattered the white dress of the unloved Frida.

Despite their divorce Kahlo and Rivera continued to appear in public. They were, after all, "Diego and Frida," the capital city's leading celebrities. The public hoped and expected to see them both on a regular basis and in character. One observer recalled the evening when they arrived late for a dance recital at the Palace of Fine Arts:

> No one paid any attention to the dance performance by Carmen Amaya. Everyone stared at Frida, who wore her Tehuana dress and all of Diego's gold jewelry, and clanked like a knight in armor. She had the Byzantine opulence of the Empress Theodora, a combination of barbarism and elegance. She had two gold incisors and when she was all gussied up she would take off the plain gold caps and put on gold caps with rose diamonds in front, so that her smile really sparkled.[22]

In May 1940 Leon Trotsky once again intruded into the lives of the two artists. Now estranged from his former hosts and relatively unprotected in his new residence, his days were numbered. Stalin had ordered his security agents in the Soviet Union's secret police, known then as the GPU, to eliminate Trotsky without delay. On June 18 his agents, accompanied by David Alfaro Siqueiros, stood in the street outside and machine-gunned the bedroom where Trotsky and his wife were sleeping. Both survived the attack. Mexican authorities arrested Siqueiros several weeks later. That panicked Diego Rivera and sent him fleeing northward to the United States. He did so with the help of actress Paulette Goddard, who was recently divorced from Charlie Chaplin and with whom Rivera was romantically involved. Traveling with them was the young Hungarian artist Irene Bohus, who was living with Rivera. The trio made their way to San Francisco, where Rivera resumed painting murals. Frida was not so lucky. When Trotsky was assassinated several weeks later, on August 20, the police arrested her as a possible accomplice in the crime. She had met Trotsky's assassin Ramón Mercader in Paris and later had hosted him at a dinner party in the Blue House. After two nights in jail and ten hours of rigorous interrogation, Frida was released. The ordeal further eroded her health. Now feeling alone and unprotected, and drinking heavily to ease the pain of her old injuries, Frida Kahlo entered into physical decline.

All her friends knew about Frida's health problems and most agreed that she would be better off with Diego Rivera than without him. After their divorce Frida continued to insist that she loved her former husband. In a letter to art collector Sigmund Firestone, she wrote: "I take care of [Diego] as best I can from a distance, and I will love him all my life even if he wouldn't want me to." Dr. Leo Eloesser, who knew more about Frida's physical condition than anyone else, was key to reuniting the couple. After Rivera spoke with Eloesser in San Francisco, telling him of Frida's problems, the physician wrote to her, "Diego loves you very much, and you love him." Eloesser went on to suggest they remarry, though with any special conditions that Frida may impose. When the couple did in fact remarry in late 1940, and Frida stipulated that she would not be bound to having sexual intercourse with her husband, Rivera responded, "I was so happy to have Frida back that I assented to everything. . . . I am going to remarry her because she really needs me."[23]

The immediate problem, though, was to get Frida out of the clutches of her physicians in Mexico City and fly her to San Francisco where Eloesser could treat her many ailments. That was done, and within a month she was back on her feet. Diego Rivera proposed remarriage to Frida during her hospitalization and she happily accepted. At about that same time, and likely with a touch of malice, Rivera introduced Frida to a young refugee from

Nazi Germany named Heinz Berggruen. When Berggruen entered Frida's hospital room, as he recalled it later, "there was a click." The young man became infatuated with Frida Kahlo, whom he remembered as "stunning, just as beautiful as in her paintings." The inevitable affair followed, with Berggruen traveling to New York with Kahlo in November 1940. The German hoped their relationship might deepen, but Frida viewed it as little more than additional therapy. Her main concern was planning for her remarriage. In late November she kissed Berggruen goodbye and returned to California never to see him again. On December 8, 1940, Diego Rivera's fifty-fourth birthday, the couple remarried in San Francisco. Soon afterward Frida wrote Sigmund Firestone, "He says he loves me more than any other girl; I am very happy."[24]

Once back in Mexico City in early 1941, the couple settled into an amicable routine lasting more than three years. They spent their nights in the Blue House in Coyoacán, rising late in the morning and having breakfast together. Frida often read aloud newspaper accounts of World War II. After breakfast Rivera would drive to his studio in the double house where he would paint and receive an endless procession of visitors. Those included young female art students from the United States and elsewhere who were eager to receive the full Diego Rivera experience: to meet and be charmed by the famous muralist, to pose for him in the nude, and to be seduced by him. Frida produced only ten paintings between 1941 and 1944. Not long after her return home her father died (her mother had died nine years earlier), sending the Kahlo family into mourning. Afterward she worked at restoring the Blue House to the way it was before being turned into a fortress to protect Leon Trotsky. In 1943 Frida accepted a government contract leading her to travel into Mexico City most weekdays to teach an art class to poor youth from the city's barrios. Her months of teaching were among the happiest of her life. She loved her students, and they revered their flamboyant professor. Several of them went on to become prominent artists. We owe some of the best descriptions of Frida Kahlo to her barrio students. For Guillermo Monroy, Frida "was like a walking flower." Fanny Rabel remembered Frida as follows:

> She had a gift for fascinating people. She was unique. She had enormous *alegría*, humor, and love of life. She had invented her own language, her own way of speaking Spanish, full of vitality and accompanied by gestures, mimicry, laughter, jokes, and a great sense of irony.... She constantly renewed the scenography of objects around her. She would wear twenty rings on one day and twenty other rings another day. Her milieu was full of things, and they were kept in order.[25]

Earning money after her remarriage to Rivera (she had vowed not to accept money from him) revealed health problems that forced her to abandon teaching in 1944. "This thing of feeling such a wreck from head to toe sometimes upsets my brain and makes me have bitter moments," she wrote to Dr. Eloesser.[26] Her *Thinking of Death* (1943) reflects her gloomy frame of mind. It shows a somber Frida Kahlo against a leafy background, and with a skull and crossbones painted within a circle on her forehead. *Roots* (1943) shows her lying on her side on a featureless plain. She wears a long Tehuana dress streaked with blood that flows into the parched earth. Lush vines covered with vivid green leaves burst from her open body cavity and envelop her. The painting, as in her *Self-Portrait with Thorn and Hummingbird*, suggests both Frida's belief in the organic interconnectedness of all things in nature and her sense that she might soon be returning to the earth.

"I NEVER LOST MY SPIRIT": FRIDA'S FINAL YEARS

In 1945 Frida's health declined further. Her right foot and spinal column brought her constant pain, fainting spells, weight loss, and low-grade fever. Her physicians had her wear steel corsets and spend lengthy periods on her back and in traction. During that time, she wrote friends in New York that she was "very thin, worn out, and completely going to hell." Her paintings of the period reflect this. In *The Broken Column* (1944) the viewer sees a weeping Frida, her hair down and her body laid open from throat to pelvis. Her spine is a cracked Doric column. Nails protrude from her right breast, spine, and right leg. The most terrible painting from this period is *Without Hope* (1945). It shows Frida in a bed, her hair down and gazing at the viewer. Vomit sprays from her mouth, forming a vile mass of bloody meat with a human skull embedded in it.

During 1945 Frida learned of a spinal bone-grafting procedure developed by a New York surgeon. Excited by its promise, she arranged to have the procedure performed early in the following year. Because her trip caused her to miss Diego Rivera's birthday party, she wrote him the following message: "Diego, my child, my love. You know what gifts I would give you not only today but always. But this year I had the bad luck of not being able to give you anything."[27]

Dr. Leo Eloesser believed many of Frida Kahlo's more than fifty surgeries were unnecessary. That led him to conclude she suffered from a rare form of narcissism related to Munchausen syndrome, defined as having operations for the purpose of attracting admiration and sympathy. Whatever the case, Frida left visual evidence of her state of mind following the risky surgical procedure. Her *Tree of Hope* (1946) shows her beautifully dressed à la Tehuana and holding a small flag bearing the inscription "Tree of hope remains strong." On the painting's left side, she depicts herself on a hospital gurney, displaying bloody surgical incisions on her back. In her painting *The Little Deer* (1946), an eight-point buck with Frida's face runs through a forest, its body riddled with arrows. The painting, a gift to the New York couple who had recommended the surgery, bears the words "In the forest of the deer the sky is brightening."

In the opinion of Frida's confidant Ella Wolfe, *The Little Deer* relates more to "the agony of living with Diego" than to her physical ailments.[28] Wolfe had urged her not to remarry Rivera, recognizing him as what is called today a sex addict. At various times in his life Rivera explained that for him sex was a natural thing, "like urinating," and wondered why people took it so seriously. He described his love of women as so intense that sometimes he worried he might be a lesbian, an outrageous statement even for Diego Rivera. Frida Kahlo believed in open marriage, but as she had suggested in her painting *The Two Fridas*, she required a more consistent love from Diego Rivera than he was capable of giving. That is why she lashed out against him in her painting *Diego and I* (1949). In the self-portrait her eyes stare almost dementedly at the viewer as her loose hair swirls around her face and throat. Her rage is explicit in *Ruin* (1947). Only Rivera's head is shown, Buddha-like and huge, shot through with cracks and fissures and encased in an ornate wooden frame, each of whose elements bears numbers running from one to twenty, thought to number his major love affairs. To the right stands a sign bearing the words "Ruin! Birdhouse. Love nest. All for nothing." In 1947 and 1949 Frida painted several allegorical paintings, two of which centered on the muralist. The first, *Sun and Life*, shows a Rivera-like sun behind which many "uterine" tropical plants shelter burgeoning life. Within their folds can be seen sperm-dripping flowers, an ejaculating penis, and a human fetus. The second, titled *The Love Embrace of the Universe: The Earth (Mexico), Diego, Me, and Señor Xolotl*, shows Frida, hair down and dressed in a flowing red Tejuana dress. In her lap she holds a large, naked "baby Diego Rivera." Both in turn are embraced by an immense Aztec deity, "Mr. Xolotl." But the deity is in fact shown as androgynous. His/her left breast drips milk, and roots extend down from the deity's enfolding arms seeking the soil below. Surrounding the three figures are desert shrubs of central Mexico. This, more than any other of her paintings, expresses Frida Kahlo's love for Diego Rivera, her homeland, and Mexico's culture and pre-Columbian past.

Women who had married Diego Rivera, or who had had significant sexual liaisons with him, invariably became friends following the experience. All agreed that Rivera was infant-like in his need for sex. He was also childlike in that he required the constant care of a responsible adult. For example, Frida could never convince him to hang up his clothes rather than throw them on the floor. Nor had Rivera's personal hygiene improved from the time she first met him. True to her promise of years earlier, she often bathed him in the bathtub in the Blue House. She gave him toys to play with, and if a visiting child was found playing with one of them Rivera would snatch it away and hide it. Rivera himself understood that he had an immature, childlike side. In his last great mural, *Dream of a Sunday Afternoon in the Central Alameda* (1948), he depicts himself as a little boy in knickers wearing a tie and straw hat. Behind him stands Frida Kahlo, looking quite maternal. Only in his fits of jealousy over Frida's love affairs did Rivera transcend his behavior as *niño consentido* (spoiled little boy). When he drove his wife's male lovers out of her bed, pistol in hand, he behaved like the typical macho male, oblivious to his own sexual double standard.

Frida's health declined drastically during the 1950s. Her New York surgery turned out to be a mortal mistake. The bone grafted to her spine had not been sterile, and she contracted an infection that was treated with every antibiotic known at the time. In 1950 her ailments sent her to the hospital for more than a year. During that time, she experienced seven spinal operations. Meanwhile her right foot became gangrenous. Only heavy doses of painkillers allowed Frida to receive visitors. The drugs permitted her to spend many days eating and partying with her friends and watching Charlie Chaplin and Laurel and Hardy movies with them. During that time Rivera spent nights in a small room next door. At last, in mid-1951, Frida was well enough to return home to the Blue House, though she was confined to a wheelchair. "I never lost my spirit," she wrote of the ordeal. "They kept me going with Demerol, and this animated me and made me happy. In the hospital it was as if it was a fiesta."[29]

Over the last years of her life Frida Kahlo painted friends and family and glorified communism, which had become her religion. When readmitted to the Mexican Communist Party in 1948, she wrote, "I understand clearly the materialist dialectic of Marx, Engels, Lenin, Stalin, and Mao Zedong. I love them as the pillars of the new world."[30] One of her last paintings, *Marxism Will Give Health to the Sick* (1954), shows a Valkyrie-like Frida casting aside her crutches as a dove of peace and Father Marx hover overhead. Extending from the head of Marx the deity is a hand shown strangling a bald eagle with an ugly Uncle Sam head. Frida Kahlo's last public appearance was at a Communist demonstration protesting the CIA-led overthrow of democratically elected and Socialist Guatemalan president Jacobo Árbenz. A photograph of the event, held July 2, 1954, shows Frida in her wheelchair, Rivera standing behind her, holding a peace sign and shouting along with the other protesters, "Out with the gringo assassins! (Gringos asesinos: fuera!)."

In April 1953, Frida Kahlo had her first exhibition in Mexico City. She arrived at the opening heavily sedated and in an ambulance. Photographers waiting for her at the Palace of Fine Arts were so shocked at her appearance that most of them set their cameras on the floor. Her four-poster bed from home had been set up in the center of the exhibition hall and from it she presided over the gala. All her friends, led by the dean of Mexican artists, Gerardo Murillo (known by his pseudonym "Dr. Atl"), came forward to embrace her. Frida had written a ballad to those who attended, its last line reading, "Well, my dear pals (*cuates*), with true friendship I thank you for this with all my heart, Frida Kahlo de Rivera." A good time was had by all. Afterward her friends gathered around her bed and sang *corridos*, including her favorite, "La Llorona." Then they sang, "Tonight I will get drunk / Child of my heart / Tomorrow is another day / and you will see that I am right." Diego Rivera pronounced Frida's opening "the most thrilling event of 1953."[31]

EPILOGUE

Frida Kahlo died on July 13, 1954, at the age of forty-seven. The coroner reported the cause of death to be a coronary embolism, though in all likelihood it was brought on by a drug overdose. The artist had been depressed since the previous August when her right leg was amputated at the knee. That led her to attempt suicide several times. Her body lay in state at the Palace of Fine Arts, and Diego Rivera, former president Lázaro Cárdenas, and David Alfaro Siqueiros figured among her pallbearers. At the end, all recognized her as one of Mexico's greatest artists. But that was not the end of Frida Kahlo's story. In 1988 Mexico declared her works to be national treasures and therefore not subject to sale or export. Outside Mexico her paintings achieved iconic status among women of the Mexican diaspora, especially Chicanas living in the southwestern United States. Today Frida Kahlo's paintings are embraced by women throughout the world for their frank portrayals of complex female reality. The final assessment of Frida Kahlo's artistic legacy is left to Diego Rivera: "Her paintings have no precedent in the history of art."[32] Rivera's words were prescient. At this moment Frida Kahlo's work is instantly recognized throughout the world. A recent survey reveals Frida Kahlo to be the best known of all Mexicans.[33]

NOTES

1. Hayden Herrera, *Frida: A Biography of Frida Kahlo* (New York: HarperCollins, 1983), 27.
2. Herrera, *Frida*, 32.
3. Herrera, *Frida*, 27–34.
4. Herrera, *Frida*, 40.
5. Herrera, *Frida*, 57–58.
6. Herrera, *Frida*, 60.
7. Herrera, *Frida*, 99.
8. Herrera, *Frida*, 128.
9. Herrera, *Frida*, 95.
10. See, for example, Helen Delpar, *The Enormous Vogue of Things Mexican: Cultural Relations between the United States and Mexico, 1920–1935* (Tuscaloosa: University of Alabama Press, 1992).
11. Patrick Marnham, *Dreaming with His Eyes Open: A Life of Diego Rivera* (Berkeley: University of California Press, 1998), 239; Herrera, *Frida*, 131.
12. Herrera, *Frida*, 299.
13. Herrera, *Frida*, 186.
14. Marnham, *Dreaming*, 279–80; Herrera, *Frida*, 199–201.
15. Herrera, *Frida*, 202.
16. Marnham, *Dreaming*, 282.
17. Herrera, *Frida*, 232.
18. Herrera, *Frida*, 235–38.
19. Herrera, *Frida*, 245.
20. Herrera, *Frida*, 261.
21. Herrera, *Frida*, 245.
22. Herrera, *Frida*, 256.
23. Herrera, *Frida*, 275, 303.
24. Herrera, *Frida*, 299.
25. Herrera, *Frida*, 329.
26. Herrera, *Frida*, 309–10.
27. Hayden Herrera, *Frida Kahlo: The Paintings* (New York: HarperCollins, 1993), 169.
28. Herrera, *Frida*, 357.
29. Herrera, *Frida*, 390–91.
30. Herrera, *Frida*, 395.
31. Herrera, *Frida*, 407–10.
32. Herrera, *Frida*, 144.
33. *Economist*, November 12, 2016, 18. The survey was conducted at the Massachusetts Institute of Technology.

REFERENCES

Delpar, Helen. *The Enormous Vogue of Things Mexican: Cultural Relations between the United States and Mexico, 1920–1935.* Tuscaloosa: University of Alabama Press, 1992.

Hamill, Pete. *Diego Rivera.* New York: Henry R. Adams, 1999.

Herrera, Hayden. *Frida. A Biography of Frida Kahlo.* New York: HarperCollins, 1983.

———. *Frida Kahlo. The Paintings.* New York: HarperCollins, 1993.

Lucie-Smith, Edward. *Latin American Art of the 20th Century.* 2nd ed. New York: Thames & Hudson, 2004. First published 1993.

Marnham, Patrick. *Dreaming with His Eyes Open. A Life of Diego Rivera.* Berkeley: University of California Press, 1998.

Rivera, Diego, with Gladys March. *My Art, My Life: An Autobiography.* New York: Citadel, 1960.

Wolfe, Bertram D. *The Fabulous Life of Diego Rivera.* New York: Stein and Day, 1963.

Chapter 7

Eva Perón, 1919–1952

INTRODUCTION

Two revolutions rocked the first half of the twentieth century: one was made by people and the other by machines. The first was attended by great human strife. In Mexico in 1910, in Russia seven years later, and yet later in other parts of the world, ordinary people undertook a violent and usually bloody reshaping of their destiny. The second revolution began when inventions brought the earth's millions face-to-face with their history and thrust them into the middle of it. Radio signals reached even the most remote mountain valley, informing people of events taking place in London, Paris, Tokyo, and their own great cities. Roads penetrated the hinterlands, unleashing a swelling flood of humanity that crowded into urban areas.

In this context of human revolution and rapid technological development, the beautiful Eva Duarte de Perón found her place. A product of the revolutionary age and a shrewd manipulator of the forces shaping twentieth-century society, she symbolized the irresistible human and technological change that has left nothing unaltered in modern times.

Eva Perón appeared in Argentine history in the mid-1930s, a time of great uncertainty the world over. The interlude between World War I and World War II gave rise, in the 1920s, to great creative expression—but this was tamped down as severe economic problems toppled civil governments, giving rise to military dictatorships in many countries. Argentina, too, experienced such change. After decades of instability, a transition to military rule was completed, and Colonel Juan Domingo Perón rose to national prominence. Soon thereafter Perón and radio personality Eva Duarte formed the alliance that would reshape the foundations of Argentine political power.

Juan and Eva could not have been better suited for the roles they chose to play. They were an attractive, exciting couple, but more important, they were of the people. They appealed to the millions of poor and disinherited Argentines as two of their own who had achieved success. Not only that, but they also held the hated oligarchs in the palms of their hands and manipulated them like puppets. The relationship between Juan and Evita Perón and the masses was an organic one. The couple played on the theme of paternal concern for their people—their "shirtless ones"—with consummate skill. And they used radio and other forms of mass communication with a flair that rivaled and in some ways surpassed contemporaries such as Franklin Roosevelt and Benito Mussolini.

Of the two Argentine leaders, Evita is by far the more difficult to judge objectively. She was literally worshipped by the masses who wanted to have her canonized even before her untimely death. Yet at the same time, her well-to-do enemies cursed her even as she lay dying of cancer. The passage of time has made it no easier to assess Eva Perón. For millions she was a saint—the incarnation of truth and hope. For others she was crude, avaricious, and corrupt. It is perhaps the better part of wisdom to accept the historical Eva as a tangle of dissonant perceptions. Yet she was no less paradoxical than the age that produced her.

A STAR IS BORN: EVITA'S EARLY YEARS

Juana Ibarguren smoothed the skirt of her black dress and turned to see that her five children, bundled against the cold July winds that swept across central Argentina, were huddled behind her, cowed as much by the weather as by the cold stares they were about to face. Juana was determined to pay her last respects to the man who had fathered her children and had looked after them faithfully for twelve years. But Juan Duarte's wife and legitimate children were so strongly opposed to the appearance of his "other" family that it was only by order of the provincial governor, a friend of Juana's, that she and her children were permitted to attend their father's wake. Quietly the six black-clad figures entered the Duartes' large house and filed past the open coffin. Terrified by the disapproval evident all around them, the children said not a word and barely looked at the familiar face that lay so still among long white candles and floral wreaths.

As soon as the wake was over, Juana left the house in the little town of Chivilcoy and led her unhappy brood back to their home in nearby Los Toldos. The determination that had taken her to Juan Duarte's funeral suddenly deserted her, and she began to wonder how she and the children would manage without Juan Duarte's protection and wealth. She could look for a job, of course, but in a small town like Los Toldos almost no decent jobs were available to an uneducated woman. It wasn't that the region was poor; it was in fact one of the richest agricultural zones in the world. But the land was owned by a few wealthy families who scarcely acknowledged the existence of the landless poor of the town. Their attention was fixed on sophisticated Buenos Aires, the great city to which provincial wealth flowed. As everything of value passed from the provinces to the capital, the countryside supported only a small middle class and a large lower class. Women like Juana were trapped on the lowest rung of Argentina's social ladder.

Juana and her children stayed in Los Toldos for three years after Juan Duarte's death. Then in 1929 they packed their possessions and moved to Junín, 130 miles west of Buenos Aires, where the family was soon established over the restaurant of a friend, an Italian immigrant. Just how Juana managed to provide for her family is not clear. Some say that she opened a boardinghouse; others, less charitably, that she began receiving male visitors on a regular basis. Be that as it may, Juana's children were successful in finding places for themselves within the rural middle class. By that time Elisa Duarte, Juana's oldest daughter, had a job as postal clerk, and Blanca was enrolled in normal school studying to be a teacher. But her third daughter was something of a problem. By the time she reached her teens María Eva Duarte, known less formally as Evita, could only be described as stagestruck. Magazines and radio programs that reached Junín from Buenos Aires seemed to feed Evita's dislike for the provincial town and cramped apartment where the family lived, and her impatience to leave home and seek her fortune soon overtook all other considerations. Her schoolwork, never more than mediocre, ceased altogether as she dreamed of life as a movie star or theater actress.

In 1934, when Evita was fifteen years old, a famous singer came to Junín on tour from Buenos Aires. Eva was not timid about meeting him. After winning his sympathies with a heavy dose of flattery, she confessed her driving ambition to enter the world of acting and begged him to take her to the capital. Such pleas from the worshipful yet self-confident girl were persuasive, but the seasoned performer hesitated, foreseeing the difficult life Evita would find there. Juana herself pleaded with him to let Evita try her luck. Perhaps she was as convinced as Eva that the future lay in Buenos Aires and in the public eye. In any case, mother and daughter finally persuaded him to take her to Buenos Aires.

Buenos Aires in the 1930s was a kind of Argentine mecca for thousands of immigrants from the interior provinces. Rural communities, as Juana Ibarguren knew well, were split into two rigid classes, one extremely wealthy, the other barely able to get along. It was from the latter group that the steady stream of job-hunting immigrants came. They settled in droves in south Buenos Aires neighborhoods like Avellaneda, Nueva Chicago, Barracas, and many others. In 1936 alone more than eighty thousand people descended on the city, most of them poorly educated, penniless, armed only with hope and, like Evita, the ambition to make their fortunes. Remarkably, 75 percent of those immigrants were women.

Evita traveled from Junín to Buenos Aires early in January 1935. At fifteen she was virtually uneducated, yet pretty in an adolescent way and full of great hopes. Her health had always been rather poor, and it suffered as she struggled to win minor parts on the stage and in radio. For four years she lived precariously on income from bit parts and radio work that paid at best thirty-five dollars a month. Yet the determination she had inherited from her mother stood her in good stead. She eagerly cultivated the friendship of powerful men who were able to help advance her career. In 1939 she won her first worthwhile part in radio and soon persuaded a wealthy soap manufacturer to become her sponsor. By 1942 Jabón Radical, another soap manufacturing company, agreed to sponsor her radio drama series.

Evita was suddenly secure. After seven long years of constant struggle, her radio career was firmly established. For the first time she indulged her taste for luxury by renting a comfortable apartment on Calle Posadas near the Radio Belgrano station where she worked. Her style of dress gradually became less adolescent and more elegant, and she happily underwent a transformation from brunette to blond. As her own wealth increased, Evita, aware of the responsibilities that money brings, searched for ways to help her family back in Junín. Never shy about using influence, she approached her new sponsor, and her older brother Juan Duarte was soon offered a position at Jabón Radical.

CHASING FAME, SEIZING POWER: EVITA AND JUAN PERÓN

As Evita was establishing herself comfortably as a radio actress, a group of army officers, unhappy with the weak conservative regimes that had ruled since 1930 and strongly influenced by fascist dictators Mussolini in Italy and Salazar in Portugal, sought to seize the reins of power in Argentina.[1] In June 1934 the military revolution became a reality, and the last vestiges of civilian rule disappeared.

Evita was well equipped to ride the wave of transition to military rule. Using an irresistible combination of flattery and personal beauty, she became friendly with several officers of the new government. A special friend was Lieutenant Colonel Aníbal Francisco Imbert, the new director of posts and telegraph. With his help Eva found it easy to secure a license for her new radio program, a series of dramatic biographies of famous women that began in late 1943.

In early 1944 a powerful earthquake devastated the town of San Juan, located far west of Buenos Aires at the foot of the Andes. In the capital, a large charity performance was planned to raise money for quake victims. The entire acting community would attend and so would the highest-ranking officials of the new government. Or January 22, 1944, the night of the performance, Evita and Lieutenant Colonel Imbert were already in their seats when a tall, amiable-looking colonel came in surrounded by a bevy of actresses. Before the evening was over, Eva and the colonel, Juan Domingo Perón, were acquainted and well on the way to becoming the most astonishing couple in Argentine history.

The details of this meeting are obscured by clouds of propaganda sent up by Peronist mythmakers. It is safe to say, however, that within a relatively short period, Perón moved to an adjoining apartment on Calle Posadas, where he and Eva settled into an ordinary sort of domestic life. The match was instantly successful. Perón at forty-eight was tall, handsome, and blessed with a charming smile. Evita, now twenty-five, was petite, blond, and expensively dressed, a perfect ornament for the ambitious widower. Perón had power and prestige, but his political ambitions were not yet satisfied. In Evita he recognized a talent for publicity that would be useful to him, and an ambition equal to his own. The two shared similar backgrounds as well: both were products of an illicit union of a wealthy man and a woman of the lowest social stratum. And above all, Evita knew how to bind Perón to her with tireless outpourings of adulation, gratitude, and praise. In later years she would compare him to Alexander the Great, to Napoleon, to José de San Martín, and even to God in an apparently successful attempt to win his trust and love.

A month after the San Juan earthquake, the military regime named Perón vice president in General Edelmiro J. Farrell's new government. The vice presidency, although an important position, was less valuable to Perón than two positions he had held since early in the military regime. As minister of war, Perón boasted in 1944 that he had on file undated retirement applications from 90 percent of all military officers. Anyone who displeased him was subject to immediate "retirement." As secretary of labor and welfare his control over employers and trade unions was less absolute, yet he had made progress in replacing union leaders with his own men—such as Cipriano Reyes of the meatpackers' union—and in urging employers to grant workers more benefits and higher wages. The successes Perón had won for labor were reflected in a leap in union membership, from 350,000 in 1943 to a million two years later. Many of the newest union members felt a personal sense of gratitude to Perón, who appeared to be an authentic advocate of the working class.

The gleam of Perón's power illuminated Evita as well. Never one to accept a free ride, however, she launched a new radio series, *Toward a Better Future*, not long after they met. Twice a week she delivered short speeches on topics like patriotism, the family, self-sacrifice—all essentially propaganda for Perón and his work at the Secretariat of Labor and Welfare. Her talent for emotional, dramatic speechmaking was clearly apparent in this series. Anti-Peronists have hinted that Perón himself stopped work at 7:00 p.m. Wednesdays and Fridays to listen to Eva's impassioned praise of him over the radio. It is certain that thousands of workers not only listened but believed her when she described Perón as a patriot and defender of the great Argentine working class.

During this period, Evita received her initiation into politics and union organization. She became president of the actors' union established in 1944. She also began to participate more and more freely in the political strategy sessions that often took place in Perón's Calle Posadas apartment.

As her political education progressed, so did her wealth. Eva's critics claim that aside from her radio career and her work in the actors' union, she became increasingly skillful at the age-old profession of graft. For a fee she would secure scarce merchandise such as unexposed film and automobile tires for eager buyers. By 1945 Eva claimed an estate of more than a million pesos, in addition to a residence some ten minutes from downtown Buenos Aires and an abundance of fine clothes and jewels. The girl from Los Toldos was suddenly a wealthy woman. But even though she thought nothing of buying magnificent gifts for her friends, she still carefully examined every bill to be sure no one dared try to cheat her.

By 1945 several of Perón's military associates began to complain that it wasn't proper for Perón to be "chasing after the actress Eva Duarte," as they phrased it. Perón, secure in his power, answered, "Well, what do you expect me to chase, actors?" The remark seems to have closed the subject. Vice President Perón's relationship with Eva did not go unnoticed by her employers at Radio Belgrano. By 1945 she was earning more than $6,000 a month, a salary related more to her association with Perón than to her talent as an actress.

By early spring 1945 Perón had become so powerful a threat to groups within the military government that General Farrell asked for Perón's resignation from his posts as vice president, minister of war, and secretary of labor and welfare. Under increasing pressure, Perón yielded to the demand and on October 9 submitted his resignation. Almost immediately Evita was fired by Radio Belgrano. Their luck seemed to have deserted them. Middle-class and professional groups staged anti-Perón rallies outside the officers' club in

Buenos Aires. Convinced that the course of wisdom lay in flight, Perón and Eva packed up their money and slipped away from the capital.

Before long they were detained by Buenos Aires police, who imprisoned Perón on an island in the Río de la Plata. Eva was allowed to return to Calle Posadas, where for four frantic days she tried to free Perón. Five years later in *La razón de mi vida* (*My Mission in Life*) she wrote the official version of those days of anxiety when she "rushed into the streets looking for friends who might still be able to do something for him." False friends in positions of power refused to help her, but, she wrote, the workers of the city opened their hearts to Perón in his hour of need. The result was the triumphant Peronist "Loyalty Day" (Día de la lealtad) on October 17, 1945, when a huge daylong strike and demonstration brought the capital to a standstill. A crowd of thousands of Argentines gathered in the plaza outside the presidential palace and, armed with banners and pictures of Perón, demanded his immediate release.[2]

Whether the demonstration was a spontaneous response to Evita's desperate pleas, or whether it was planned in advance by labor organizations, the Loyalty Day was something the military government could not ignore. Perón was brought quickly to the presidential residence, the Casa Rosada. As he stepped out on the balcony he was greeted by a roar of delight from thousands of meatpackers, railway employees, and textile and garment workers, many of whom were women. All of them viewed Perón as their savior. President Farrell embraced him on the spot, and Perón turned to the crowd with his arms outstretched. In the warmest, most fatherly terms, Perón thanked them for supporting him in his hour of need. In answer to shouts from demonstrators asking where he had been, Perón claimed to have already forgotten. But a man who cannot forget bad memories does not deserve the respect of his fellows, he said, and he wanted to be loved by those gathered together that day. For did he not love and understand them because they had suffered as his old mother had suffered? Longing only to be one of them, he announced his resignation from the army and melodramatically handed over his sword and sheath to General Farrell. Then, cautioning the people to disperse quietly because there were ladies in the crowd, he begged them to stand before him just a moment longer so that he might feast his eyes on them.

Perón's great success on that day was owed at least in part to Evita's faithful efforts on his behalf. In gratitude—and because it was prudent for both of them—Perón returned with her to Junín, where they were married in a secret civil ceremony witnessed only by Colonel Domingo Mercante, a loyal supporter from the Secretariat of Labor and Welfare, and Eva's mother and brother. Almost immediately Perón announced that he would run for president, and with Eva at his side he plunged into the campaign.

The campaign was a battle between candidates of the National Democratic Union Party and Juan Domingo Perón. Mass media were used constantly, but Perón, with Eva at the microphones of Radio Belgrano, was easily more effective than Democratic Union–controlled newspapers. Eva and Perón traveled by rail throughout Argentina, appealing to nationalist and class sentiments, distributing small gifts and pictures, and arousing the admiration of rural as well as urban workers. Emphasizing their own humble backgrounds at every opportunity, Eva, dressed in extravagantly expensive clothes and jewelry, and the genial Perón spoke to working-class Argentines in terms that appealed strongly to a group long ignored by national institutions.

Traditional government had looked to wealthy landowners and industrialists—the oligarchs—for support and had treated powerless segments of society with contempt, if it paid attention to them at all. Trade unions established before Perón's rise appealed mainly to European immigrants who understood their socialist, syndicalist appeals. The recent wave of migrants from Argentina's own rural provinces had been left by the new regime to sink or swim as they might. Evita and Perón, however, not only recognized the existence of these new classes but seized on the old disdainful names privileged Argentines had given them—terms such as *cabecitas negras* (little black-haired people) and *descamisados* (shirtless ones)—and turned them into symbols of unity. Perón spent long hours being photographed in his shirtsleeves, and Eva, with her beautiful clothes and sparkling jewelry, came to represent a poor girl who had made good.

About halfway through the campaign, the US government published a "blue book" that was highly critical of Argentina's military regime. While intended as a warning to Argentines, it had exactly the opposite effect. Perón increased his nationalistic appeals, and Argentines, offended by US interference in their affairs, rose to his defense. The election took place on February 24, 1946, and, most observers agree, was relatively fair. Perón won over 52 percent of the nearly three million votes cast. In the Chamber of Deputies Peronists won two out of every three seats, and in the Senate there was virtually no opposition. One of the Congress's first acts was to impeach every member of the conservative Supreme Court, so that by the end of his first year as president, Perón had ironclad control over Argentina's three branches of government.

BREAKING FROM THE PAST, BRANDING PERÓN

Perón's inaugural celebration of June 4, 1946, was in many ways indicative of things to come. Eva, especially, seemed to enjoy flouting long-established custom by behaving in ways no president's wife had ever done before. During the ceremony her friends the Doderos occupied a place of honor close to Perón himself, even though Alberto Dodero was an industrialist with no official connection to Argentina's new government. In a gesture that was almost insulting to staid members of Argentine society, Eva chose to wear a gown so low-cut that Cardinal Copello, seated next to her during the banquet, was literally afraid to glance her way.

Evita's iconoclastic behavior left wealthy Argentina aghast. The president's wife was traditionally offered a place of honor in the highest social circles. But the wealthy matrons of Buenos Aires were horrified at the thought of receiving Madame Perón in their homes. To them, Eva was a person of shady reputation who had risen from the dregs of society. Her wealth and power were won through the most questionable means and certainly could not make up for her lack of breeding, education, and family connections.

Once Perón became president, war broke out between Evita and the ladies of the oligarchy. The first battle was waged over the presidency of the Sociedad de Beneficencia, a social service organization that had received high-society support for many years. Custom dictated that the president's wife should preside over the Sociedad de Beneficencia, but Eva's wealthy enemies refused to offer her the position. When she demanded to know why, they responded that she, at twenty-seven, was too young. At that Eva kindly offered the services of her mother, Juana Ibarguren, who was, if possible, less acceptable than Evita herself.

Her rejection by Argentina's social circles appeared to hurt Eva deeply. Although she reacted to the experience with outward scorn, she took every opportunity to humiliate the women who had humiliated her. On one occasion when a group of wellborn ladies gathered to protest her opposition to the Sociedad de Beneficencia, she ordered them arrested and hauled away weeping in police vans. After they endured several days of imprisonment alongside prostitutes and petty thieves, the first lady permitted their release. On other occasions, elderly matrons were forced to receive her in their homes in exchange for special favors that only the president could grant.

In *My Mission in Life* Evita later claimed that it was she who rejected Argentine society, not vice versa. "The oligarchy has never been hostile to anyone who could be useful to it," she writes. "Power and money were never bad antecedents to a genuine oligarch." Yet her later vindictiveness toward those same oligarchs is compelling evidence that she was in fact wounded by them. Perhaps for that reason she dressed defensively—even extravagantly—during the early years of Perón's presidency. Her hair, her jewels, her clothes all betrayed a deep insecurity as well as the desire to seem wealthier than the wealthiest aristocrat.

Yet Evita's actions during her six short years of glory cannot be fully explained in terms of vengeance or mere ambition. In her autobiography, she claimed that she could never have been satisfied with the passive role normally played by the president's wife. This was undeniably true. Coupled with energy and vitality that seemed at odds with her physical frailty was a body of ideas, simplistic perhaps, but founded in personal experience, leading her to choose a path of action no Argentine first lady had followed before. Principal among those ideas was the view of society as composed of two groups—the privileged rich and the downtrodden poor. The former class was proud, cold, and, in a word, bad; the latter, from which she herself had come, was good. The evil committed by the wealthy and the suffering of the poor could only be addressed by reversing the balance of power, redistributing wealth by cunning and force, if need be, so that the workers and rural poor could gain benefits they had never before enjoyed.

The methods Evita chose to use in her campaign for the Peronist brand of social justice were highly personal, arbitrary, and haphazard. Soon after Perón was inaugurated, she set up an office at the Ministry of Labor and Welfare, where she quickly overshadowed the minister himself. From her office she also organized and directed the Social Aid Foundation, a successor to the more traditional Sociedad de Beneficencia (see figure 7.1). From her double position of power, she forced employers to grant benefits and salary increases to trade unions while at the same time she demanded—and received—huge

Figure 7.1. Evita Perón (lower left) working at the Eva Perón Foundation

donations from all sectors of Argentine society. The monies were then distributed almost at random to the poor and needy. Evita's position gave her a rare opportunity to exercise unchecked power. No laws had been written to govern the activities of a president's wife, so Eva found herself in a kind of legal vacuum. Only Perón could have controlled her, and he chose not to. So she forged ahead with her grandiose social welfare plans and with her largely successful attempt to convert the labor unions into her devoted followers.

At its height the Social Aid Foundation annually took in $50 million—some say $100 million—from donations, wage deductions, and "voluntary" contributions. None of this money was taxable because the foundation was considered a government agency. At the same time, it was free from external control so that no accounting of funds was ever required. Hospitals, schools, and children's homes were built by Eva's foundation, and help was made available to any disaster victims who caught her eye. Under the blotter on her desk was a stack of hundred-peso notes that Evita gave out one by one to the thousands of people who came to her for aid.

Critics claim that the public facilities she built were hollow shells used for propaganda purposes rather than for the benefit of the needy. The large hospital named after President Perón was found to be immaculate but empty. The Children's City in Belgrano and the Working Girls' Home were expensively furnished but hardly used. Some even suspected that Eva's welfare work was largely mythical, a kind of private fantasy designed to please her alone. The operations of the foundation were so well protected from the public eye that no one really knows what goals it achieved.

WOMEN'S RIGHTS: PUSHING FOR REFORM

In one area, however, Evita's activities were highly visible. The movement for women's rights had long existed in Argentina. Yet at the same time Eva was wielding power as de facto minister of labor, women were still denied the right to vote. Married women occupied much the same legal position as children under Argentine law, and female workers, numbering almost one million in 1944, were paid an average of 40 to 60 percent less than men performing the same job. Unlike most military officers, and in direct opposition to the sexist concept of women's proper role, Perón was sympathetic to the feminist movement. Soon after his inauguration, he and Evita established a "right to vote" association and began a forceful campaign for female suffrage. These efforts were rewarded with success in September 1947, when the largely Peronist Congress granted Argentine women the right to active citizenship. Eva was not satisfied with this victory alone. Through the newly formed Peronist

Women's Party, she campaigned for equal pay for equal work, divorce, and civil equality, all basic feminist goals. In 1949 women in the textile industry won substantial pay raises. A minimum wage law guaranteed that women's wages would never be more than 20 percent less than those earned by men.

Eva's successes in the feminist movement rested on her ability to make women's rights palatable to most Argentines. Unlike the upper-middle-class feminists of preceding decades, Eva was able to persuade the great mass of her countrymen that the time had come to grant women equal rights. Yet her arguments were curiously conservative and traditionalist. She argued that women are basically different from men, moved by emotion and intuition rather than intellect. For that reason, they would have a positive, softening effect on national politics. Those who claim that women should not be paid the same wage as men are wrong, she said, because a woman who is paid less has an unfair advantage in getting jobs. And because the family as an institution is so important, she proposed that mothers and housewives receive the same wages paid to factory workers in recognition of their valuable contribution to society.

Through the Peronist Women's Party she organized *unidades básicas* (basic units), small women's clubs located throughout Buenos Aires and the provinces. In addition to instilling loyalty to Perón in their members, the clubs urged women to become aware of their need for economic and political independence from men. The positive contribution women can make to society was emphasized, as when Eva said, "I should rather say that the world at the moment suffers from a lack of women. Everything, absolutely everything in this world, has been conducted on men's terms."[3] Eva's feminism conceived of women in their traditional roles as wives and mothers, yet within that framework she supported programs that went far beyond anything Argentina had seen before.

While occupied with her work at the Ministry of Labor, the Social Aid Foundation, and the Peronist Women's Party, Eva maintained a daily work schedule that stretched from eight in the morning to midnight and placed her under constant pressure. Nothing in her background had prepared her to deal effectively with the labor disputes and social problems she tried to settle, and her intervention was often shallow and capricious. Businessmen who claimed that they would go bankrupt if employees were granted wage increases were forced to raise salaries anyway. Poor children from the country were brought to Buenos Aires, lodged in the best hotels, and treated like royalty for several weeks, only to be sent back home to the same hard existence. On many occasions Evita prescribed medicines for people who came to her for help, unconcerned by her lack of any medical training. Worrisome as her activities were to others in Perón's government, to the thousands of men, women, and children who came to her for help, she was nothing less than a good fairy, a kind of Argentine Virgin Mary who answered the prayers of the Peronist faithful.

IN POLITICS AND IN HEALTH: EVITA'S DECLINE

Involved as she was in social welfare and union affairs, Evita continued to cultivate power, both economic and political. With Perón and her shrewd businessman friend Miguel Miranda, Eva accumulated vast sums of money through questionable import deals. Soon after he became president, Perón established the Banco Central, which controlled most banking operations in the nation, and the Argentine Institute for the Promotion of Trade. Both agencies were directed by Miguel Miranda, who bargained with foreign buyers so that Argentina's raw materials, meat, and grain would bring higher prices than in the past. In this he was highly successful during the post–World War II years, when Western nations, their agricultural production diminished by war, were desperate for food at any price. It was rightly claimed, however, that the benefits of higher international prices did not reach Argentina's ranchers. As a result, cattle production declined, and with it the nation's economy.

In the fall of 1947, from April to early June, when Argentina's beef and grain were in greatest demand in western Europe, Evita left Buenos Aires and began a semiofficial tour of Spain, Italy, Switzerland, and France. It was dubbed her "Rainbow Tour." For two and a half months she, with a large entourage that included her friends the Doderos, was feted, decorated, wined, and dined. In Spain, Generalissimo Francisco Franco awarded her the Great Cross of Isabel the Catholic as Evita, dressed in a long mink coat, stood perspiring in the summer heat of Madrid. Along the way, she delivered radio addresses to the women of each nation she visited. After the pope failed to decorate her for her welfare work and instead sent warm greetings to the ladies of the Sociedad de Beneficencia, Evita showed her disappointment by delivering a rather acid speech to Italian women. In France she was received graciously and accorded the attention the French traditionally give beautiful women. One Parisian commentator was heard to remark, however, that "beautiful as Madame Perón is, she would be more welcome dressed as a frozen side of beef." But the lure of Argentine food was not enough to persuade Great Britain to receive her with the honors Eva demanded. After negotiating with Buckingham Palace from Paris, Evita decided to skip England altogether and sail for Brazil and Argentina.

While she was gone, forces within the military tried to persuade Perón to curtail Eva's activities. He refused, but Evita became more determined than ever to consolidate her political power. Anyone who posed a threat to her control quickly disappeared, either exiled to Uruguay or imprisoned. Cipriano Reyes, Perón's supporter in the meatpackers' union, was accused of plotting to assassinate the Peróns and suffered immediate imprisonment. Colonel Domingo Mercante, the witness at the Peróns' wedding, went into exile when his vice-presidential ambitions became known. Juan Atilio Bramuglia, a loyal Peronist, was exiled when he won international acclaim as Argentina's delegate to the United Nations. Even Miguel Miranda, the Peróns' financial adviser, had to flee secretly to Uruguay when a remark he made at a party aroused Eva's anger.

At the same time Evita was busy banishing officials who seemed either too successful or disloyal, she surrounded Perón with people whose allegiance to her was absolute. Her mother's friend from Junín was named director of posts and telegraph, giving Eva almost complete control over all radio licensing in the country. Juancito Duarte, Eva's brother, left his job as a soap salesman to become the president's private secretary. Each of her brothers-in-law was given a position in government. Blanca's husband, a lawyer, was appointed governor of Buenos Aires Province and later named to the Supreme Court. Elisa's husband Major Arrieta was elected to the Senate. And Herminda's husband, a former elevator operator, became director of customs.

By 1951 Peronist control over Argentina's communications system was complete. In 1947 Eva had bought *La Democracia*, a daily newspaper published in Buenos Aires, and began writing a regular political column. Soon after that, she acquired Radio Belgrano, the station where she had once worked for thirty-five dollars a month. Independent newspapers like *La Nación* and *La Prensa*, owned by wealthy Argentines who were highly critical of the Peróns, were muzzled through government control of newsprint. *La Prensa* was gradually reduced from thirty-two to twelve pages a day. In the wake of labor disputes that closed the paper down in early January 1951, Perón bought *La Prensa* for 5 percent of its real worth. In October *La Prensa*, once an outspoken enemy of Peronism, became the official voice of Eva's national labor federation.

Evita's power peaked sometime in 1950. From then on forces far beyond her reach, forces that she was powerless to control, began to be felt. By July 1950 her lush beauty had faded somewhat, replaced by a pale, tired look that was reinforced by dark, tailored suits and blond hair that she wore pulled back tightly in a bun. At about that time, she decided to run for the vice presidency. Reasoning that women had won equal citizenship and that she already functioned as an unofficial vice president, Eva persuaded Perón to support her candidacy. The movement steadily gathered momentum, and on August 22, 1951, the Perón-and-Perón ticket was officially announced. Eva was so confident of her nomination that she planned a huge demonstration in Buenos Aires to span four days in late August. She boasted that two million people would come to cheer her. But in spite of the free transportation, food, lodging, and entertainment promised by the government, the rally was a disaster. Scarcely a quarter million people came, and the demonstration was abruptly canceled after the first day.

Opposition to Eva's vice-presidential ambitions was as widespread as it was unexpected. Argentina's military establishment was especially horrified at the thought that in the case of Perón's death, the commander in chief would be not only a woman but Evita. Under irresistible pressure from high-ranking officers, Perón persuaded her to withdraw her candidacy. On August 31, Eva delivered an emotional radio address to the nation claiming that because she was only twenty-eight, she could not legally run for the vice presidency. At that time she was thirty-two, as most Argentines knew. Soon after the broadcast she suffered a severe emotional and physical collapse from which she never recovered.

A dismal parallel can be drawn between Evita's health and that of Argentina's economy. The years of Peronist extravagance plus a run of ill fortune had as devastating an effect on Eva's frail body as it had on national finances. Through gross mismanagement, widespread graft, and two years of drought, Argentina's cattle production had dropped and its financial reserves disappeared. More and more money was printed to cover government expenses—including huge outlays for Peronist propaganda—and the resulting inflation wiped out many of the workers' wage increases. Food that had always been abundant and cheap was suddenly scarce. Another symptom of Argentina's economic ill health was the drop in the value of the peso. In the postwar flush of prosperity, the peso was valued at 4.8 to the dollar. Two years later, in December 1949, it dropped to almost sixteen pesos to the dollar, and by 1951 it plunged to twenty.

Shortly before the November 1951 presidential election, Eva was discovered to be suffering from cancer. She underwent surgery in early November, and very shortly thereafter Perón was reelected by a 62 percent majority. Almost two million women voted for the first time in an extremely emotional atmosphere. Prayer vigils were organized outside Eva's hospital, and throughout the nation open-air masses were said for her recovery. During the campaign, Eva's picture and name appeared as often as Perón's even though she was no longer politically active.

The course of the disease was not long delayed by the November operation. During her last months, Eva received every honor Perón could bestow on her, among them the titles of "Spiritual Leader of the Nation" and "Capitana Evita." In December 1951, her autobiography *La razón de mi vida* appeared and became a bestseller, as well as required reading for all schoolchildren and university students. On May 1, 1952, she made her last speech, and in June Eva stood in an open limousine and traveled the distance from the Capitol to the Casa Rosada, where Perón was to be inaugurated for the second time. The experience so taxed her strength that she collapsed during the ceremony. Less than two months later, on the evening of July 26, 1952, Evita died.

The Argentinian response to Eva's death manifested in spontaneous, overwhelming, and public demonstrations of grief. Her embalmed body lay in state for the three years that Perón managed to stay in power without her. By 1955 economic stagnation and opposition from the church brought Juan Domingo Perón's downfall. Such was the power of Evita's memory that her body was secretly moved during the anti-Peronist revolution, only to reappear years later when Comrade Evita had become a symbol of leftist militance.

During her few years in power Eva was an important force for change. She recognized broad-based groups in society—women, workers, lower-middle-class families—that had never been considered important by traditional governments. Her impassioned advocacy for the rights of Argentina's disadvantaged was genuine, for it sprang from her own experience as a woman who grew up without the benefit of money or prestige in a society ruled largely by and for men.

It is only partially ironic that leftist groups active twenty years after her death chose Eva as their symbol. Eva Perón's devotion to power and lust for wealth at almost any cost diminish her reputation as an advocate of the poor and downtrodden. Yet in her few years on the national political stage, she was able to express the kind of anti-aristocratic militance echoed by those who wish to take power from established groups. In a speech delivered nine months before her death, she urged Peronist workers to bear their party's flag forever to victory. For the poor of Argentina, Evita Perón's name has indeed become symbolic, not so much of absolute victory, as of the ongoing battle between tradition and change in their divided nation.

EPILOGUE

Juan and Eva Perón revolutionized Argentine politics. Sharing humble origins and a populist mindset with, for example, the iconic Mexican revolutionary leader Emiliano Zapata, the Peróns demanded a place at the political table for people like them. What the two preeminent left-populists demanded above all was justice for their rank-and-file fellow citizens. The Peróns achieved their goal through the creation of a political party, the Justicialist, or Peronist,

Party. During the 1980s it emerged as Argentina's dominant political party, and it has remained so into the twenty-first century.

Of the two Argentine politicians, Eva Duarte de Perón was the more passionately committed to the cause of the poor. She, after all, had been one of them, rising to power only by dint of drive, determination to succeed, and, at the end, good luck. When she teamed up with Colonel Juan Perón, Eva Duarte ensured that she and her husband made the cause of the poor their own. That cemented their remarkable success as political leaders.

Not long before her death, Evita Perón explained in colorful and romanticized terms her pledge to stand by her husband to the end. In crafting the outline of her ghostwritten autobiography *My Mission in Life*, she made sure the following passage appeared in its early pages: "I put myself at his side. . . . And when he had time to listen, I said to him: "If, as you say, the cause of the people is your cause. . . I will not leave your side until death."[4] Her autobiography was published in December 1951, seven months before cancer claimed her life.

Eva Perón was the first consequential feminist in Latin American history. She, as no other had done before her, led the women of her country along the path to political power. Thanks to her, Argentine women were in fact empowered at the political level—and this in what is arguably one of Latin America's most sexist and *machista* nations. Her signal political achievements were helping enfranchise Argentine women in 1947 and forming the Peronist Women's Party later that same year. As she lay on her deathbed a smile would surely have brightened Eva Perón's face had she known that in forty-five short years her country would elect its first female president, a left-populist Peronist of her own kind.[5]

NOTES

1. Alberto Spektorowski, "The Ideological Origins of Right and Left Nationalism in Argentina, 1930–1943," *Journal of Contemporary History* 29, no. 1 (1994): 155–84, http://www.jstor.org/stable/260959.

2. Eva Duarte de Perón, *My Mission in Life*, trans. Ethel Cherry (New York: Vantage Press, 1953), 27.

3. Perón, *My Mission in Life*, 43.

4. John Barnes, *Evita, First Lady: A Biography of Eva Perón* (New York: Grove Press, 1978 (first published 1954), 25.

5. She was Cristina Fernández de Kirchner, whose presidential term was 2007–2015.

REFERENCES

Barnes, John. *Evita, First Lady: A Biography of Eva Perón*. New York: Grove Press, 1978. First published 1954.

Cowles, Fleur. *Bloody Precedent*. New York: Random House, 1952.

Crasweller, Robert D. *Perón and the Enigmas of Argentina*. New York: W. W. Norton, 1987.

Fraser, Nicholas, and Marysa Navarro. *The Real Life of Eva Perón*. New York: W. W. Norton, 1996. First published 1980.

Naipaul, V. S. *The Return of Eva Perón*. New York: Alfred A. Knopf, 1974.

Patroni, Viviana. "A Discourse of Love and Hate: Eva Perón and the Labour Movement (1940s–1950s)." *Canadian Journal of Latin American and Caribbean Studies / Revue Canadienne des Études Latino-Américaines et Caraïbes* 24, no. 48 (1999): 153–75.

Perón, Eva Duarte de. *My Mission in Life*. Translated by Ethel Cherry. New York: Vantage Press, 1953.

Spektorowski, Alberto. "The Ideological Origins of Right and Left Nationalism in Argentina, 1930–1943." *Journal of Contemporary History 29*, no. 1 (1994): 155–84. http://www.jstor.org/stable/260959.

Chapter 8

Celia Cruz, 1925–2003

INTRODUCTION

Set against the sweep of global music history, Latin America's musical tradition is especially rich, uniting three distinct ethnic strands: European, African, and Indigenous. Native peoples played flutes, maracas, and a range of percussion instruments that they used to accompany ritual chanting and to enliven festive occasions. Spanish and Portuguese conquerors brought their music with them, along with European instruments such as the laud, which evolved into the guitar. Enslaved Africans contributed drums and twin strikers of resonant wood called *claves* (keys), used to call forth tribal deities, or orishas. Following Europe's conquest of America these three ethnicities blended their musical traditions to create instrumentation, song, and dance unique to the region.

In the last century, the global diffusion and appreciation of Latin American music has transcended and connected cultures like no other. Even the United States, long dominant in the economic and military spheres, has embraced Latin America's lively tropical sound. By the early twentieth century Anglo-Americans were dancing Cuban rumbas and Brazilian sambas—and tangos from nontropical Argentina. North Americans embraced mambo and cha-cha at midcentury and found themselves intoning soulful Mexican boleros. At century's end young people danced salsa while their elders struggled to master the macarena. Many who made the Latin sound became famous. By the mid-twentieth century these musicians included Tito Puente, the King of Percussion, and Mambo King Pérez Prado. Singer and conga virtuoso Desi Arnaz took America by storm, going on to become a television star in the sitcom *I Love Lucy*. These artists were notable incarnations of the cultural capital that Latin America joyfully exported beyond regional boundaries.

Cuba was the heartland of Latin music popular in greater America—and for a long time, the world of Cuban dance music was mostly masculine. All-male bands featured Afro-Cuban beats laid down against a backdrop of drums, guitars, flutes, and sinus-clearing trumpets. These bands made music in the tradition of the son, an Afro-Cuban form possessing a near-perfect balance of African and Hispanic elements. Cuban sons were ballads telling stories of lost loves and of mundane episodes in the lives of ordinary people. Some of the most popular ones evoked the calls of street vendors. Dance bands and orchestras typically had one or more male vocalists, though larger ones featured a female vocalist as well.

Within such settings it is remarkable that a woman would be the iconic figure of twentieth-century Cuban popular music. Celia Cruz, a native of Havana, began her career early in the 1950s, rising to become her country's leading vocalist in just ten years' time. In the words of one music historian, "Her diaphanous contralto voice was so rich in timbre and nuance that it seduced everyone who heard it."[1] When Celia Cruz sang her voice rose above all else, riveting the attention of her listeners. And as she sang, she radiated a delight that infected dancers and concert audiences alike. Well before her career reached its midpoint, the singer's fans in the Americas and elsewhere acclaimed her the diva of tropical music and the Queen of Salsa.

USING HER GIFT: THE EARLY YEARS OF CELIA CRUZ

Úrsula Hilaria Celia de la Caridad Cruz Alfonso was born on October 12, 1925, in a ramshackle tenement in the Santos Suárez neighborhood of central Havana. Her father was a railroad fireman and her mother presided over a home filled with her own children and a mix of relatives. Theirs was an urban Afro-Cuban family rooted somewhere in the lower stratum of the island's large middle class. Celia, as she came to be known, attended a nearby public school, did chores around the house, and helped take care of her younger siblings. A radio was always on somewhere in the house, tuned to one of Havana's many AM stations. When her father, Simón Cruz, returned home after work he liked to smoke a cigar on the patio and sing popular tunes of the day. Daughter Celia remembered that one of his favorites was "¿Y tú, qué has hecho?" (And you, what have you done?). Other favorites were "Blancas azucenas" (White lilies), and "Las calles de San Juan" (The streets of San Juan).

Music and dance swirled around the barrio of Santos Suárez. Throughout the year many people in the neighborhood worked on their carnival floats. At carnival time nubile young women walked alongside the float, performing dance routines, singing, and dancing the conga. Celia Cruz sang too, and when she did so she turned heads. Hers wasn't a little girl's voice. Rather, it was vibrant, a bit loud, and lower in pitch than normal for someone of her age. This explains why her mother, Catalina "Ollita" Alfonso, tasked her with singing lullabies to her younger brother and sister. That unfortunately had the effect of keeping her siblings awake and attracting neighbors who gathered around the open front door to listen. When Simón Cruz closed the door, they moved down the sidewalk and continued listening beneath the bedroom window. When there were visitors Celia's parents invariably called on her to sing. Grandmother Delores Ramos was one of the first to opine that singing was Celia's destiny. Ollita wasn't convinced until the day she and her daughter were window-shopping in downtown Havana, Celia singing happily at her side. One day, when a passing American tourist asked whether the little girl would sing a song for her, Celia obliged with a spirited rendition of "¿Y tú, qué has hecho?" The woman was so impressed that she took her into a shop and bought her a pair of shoes. For Ollita the event was an augury instructing her that her daughter would indeed become a singer. She resolved to do everything in her power to make sure that happened.

The Afro-Cuban Cruz family were all devout Roman Catholics, straitlaced and upwardly mobile. As a member of a population group not far removed from slavery, Simón Cruz was determined that his children do well in life. Celia, he resolved, would not become a professional singer, but rather a schoolteacher. From his experience women who sang for a living were invariably *mujeres de la vida,* or prostitutes. Accordingly, Simón Cruz sacrificed to ensure his daughter the best possible education as a pathway to the honorable profession of teacher. When Celia graduated from elementary school he sent her to study at the Academy of Oblate Nuns, located at the edge of the Santos Suárez neighborhood. After her high school graduation he enrolled her in the National Teachers' College in Havana, proudly witnessing her graduation in 1947 as a certified teacher. Simón Cruz was satisfied. His family now had a member who could proudly claim membership in Cuba's middle class.

During her school years Celia Cruz was constantly called on to sing. She sang for teachers and schoolmates, specializing in emotion-filled renditions of the national anthem along with other patriotic songs. She sang at family gatherings, at baptisms and weddings, and anywhere else a song was called for. Her talent was so obvious that on the day she graduated from normal school her academic adviser took her aside and said, "Celia, God gave you a wonderful gift. Don't waste your time trying to become a teacher. You were put on earth to make people happy—*by using your gift.*"[2]

During the long days when Simón Cruz was away at work his family members helped Celia make use of her gift. One day in 1947, toward the end of her college years, her cousin Serafín appeared at her door announcing that he had signed her up for a Saturday afternoon radio talent show called *Tea Time*. He ordered her to put on her best dress and sing her best. "Am I making myself clear?" said Serafín in a slightly menacing tone of voice. Years later Celia Cruz recalled that she was both overjoyed and nervous about the chance to perform competitively. She won the contest easily, received a cake as her prize, and took it home, where her family members consumed it with gusto. After that she entered talent competitions all over Havana, winning most of them. Sometimes she received little or nothing for her effort. At other times she was awarded a box of store-bought delicacies not often seen in her household. Occasionally she won small cash prizes that she used to pay for textbooks. Following one contest she did not win, her favorite aunt Ana complained that during the competition she stood onstage "like a stick." "Celia," she added, "why don't you shake it a little, honey?" Her niece took her advice, recalling it as the moment "when I added the famous 'zing' to my performance." Celia was concerned that her father would not be pleased with the "zing," but her mother advised her not to worry, saying, "He's just a grumpy old black man."[3]

A STAR IS BORN

By her early twenties everyone around Celia Cruz, excluding her father, understood that her future lay in singing. After college graduation she devoted herself entirely to music. She earned a precarious living as one of many itinerant musicians and actors freelancing at Havana's radio stations. These aspiring artists were called *bolos*, and they shared long hours sitting together on benches located in station reception areas. Some days they were called in to perform, earning a few pesos; other days there was no work and they returned home hungry. Radio station CMQ was the favorite gathering place for Havana's *bolos* because its signal reached all parts of Cuba and countries bordering on the Caribbean as well. In this way it gave them exposure to both national and international audiences. The ambitious young artists thus sat patiently on the Radio CMQ's "bench of dreams" hoping for a chance at stardom. Celia Cruz made many friends while waiting for the call to perform. Her fellow *bolos* admired her dignity and good posture, giving her the nickname the "Black Swan." Another of her nicknames was the "little chocolate doll."

One day at the end of 1949 her hard work began paying off. She signed contracts with several nightclubs in Havana where she performed during their run-up to the Christmas holidays. Early the following year she was invited to sing at a nightclub in Caracas, Venezuela. While there she accepted a side engagement in Maracaibo with an all-female Cuban band called Anacaona, named for the ill-fated queen of Hispaniola's Taíno people. Not long after returning to Havana, she found herself once again headed to Caracas, signed to what turned into a four-month engagement at a club called the Quiet Tavern. Her all-female show featured Celia singing before a dance group called Las Mulatas de Fuego (the Blazing Mulatto Women). The Mulatas were four statuesque showgirls who wore skimpy feathered costumes. In their act Celia, dressed in a sequined, form-fitting evening gown, entered the stage with the Mulatas gliding along behind her. Celia sang, the showgirls danced, and the largely male audience went wild. Their show played to packed houses in Caracas before moving on to Mexico City, where it was equally well received at the city's Zombie Club. Back in Cuba once again, and now a known quantity, Celia Cruz started singing at dance clubs across the island. Newspapers began reporting on her. One day at the railyard a fellow worker showed Simón Cruz a glowing newspaper feature on the talented young singer named Cruz, asking whether they were related. Suddenly Simón Cruz understood that his daughter was not a prostitute but rather a rising musical talent. Following work that day he sat down with his daughter and told her of his change of heart. "He finally told me," she wrote in her autobiography, "that he trusted me from that moment on and would never again deny that I was his daughter."[4]

Despite her recent successes Celia Cruz was still not earning much money. Between gigs she rejoined her friends on the "bench of dreams" at Radio CMQ. It was there that she had her first big break, through her friendship with a choreographer named Rodney Neyra. Neyra invited her to join a show he was producing for the Tropicana, at the time one of the world's most famous nightclubs. Its performance area boasted three stages, known collectively as the Paradise under the Stars. Neyra titled his show *Sun Sun Ba Baé* (Pretty hummingbird of dawn). Both the title and all songs in the ninety-minute extravaganza were in Lucumí, the Cuban dialect of Yoruba, the West African language of the Santería religion. Celia Cruz did not speak Lucumí. But she had grown up hearing it both spoken on the street and used in the lyrics of Cuban popular music. She had no trouble memorizing the lyrics of the show tunes, which she sang to standing ovations at the Tropicana for the better part of two years. She recalled that singing in the language of Santería was "a beautiful way of expressing my African roots." *Sun Sun Ba Baé* made Rodney Neyra famous both in Cuba and in greater Latin America.[5]

Celia Cruz had her second big break during rehearsals for Rodney Neyra's show. In late 1950 one of Cuba's top dance bands, Sonora Matancera, lost its female soloi, a blond named Myrta Silva, who retired and moved back to her home in Puerto Rico. At that moment Celia was working full-time at Radio

Figure 8.1. Celia Cruz and La Sonora Matancera (1950s). Narcy Studios, Montserrat y Empedrado, Havana

Cadena Suárez, barely making ends meet. One day a man named Sotolongo walked into the station and asked if she was interested in trying out with Sonora Matancera. The implications for her were tremendous. Joining a well-known band meant steady work and no more lean times pinching pennies between short-term engagements. Her audition was successful and within the week Sonora's bandleader Rogelio Martínez hired her as the group's female vocalist. That marked the beginning of a mutually beneficial fifteen-year relationship (see figure 8.1).

Throughout the 1950s the slim, dark-skinned singer with the unique and dominating voice toured with Sonora Matancera throughout Cuba and countries bordering the Caribbean basin. A year after joining the band Celia began recording with the band, eventually releasing seventy-four albums with it. That worked out to one new album every three months. Initially, though, Rogelio Martínez had a hard time convincing Sonora's label, New York–based SEECO Records, to record his female singer. Sidney Siegel, the company's owner who was based in New York, told Martínez that record sales were poor for female soloists, even for Argentine diva Libertad Lamarque. Martínez insisted that Siegel was comparing apples and oranges, that Celia

Cruz was no Libertad Lamarque. The New Yorker finally agreed to promote one album with the new singer on the condition that if it did not turn a profit, neither Sonora nor Cruz would receive a dime for their effort. One of the record's tunes, "Cao, cao, maní picao," known as "the peanut vendor's song," became a hit throughout Cuba. From that moment, and for many years afterward, Celia Cruz figured among SEECO's most successful artists.

In 1957 Celia Cruz recorded her first gold single for SEECO, "Burundanga." She was invited to New York City to receive an award for the song, and then to perform in a concert following the award ceremony. Unfortunately, Saint Nicholas Arena in the Bronx oversold tickets, leading to a riot and to police clearing the arena. The following day a New York newspaper carried the headline "Anarchy at a Cuban Singer's Concert."

By the late 1950s Celia Cruz was famous in Cuba and known throughout the Caribbean and in parts of the United States. For the first time in her life, she was financially secure. Through her work with Sonora Matancera she had become a sought-after singer of television jingles advertising products such as Coca-Cola, Bacardi Rum, and H. Upmann cigars—though the woman shown on-screen was invariably a blond White woman lip-synching the lyrics. These successes allowed Celia Cruz to realize her dream of moving her mother out of the old Santos Suárez tenement and into a new house she had built in the middle-class Lawton neighborhood in suburban Havana. In late 1958 the house was complete and filled with all-new furniture bought by Celia at Havana department stores. In its front yard the house boasted a shrine to Our Lady of Charity, the patroness of Cuba. On Christmas Eve the Cruz Ramos clan gathered around grandmother Delores for a festive housewarming. After taking photos in front of a modest Christmas tree, they all walked to a neighborhood church for midnight mass. It was to be one of the last carefree moments for the close-knit family.

CUBAN REVOLUTION: EXILE TO MEXICO

On January 1, 1959, troops of revolutionary guerrilla leader Fidel Castro occupied Havana. As Castro's forces approached the city, Cuba's dictator Fulgencio Batista and his top supporters fled the island by air and sea. Within a week Castro and his forces were moving toward achieving full control of Cuba. Castro and his lieutenants made it known that they planned to bring wide-ranging social and economic reforms to the island. Land reform was highest on their agenda. Land redistribution had been a dream of Latin American reformers throughout the twentieth century. At last, a thirty-four-year-old lawyer-turned-revolutionary named Castro was carrying it out. Initially those in Cuba and elsewhere praised Castro for attacking widespread poverty in rural areas by breaking up the island's many large sugar-growing plantations. Even Celia Cruz approved. Touring in Mexico during January 1959, she recorded a ballad that included the following lyrics:

Guajiro, ya llegó tu día, ya llegó tu día.
¿Para qué tantos con tanto, y por qué tantos sin nada,
si esta es la tierra Sagrada?
Porque Dios mandó a Fidel.[6]

(Campesino, your day has come. Why do so many have so much, and others nothing, if this is the sacred land? [This is why] God sent Fidel.)

Within weeks the singer started changing her good opinion of the new regime. Arriving at the Havana airport in late January 1959, she discovered it was now run by hard-eyed soldiers who demanded her passport and examined it carefully. Soon she saw her main source of income vanish when Havana's nightclubs and casinos were closed through revolutionary decree. Although the city's glitziest casinos had been controlled by a mix of Cuban gangsters and members of the US mafia, they offered the island's entertainers their most lucrative employment. Before long it became clear that singers such as Celia Cruz and bands like Sonora Matancera were threatened by poverty. The closing of nightclubs and casinos took place against the backdrop of revolutionary actions that included the execution by firing squad of scores of Batista supporters and army officers. By late 1959 Celia Cruz and many other Cubans were intensely unhappy over this state of affairs.

Fidel Castro, however, was a fan of Celia Cruz—though not for long. One day Castro arrived at a reception given in his honor by Miguel Ángel Quevedo, editor of *Bohemia* magazine. When told that Celia Cruz was entertaining there, Castro remarked that he had often cleaned his rifle to the rhythms of "Burundanga." He asked that the singer come greet him when he arrived. An annoyed Celia Cruz sent word that if Castro wanted to meet her, he should come to where she was performing. Offended, Castro refused. That was the beginning of bad blood between Celia Cruz and Cuba's revolutionary leader.

Their animosity deepened several months later when the new regime organized a concert at Havana's Blanquita Theater. When Castro arrived for the event, most of the performers rushed out to have their pictures taken with him. Not only did Celia Cruz remain backstage but she refused to sing "Burundanga." Following her performance, she left by a side entrance to avoid having to meet Castro. As she departed, a Castro aide hissed, "You are the only one who hasn't shown El Comandante the respect he deserves."⁷ Part of her distaste for Castro may have been race based. All her life Celia Cruz had been reminded of her dark skin by Creoles, American-born people of Spanish descent, who usually treated her dismissively. Fidel Castro was a Creole from a well-to-do family. White Cubans were accustomed to having Black people at their beck and call—and despite Castro's status as revolutionary leader of Cuba, Celia was not about to continue this tradition.

Providentially for Celia Cruz and Sonora Matancera, in early 1960 both received offers to perform in Mexico City, Celia at the Club Terraza and Sonora at the Lyric Theater. Although never formally a member of the band, but rather its invited lead vocalist, Cruz traveled with the musicians whenever possible. When traveling outside the country she let Rogelio Martínez handle the paperwork. On July 15, 1960, Celia Cruz and Sonora Matancera rode together to the Havana airport. There they said goodbye to friends and family members who had come to see them off and proceeded through customs to their plane. Once it cleared Cuban airspace Martínez rose and turned to face his group. "Guys," he said, "this is a one-way trip."⁸

None of those who boarded the plane in Havana that July morning suspected it was the last time many of them would ever return to the city. Yet that proved to be the case. Worsening relations between Cuba and the United States made the island a fortress nation. On April 17, 1961, CIA-trained and equipped exiles stormed ashore at an inlet called the Bay of Pigs. Their intent: to overthrow Fidel Castro. That military operation was similar in many ways to the one that drove Guatemala's Socialist president Jacobo Árbenz from power seven years before. But unlike what had happened in Guatemala, the Bay of Pigs invasion ended disastrously for the invaders, most of whom were either killed or captured by Cuban forces. The failed US-sponsored attack had the effect of driving Cuba into the arms of the USSR (Union of Soviet Socialist Republics). In December 1961 Castro proclaimed himself to be a Marxist-Leninist, signaling his alliance with the USSR. The United States severed relations with Cuba and placed an embargo on the island destined to endure for many decades.

Not long after arriving in Mexico, Celia Cruz fell in love. Earlier, while living in Cuba, the proper young woman with regal posture and an incomparable voice had not had any serious romantic involvements, at least not as far as anyone knew. Over her first ten years performing with Sonora Matancera, the band's eight male members protected her as if she were their little sister. That was clear on occasions when some man followed her into an unlit parking lot after a late-night performance. The potential assailant invariably stopped short when finding himself staring into the stony faces of the men of Sonora Matancera who were lined up alongside the band's bus.

Among the band members, Celia Cruz was closest to trumpeter Pedro Knight. Knight had been the first member of the band to greet her on the morning in 1950 when she showed up to audition for the job with Sonora. Over the years the two developed a "best friend" relationship. It could hardly have been otherwise. Pedro Knight was three years her senior, twice married, and the father of at least six children. He was also known to be a womanizer. Arriving in Mexico, though, Celia Cruz and Pedro Knight started thinking of each other in a new way. By that time the trumpeter was divorced from his second wife, and both he and his best friend were feeling unhappy and stateless. One day as the two strolled through a park in Mexico City, Pedro Knight stopped and said, "Celia, I have a problem. I think I'm falling in love with my best friend." She replied that friendship and love are not mutually exclusive, adding that she too had been feeling that way. This cool exchange marked the engagement of Celia Cruz and Pedro Knight. Despite her outward calm it was a moment of high emotion for Celia Cruz. As she later described it, when she heard her best friend's declaration of love,

> my heart began to pound in my chest. Pedro took my hand and kissed me for the first time right there. He then embraced me and then I remember feeling as if I was going to faint. My stomach did flips; and it felt like thousands of butterflies fluttered inside me. I stood there with my head on his shoulder, the tears streaming from my eyes.[9]

The two married a year later, on July 14, 1962. Celia Cruz and Pedro Knight remained inseparable until parted by death forty-two years later.

An immediate problem facing the newlyweds was where they should make their home. Both Cruz and Knight were happy in Mexico, a Hispanic country full of friends they had made over the years. Before long they found a spacious apartment in Mexico City where both lived contentedly. But several problems arose, the first and most serious being the inordinate amount of time Celia spent touring in the United States. Large numbers of Cubans lived there, concentrated in and around New York City and southern Florida. Whether exiles like her or Cubans who emigrated to the United States prior to the revolution, they made up her most steadfast fan base. For that reason, she was constantly being invited to perform in the United States, meaning that she and her husband needed somewhere to live during engagements that sometimes stretched into weeks or months. The solution they found was to rent a small apartment in Lower Manhattan, relatively close to the city's major performance venues. While in New York in 1962 Celia Cruz became the first Hispanic woman to perform in Carnegie Hall. During the 1960s she was also booked to perform in Radio City Music Hall and Harlem's Apollo Theater.

Two things hindered the Cuban singer's initial time spent in the United States. The first involved English. The second concerned her hair—specifically, her struggle to find a hairdresser. In her early weeks in New York City Celia Cruz scheduled appointments to have her hair done and then found herself waiting for hours as the beautician let her regular customers butt into line ahead of her. The Spanish-speaking performer was forced to sit there mute, unable to protest. Still, the experience had two beneficial effects. First, it gave Celia Cruz both time and incentive to learn English. Second, it permitted her to study advances in dressing African American hair. These included the technique of relaxing hair and then weaving straight hair into it. Eventually the singer found a full-time hairdresser who traveled with her on tour, both helping with makeup and tending the wigs that she increasingly preferred wearing during performances. As for her English, she never mastered it. As she always said, "My English is not very good-looking."[10]

Throughout the early 1960s Celia Cruz and Pedro Knight continued touring throughout Mexico with Sonora Matancera, always playing to enthusiastic audiences. It was a grueling routine, but at the end of each tour the couple could return to their comfortable apartment in Mexico City. It was not long, though, before two problems arose that kept them from making Mexico their permanent residence-in-exile. The first involved a Mexican law prohibiting foreigners from buying property in the country. The second was that, proud of its own revolutionary tradition, Mexico maintained cordial relations with Cuba. Celia Cruz thus found herself under increasing pressure to share the stage with visiting Cuban artists. This she refused to do. Within this setting there was a powerful third force arguing for making the United States, not Mexico, the artists' preferred residence. That was the US policy of reaching out to Cuban exiles for help in strengthening domestic support against Fidel Castro and Communist Cuba. All these considerations, and others as well, led Celia Cruz and Pedro Knight to accept the reality that the United States, not Mexico, was the logical place for them to live.

Throughout the 1960s Celia Cruz and Pedro Knight continued to divide their time between performance in Mexico and the United States, although professional considerations pushed them in the direction of the latter country. By mid-decade Celia Cruz had tired of the incessant touring throughout Mexico, singing the same set of Cuban standards frequently accompanied by mariachi bands. Even performing with Sonora Matancera had grown stale. At the same time her record sales had started to fall. It was clearly time for a change. Luckily that suddenly became possible when New York–born bandleader Tito Puente asked Celia Cruz to both join his band and record for his company, Tico Records. She instantly accepted the offer. At first Sidney Siegel refused to release her from her contact with SEECO Records. But at last, he agreed to do so, thereby ending their long relationship. Cruz reported to her husband, "The poor man started to cry."[11]

During the late 1960s Celia Cruz recorded fifteen albums with Tico Records. In one of her first performances with her new band she celebrated the event with the following improvisation:

Luego me fui a Nueva York en busca de otro ambiente.
Y al llegar tuve la suerte de grabar con Tito Puente.[12]

(Then I went to New York looking for a different scene.
When I arrived, I had the good luck to record with Tito Puente.)

AFRO-CUBAN MUSIC AND POLITICS BEYOND THE 1960s

Despite her break with both SEECO Records and Sonora Matancera, all was not well with Celia Cruz—and Afro-Cuban music generally. In terms of her own career, the singer's record sales did not pick up in any notable way when she started singing with Puentes's band, which was so large that at times it almost drowned out her voice. Meanwhile Afro-Cuban music, often called Caribbean or tropical music, found itself competing with an explosion of musical genres in the United States of the late 1960s. Young record-buying Latinos were drawn away from their traditional music by rock and roll, doo-wop, rhythm and blues, and the Motown sound. There were jazz and folk music revivals during the decade, and bluegrass, country and western, blues, and delta blues were growing in popularity. When the 1970s dawned, disco became the rage throughout the United States. Latin American music remained popular only in states bordering Mexico, and in Hispanic enclaves on the East Coast. By the early 1970s Celia Cruz was noticing a troubling decline in the number of fans attending her concerts. That came through to her forcefully one evening in 1972 while she was performing at Radio City Music Hall. During the concert she noticed a near absence of young people in the audience. "Everyone there was older," she told Pedro Knight, adding, "I've begun to think Cuban music is doomed."[13] Celia Cruz and her husband were resigned, even melancholy, on their flight back to Mexico City.

Celia Cruz may not have known it at the time, but Afro-Cuban music was experiencing a rebirth destined to take it far beyond the Cuban American exile community. In the musical melting pot that was New York City, a hybrid pan-Caribbean music called "salsa" was being created. It soon drew Celia Cruz to it and made her its foremost star.

Salsa's vehicle was a band called the Fania All-Stars. Fania was founded by three men: New York cop-turned-lawyer Jerry Masucci, Harlem-born pianist Larry Harlow, and Dominican-born-but-New-York-raised flutist, composer, and bandleader Johnny Pacheco. Masucci and Harlow met in 1964 at Havana's Fania Bar. Masucci was in Havana researching Santería, and Harlow was there studying Afro-Cuban music. Both knew Pacheco from the New York music scene. Two years later the three met by chance at a party at Jerry Masucci's New York City apartment. During a conversation lasting until dawn, they agreed to form the Fania All-Stars and to promote its hot sound in the Latin dance clubs of Lower Manhattan and surrounding boroughs of the city. Over the late 1960s Fania hired the brightest young talent on the Latin music scene, going on to hire promoter Ralph Mercado in 1971 to help them popularize salsa. The result was a series of well-advertised bookings in Manhattan's most popular dance venues, one of which was the Cheetah Club and Casino. A sold-out performance there in 1971 resulted in the two-disc album *Live from the Cheetah*, which quickly became one of the best-selling salsa albums of all time. In the words of Latin music historian Ed Morales, the album "awakened ancestral memories and nostalgia" among young New Yorkers. Young Puerto Ricans, he wrote, loved the album's track "Anacaona." In Morales's words, as they listened to the song, "they riffed barrio memories and salutes to the Taíno goddess in the declamatory style of décima poets."[14] Although salsa was rooted in the Afro-Cuban music that Celia Cruz and her fans knew so well, the new-yet-old sound was pitched to, and clearly resonated with, the young and the hip.

By 1972 Masucci, Harlow, and Pacheco had agreed their all-male band required a female vocalist. They also agreed that she must be Celia Cruz. In early 1973 Larry Harlow contacted the singer in Mexico City, inviting her to join the Fania All-Stars and to star in three major projects that the band had scheduled for later in the year. The first of them was Harlow's Spanish-language rock opera, *Hommy: A Latin Opera*, to open in New York City in April. He offered Cruz the starring role of Gracia Divina (Divine Grace). Ralph Mercado wanted her to headline a midsummer Fania concert to be held in Yankee Stadium. And Johnny Pacheco wanted her to record an album with him. Celia Cruz happily accepted the three proposals, effectively becoming a starring member of the Fania All-Stars. That association led Cruz and her husband to leave their Mexico City apartment and permanently relocate to New York City.

The album *Celia and Johnny*, with Johnny Pacheco, released in late 1973, became the most important album in Celia Cruz's career. In its liner notes Juan Moreno Velásquez describes the album as having "opened the doors of success for the famous Cuban singer with the force of a raging bull." It in effect marked the beginning of a second career for Celia Cruz, introducing her to a new generation of listeners. Its tracks "Toro mata" (The bull kills), of Peruvian origin, and "Quimbara," featuring a series of drums talking with one another, became instant hits.

The August 24, 1973, Yankee Stadium concert was a phenomenon. Forty-four thousand people jammed the venue and went wild when Celia Cruz burst onto the stage dressed in African style, big gold hoops in her ears and sporting a similarly oversized Afro. The crowd gave her a standing ovation when she sang her signature song, "Bemba colorá" (Thick red lips). As she sang, an ecstatic Cruz turned to Johnny Pacheco and improvised some lyrics: "I've met the great Johnny Pacheco, my brother. This doesn't end here. The best is yet to come." As soon as she left the stage the supercharged crowd flowed out of the stands and rushed the stage to hug and kiss the performers (some of them also made off with instruments and sound equipment). Altogether the Yankee Stadium concert of 1973 was a stellar moment in salsa history.[15]

A steady stream of bookings followed for Celia Cruz. The year 1975 found her on a plane bound for Kinshasa, Zaire, along with other entertainers invited to perform over the days preceding Muhammad Ali's "rumble in the jungle," his championship heavyweight fight with Joe Frazier. Johnny Pacheco traveled with the Cuban singer. Together they "turned the plane into one big party" when they gave their fellow performers an extemporaneous concert. Among those joining in the fun were James Brown, B. B. King, and Sister Sledge. Johnny Pacheco, who had recently released his hit album *Viva África*, was mobbed when the plane landed in Kinshasa. Celia Cruz remembered him as the most popular of the American performers there, though she also recalled the crowd exploding over her renditions of "Quimbara" and "Guantanamera." "A sea of Black faces dancing is a great thing to see," she later wrote.[16]

At last Celia Cruz was comfortable living in the United States. No longer was she an anonymous Latina unable to speak a word of English. Beyond that, as a celebrity and a Cuban American she benefited from the United States' anti-Cuba policy. That led her to apply for US citizenship, which she received in 1977. Celia Cruz was never one to hide her feelings. Following her swearing-in ceremony in a downtown Brooklyn courthouse, walking down the street with her naturalization papers in hand, she literally jumped. Not long before her death Celia Cruz told an interviewer, "Becoming an American citizen is one of the things in my life I'm most proud of."[17]

By the 1980s the second career of Celia Cruz was in full flower. Although she turned sixty in 1985, she maintained her astonishing average of seventy concert performances per year. Among the highlights of the decade were a sold-out Madison Square Garden tribute concert in 1982, the receipt of her first Grammy in 1983 (for her album *Ritmo en el corazón* [*Rhythm in the heart*]), a White House reception and award from President Ronald Reagan, and the awarding of her star on Hollywood's Walk of Fame. His wife's stamina amazed Pedro Knight. During a European tour that took the singer to nineteen countries in six weeks' time, she broke a toe. Yet later the same day she was onstage singing and dancing as if nothing had happened. "You had to see it to believe it," said Pedro Knight.[18]

Celia Cruz was superstitious. She feared flying, so when she boarded a plane she prayed to Saint Christopher, the protector of travelers. When checking into a hotel she always avoided the thirteenth floor—and any room having thirteen in its number. She never wore pearls because she believed they brought her bad luck. When performing on a new stage she always wore something white to honor the Virgin of Mercy, Peace, and Prosperity (and perhaps, too, Obatalá, the Santería counterpart of the Virgin of Mercy). Whenever the diva traveled she brought along her personal pantheon of Catholic saints. Among her favorites were Saint Lazarus, for protection against disease (Babalú-Ayé, his counterpart Santería deity); Saint Gregorio Hernández, an anointed Venezuelan physician believed to stop pain; and Afro-Peruvian Saint Martín de Porres, revered for his healing powers and ministry to the poor.

An important saint for devout Cubans is the Black Virgin of Regla, whose intercession brings calm seas and fair weather (whose Santería counterpart is Yemayá, queen of the waters). Celia Cruz always prayed to the Virgin of Regla prior to an outdoor concert, frequently with the hoped-for result. The best evidence of such weather-related divine intervention came the evening of March 3, 1987, at an open-air concert in Tenerife, capital of the Canary Islands. The night was cool and the sky cloudless as an enormous crowd flowed into the concert venue. "There was a sea of people in front of me," the singer recalled. When she sang "Bemba colorá" the ground shook as 240,000 happy fans sang along with her.[19] The *Guinness Book of World Records* lists it as the largest concert audience in world history.

The 1990s were a time of awards and recognitions for Celia Cruz, both in the United States and abroad. First came Colombia's award to the singer of its Presidential Medal of the Arts (1990). A year later Miami's Cuban American community renamed Calle Ocho Celia Cruz Way. A few months after that President Bill Clinton awarded her the Congressional Medal of the Arts. In 1994 the Dominican Republic named Celia Cruz its artist of the year, and the Smithsonian Institute awarded her its Lifetime Achievement Award and honored her with a permanent exhibit. In Colombia the Cali Music Festival chose her hit "La vida es un carnaval" (Life is a carnival) as its theme in 1999, and the city of Cali awarded her its highest honor, the Cross of Sebastián de Belalcázar. At decade's end Telemundo named her Artist of the Millennium.

In her autobiography Celia Cruz assessed her prospects for the approaching twenty-first century: "The millennium may have been coming to a close, but my career was entering an entirely new phase and the future seemed brilliant."[20] What she had in mind may have been the Latin pop music explosion of the late 1990s and the seemingly effortless way she lent her musical talent and showmanship to it. Latin pop won Celia Cruz new fans, especially through her collaboration on a 1998 album with Wyclef Jean and Santana. The album also contained Puff Daddy's single "Señorita," and "Dáme espacio," (Give me space) by Puff Daddy's protégé Black Rob.

These successes and innovative collaborations were played out against a backdrop of steadily worsening US-Cuba relations. Cruz remained a relentless critic of the Castro regime. In 1993, when both she and Fidel Castro were visiting Colombia, that nation's president, César Gaviria, asked her opinion of her countryman. She snapped, "He's nothing but a tin-pot dictator," adding, "Have you by any chance asked [Castro] what he thinks of me?" Invited to perform at Bill Clinton's 1994 Summit of the Americas, aimed at creating an Americas-wide free trade zone, Celia Cruz stopped in midperformance, turned, and lectured the assembled dignitaries: "Stop aiding and abetting Fidel Castro. Support the embargo and make him give up power."[21]

Her hostility toward Castro earned Celia Cruz the ire of many supporters of the Cuban regime. This came to a head in early 2000 when hecklers disrupted her performance and forced her from a stage in San Juan, Puerto Rico. The background of the unprecedented incident lay in an event that occurred three years earlier, in Miami, when Puerto Rico's leading *salsero*, Andy Montañez, was not allowed to participate in the city's annual Calle Ocho Carnival. Celia Cruz supported the action. The Puerto Rican entertainer's offense was his friendship with Cuban singer Silvio Rodríguez. Rodríguez was a leader of the Nueva Trova movement, dedicated to keeping Cuba's revolutionary spirit alive. The Cuban Americans of South Florida anathematized the music of Nueva Trova (roughly translated as "new troubadour"), especially as performed by Rodríguez. As a consequence, Puerto Rican *salseros* sympathetic to the Cuban regime boycotted Celia Cruz and her music after 1997, despite the claim by Andy Montañez that his friendship with Silvio Rodríguez was in no way political. Cruz was pointedly not invited to the World Salsa Festival in San Juan in late 1997. When she performed in Puerto Rico three years later, she was punished yet again. Pro-Cuban *salseros* packed San Juan's Bithorn Stadium for a Fania All-Stars concert held on April 29, 2000. They drove Celia Cruz from the stage in tears. It was the low point of her career. Such were the passions running beneath the surface of Afro-Cuban music in the years following Fidel Castro's Cuban Revolution.

Despite these sad events in San Juan, Celia Cruz moved through the remainder of that year with her usual vigor. In January she vacationed with her husband in Punta del Este, Uruguay, performing in concerts held across the Southern Cone. Later in the year she collected her second Grammy for Best Salsa Performance. Following the award ceremony, the diva, then seventy-four, partied the night away with her husband, José Feliciano, Jennifer Lopez, and others. At the end of 2000, and in quick succession, *Billboard* magazine devoted an entire edition to her fifty years onstage, and Whoopi Goldberg asked for and received permission to pitch and star in a biopic about her. Shortly thereafter she sang "Las Mañanitas" at a holiday service at Mexico's shrine of the Virgin of Guadalupe. The performance was broadcast throughout the Spanish-speaking world via television and radio.

Many wondered how the Cuban entertainer kept up a pace that drove other touring artists into early retirement. The answer lay both in her love of her work and her temperate lifestyle. When she and her husband checked into a hotel she granted just one interview, usually to a reporter she had known for years and who effectively publicized her concert. She and Pedro Knight took their meals in their room and washed laundry in the bathroom. Once settled in her hotel she set to work on correspondence, writing notes and letters to friends, relatives, and colleagues. Many of her notes went to children and young people. She and her husband were never able to have children of their own, but they became the godparents of scores of her friends' children, and their children's children. Cruz traveled with a fat datebook that helped her remember a myriad of birthdays, christenings, saint's days, first communions, graduations, and marriages. She commemorated these through personal notes. One section of the datebook contained contact information, arranged by geographic region, for the hundreds of friends she had made during decades of touring, along with publicists she kept current on her activities. This regimen of note writing both rested her voice and relaxed her prior to performances. It was also an exercise she enjoyed.

When in the United States Celia Cruz was generous with her time. Miami was a home away from home for her, and she visited the city every year to host the city's annual League Against Cancer telethon produced by Telemundo Miami. The event was built around live entertainment provided by its mistress of ceremonies. Children dubbed *cangrejitos* (little crabs) collected donations by passing "Celia's Buckets" through the audience, while phone-bank volunteers recorded the donations that flowed in. The first time the event passed the million-dollar mark was 1983, when it was helped along by the MC's performance of her merengue "El Guabá" (The little black spider), that she had recently recorded with Johnny Pacheco. The song was so popular that she sang it four times over the course of the event, which lasted from 10:00 a.m. to 2:00 a.m. the following morning. Celia Cruz said that the daylong telethons left her invigorated rather than tired, in part because she felt she hosted the fundraisers in honor of her mother Ollita, a cancer victim.

Toward the end of the Clinton presidency (1993–2001) restrictions eased for US citizens traveling to Cuba, but increased cultural exchange led to new tensions. During this time, the film *The Buena Vista Social Club* recalled Afro-Cuban music of a bygone era and created new appreciation of the island's unique Latin sound. The film also had the effect of reviving the careers of musicians who had been forgotten in Castro's Cuba. The young Cuban singer Halia Mopié even released a tribute album dedicated to the music of Celia Cruz. None of that, however, lessened the diva's loathing of Fidel Castro. So when Miami was selected to host the 2001 Latin Grammy Awards, Cuban Americans there forced the event's relocation to Los Angeles. Their action was for the usual reason: they refused to allow Cubans to perform in their midst. Celia Cruz reacted to the change of venue in typical fashion: "Again Fidel's evil grasp [has] complicated our lives."[22] Those complications turned out to be greater than Cruz had suspected. The award ceremony was set for September 11, 2001.

The 9/11 terrorist attacks led to the cancellation of the Latin Grammy Awards, disrupting the entertainers' return trips home. After being stranded in Los Angeles for three days, Celia Cruz and her husband caught a ride back to New York on a jet chartered by Sony Records. The Colombian star Shakira—like Cruz also under contract with Sony—was on the flight. A political opposite of Celia Cruz, Shakira refused to speak with, or even to look at, the Cuban singer. Doubtless hurt by the younger woman's hostility, Celia Cruz could only remark, "I guess I wasn't her cup of tea."[23]

When 2002 began, Celia Cruz threw herself into her usual whirlwind of activity. She spent the first six months of the year touring in Europe and South America, returning to the United States only briefly to emcee Miami's League Against Cancer telethon. Meanwhile she released *La negra tiene tumbao* (The Black lady's got party), which earned her a second Latin Grammy Award as the year's best salsa album. In midyear Telemundo proposed an early-2003 tribute to her in recognition of her fifty years onstage. Then, in August, she and Pedro Knight returned to New York for their annual medical checkups. A few days after the examination the tests revealed that Celia Cruz had breast cancer. The diagnosis came two months before her seventy-seventh birthday.

In late September the singer had a single mastectomy. The procedure went well, and Cruz attempted to carry on as before. The day before her operation she appeared in a daylong photo shoot with Mexican writer and fan Ana Cristina Reymundo for an article to appear in the in-flight magazine of American Airlines. A week after her surgery Celia Cruz flew to Miami for yet another program given in her honor. All the while she prepared for a November 27 concert in Mexico City, organized to celebrate high points of her career.

Although Celia Cruz recalled that she enjoyed the Mexico City event, which was attended by many of her oldest friends, along with celebrities such as Colombian novelist Gabriel García Márquez, all was not well with the honoree. The morning of the concert she fought with her husband in their hotel room. She complained of headaches. And when at the end of the program she sang the Cuban standard "Usted abusó" with Pedro Knight, she could not remember some of the lyrics. Several people at the event noticed that she babbled, and that some of her sentences lacked coherence. Following her return to New York, tests confirmed the worst: cancer had spread to her brain. On December 6 Celia Cruz underwent six hours of surgery to remove a malignant tumor. Soon afterward, other tumors were discovered in her brain.

The singer's repeated hospital stays convinced some of her fans that Celia Cruz was undergoing plastic surgery. When told that she laughed, saying, "This face, this smile, and these fat black lips are part of my personality."[24] Clearly, though, it was time to make her condition public. On December 7, 2002, Cruz released a statement thanking her fans for their support over so many years. She went on to describe the reasons for her recent surgeries. She did not mention in the letter that her brain tumors were inoperable and that she had only a short time left to live.

Incredibly, early 2003 was full of activity for Celia Cruz and those around her. January was dedicated to two projects. First was the sale of her New York apartment and a move across the Hudson River to Fort Lee, New Jersey. It was a cost-cutting measure to help pay medical bills. Second was work on an autobiography with Ana Cristina Reymundo. In February she labored to complete her last album, *Regalo del alma* (Gift of the heart). Weakened by chemotherapy and radiation therapy, she was forced to record each of the album's eleven songs line by line, and with extensive technical assistance (all the while assuring everyone, "I feel fine"). Next it was on to prepare for the March 13 Telemundo program in Miami, which was given the title *Celia Cruz: ¡Azúcar!*. That evening all the greats from the Latin music recording world were present. The honoree was resplendent in a form-fitting red dress, a blond wig with curls reaching to her shoulders, and a diamond choker. There was not a dry eye in the house when Pedro Knight serenaded his wife with "Quizás."

Celia Cruz spent the last three months of her life at her New Jersey apartment surrounded by family and friends. The end came on July 16, 2003. Pedro Knight and Johnny Pacheco were at her side when she took her last breath. Two days later her body was flown to Miami, where her casket was taken to the city's Freedom Tower. During the two-day wake, 150,000 mourners filed past to pay their respects. The scene was repeated two days later in New York City, where more than 200,000 mourners filed past her casket. On July

23 a horse-drawn carriage transported her body to St. Patrick's Cathedral for a funeral mass. The hearse proceeded to Woodlawn Cemetery followed by a throng of mourners. A loudspeaker near graveside played her songs, including her last recording, "Yo viviré" (I will live). Non-Spanish-speaking police on duty there were startled when the crowd suddenly shouted an ovation. They were responding to lyrics from Celia Cruz's last hit song, "Ríe y llora" (Laugh and cry):

Ríe y llora,
que a cada cual le llega su hora.
Ríe y llora,
vive tu vida y gózala toda.

(Laugh and cry,
the end comes to everyone.
Laugh and cry,
live your life, and enjoy all of it.)

EPILOGUE

Celia Cruz was an uncomplicated person with a gift—her voice. Throughout her life she used it to bring joy to her listeners. Up to the time of her passing it seemed that the Queen of Salsa would go on forever thanks to her stamina, determination to entertain, and relentless performance across the world's inhabited continents. She seemed an eternal presence on the Latin music scene. Cruz suggested as much in the songs she chose for her last album: "Ella tiene fuego" (She's got fire), "Me huele a rumba" (I smell a party), and "Yo viviré" (I will always live).

Yet there is a sadness in the story of Celia Cruz. Her love of Cuba was all-consuming. But because of the island's centrality in the nuclear superpower standoff between the United States and USSR, she was denied the right to walk the streets of Havana and visit the graves of her parents. All Cubans, whether they remained on the island after Castro or removed themselves from it, were pawns—peripheral ones at that—in a great-power game having life-and-death consequences. There is no missing the lament in one of her last songs, "Diagnóstico" ("Diagnosis"), the fifth track on *Regalo del alma*:

Yo tengo el son en el corazón
Yo tengo azúcar, yo tengo son
Yo tengo a Cuba en el corazón

(I have the son in my heart
I have sugar, I have son
I have Cuba in my heart)

Talent, perseverance, and circumstances helped Celia Cruz and her fellow musicians offer Afro-Cuban dance music to greater America and to the world. Hers was the enduring gift of liveliness, happiness, and fun. Sharing it is what made her happy.

NOTES

1. Eduardo Marceles, *¡Azúcar! The Biography of Celia Cruz*, translated by Dolores M. Koch (New York: Reed Press, 2004), 44.
2. Eduardo Marceles, *¡Azúcar!*, 32.
3. Celia Cruz, with Ana Cristina Reymundo, *Celia Cruz: My Life. An Autobiography*, trans. José Lucas Badué (New York: Saro Books, 2004), 36–37.
4. Cruz, *Celia*, 50.
5. Cruz, *Celia*, 44.
6. Marceles, *¡Azúcar!*, 105.
7. Salserísimo Perú, "Celia Cruz y Fidel Castro, una historia de odio y revancha," YouTube video, 8:04, April 10, 2020, https://www.youtube.com/watch?v=VvNoyaBfx6I&ab_channel=Salser%C3%ADsimoPer%C3%BA.
8. Cruz, *Celia*, 67.
9. Cruz, *Celia*, 99.
10. Cruz, *Celia*, 102.
11. Cruz, *Celia*, 109–10.
12. Marceles, *¡Azúcar!*, 65.
13. Cruz, *Celia*, 130.
14. Décima is a ten-line poetry form used in songs. Ed Morales, *The Latin Beat: The Rhythms and Roots of Latin Music from Bossa Nova to Salsa and Beyond* (New York: Da Capo Press, 2003), 65. See: James D. Henderson, Linda R. Henderson, and Suzanne M. Litrel, *Ten Notable Women of Colonial Latin America* (New York: Rowman & Littlefield, 2022), 13–39: Anacaona, 1464?–1503.
15. Morales, *Latin Beat*, 74; Marceles, *¡Azúcar!*, 144–45.
16. Cruz, *Celia*, 141.
17. Cruz, *Celia*, 124–25.
18. Marceles, *¡Azúcar!*, 81.
19. Cruz, *Celia*, 154.
20. Cruz, *Celia*, 195.
21. Cruz, *Celia*, 179.
22. Cruz, *Celia*, 208.
23. Cruz, *Celia*, 210.
24. Cruz, *Celia*, 223.

REFERENCES

Bastide, Roger. *African Civilizations in the New World*. New York: Harper & Row, 1971.

Bolton, Herbert Eugene. "The Epic of Greater America." Presidential address. American Historical Association, 1932.

Cruz, Celia, with Ana Cristina Reymundo. *Celia: My Life. An Autobiography*. Translated by José Lucas Badué. New York: Saro Books, 2004.

Henderson, James D., Linda R. Henderson, and Suzanne M. Litrel. *Ten Notable Women of Colonial Latin America*. New York: Rowman & Littlefield, 2022.

Marceles, Eduardo. ¡*Azúcar! The Biography of Celia Cruz*. Translated by Dolores M. Koch. New York: Reed Press, 2004.

Morales, Ed. *The Latin Beat: The Rhythms and Roots of Latin Music from Bossa Nova to Salsa and Beyond*. New York: Da Capo Press, 2003.

Pérez, Jr., Louis A. *Cuba. Between Reform and Revolution*. 2nd ed. New York: Oxford University Press, 1995.

Roberts, John Storm. *The Latin Tinge: The Impact of Latin Music on the United States*. 2nd ed. New York: Oxford University Press, 1999.

Salserísimo Perú. "Celia Cruz y Fidel Castro, una historia de odio y revancha." YouTube video, 8:04. April 10, 2020. https://www.youtube.com/watch?v=VvNoyaBfx6I&ab_channel=Salser%C3%ADsimoPer%C3%BA.

Valverde, Umberto. *Celia Cruz: Reina Rumba*. 2nd ed. Bogotá: Tercer Mundo, 1995.

Chapter 9

Rigoberta Menchú Tum, 1959–

INTRODUCTION

In colonial times the region known as Central America formed the southernmost part of the sprawling viceroyalty of New Spain. Central America extended from the southern border of present-day Mexico to the Isthmus of Panama. Following independence from Spain in the early 1800s, the region broke into the five republics of Guatemala, El Salvador, Honduras, Nicaragua, and Costa Rica. At first, they tried to form a federal union similar to that of the United States. But soon they agreed to go their separate ways as sovereign republics. Geographic location placed them firmly in the economic orbit of the United States. The United States purchased not just their bananas but their other exports as well: coffee, sugarcane, and cattle.

Central America also fell within the strategic sphere of the United States. The overwhelming power of the United States together with the instability and small size of the Central American states made their relationship with the North American powerhouse something like that of the children of a stern father. When one or another Central American nation stepped out of line it was speedily disciplined by the United States. By the early twentieth century the United States exercised "Big Stick" diplomacy throughout the Caribbean basin region. That meant it never hesitated to use military power to enforce its will there. Nicaragua provides an example. A succession of US presidents sent troops to occupy Nicaragua from the second through the fourth decades of the twentieth century. At length the United States succeeded in putting a pro-US strongman, Anastasio Somoza, in power. Somoza and his family ruled Nicaragua with an iron fist from 1934 to 1979.

Guatemala had perhaps the closest relationship with the United States. Abundant lowlands on the country's Caribbean side were ideal for banana

Figure 9.1. Rigoberta Menchú in the March 2009 march commemorating the anniversary of the signing of the Treaty on Identity and Rights of Indigenous People. By Surizar, March 31, 2009. Wikimedia Commons. CC-BY SA 2.0

cultivation. As American demand for that fruit grew, US businessmen set up companies dedicated to producing bananas on company-owned plantations and shipping them northward. Among these firms the greatest of all was the United Fruit Company. Incorporated in 1898, United Fruit transported a swelling flood of Guatemalan-grown bananas to US consumers. This mutually beneficial economic relationship among fruit companies, Guatemalan elites, and the army, which protected both, was not seriously questioned until the mid-twentieth century. Then, the country's first-ever free elections brought two social democratic presidents to power, Juan José Arévalo

(1945–1950) and Jacobo Árbenz (1950–1954). Both men were committed to aiding Guatemala's impoverished majority, most of whom were landless peasants. Their chief way of doing this was by turning the peasants into small landholders by purchasing fallow property from large landowners and selling it to the landless on easy terms. Guatemala's land reform reached its peak during the presidency of Jacobo Árbenz. It brought him into conflict with the United Fruit Company, which possessed 234,000 acres of unused land in eastern Guatemala. A law from January 1954 ordered this land sold to the government for the purpose of redistribution. This law, and the fact that some of those working for Árbenz were members of the country's small Communist Party, moved the United States to act. It tasked its newly created Central Intelligence Agency (CIA) to overthrow Árbenz and replace him with a junta of anti-communist army officers. CIA actions caused Jacobo Árbenz to flee Guatemala in June 1954. A purge of his supporters followed, with many of them driven into exile, jailed, or killed.

A significant footnote to Guatemalan history involves an incident that took place in the days following the coup. When Argentine diplomat Nicasio Sánchez learned that a young countryman was in danger, he soon located Ernesto "Che" Guevara in Guatemala City and escorted him to the Argentine embassy. A few days later Guevara slipped across the border into Mexico, where he soon met Cuban exile Fidel Castro, who at the time was planning an armed expedition to overthrow the island's dictator, Fulgencio Batista.

Fidel Castro's overthrow of Batista on January 1, 1959, was far from the minds of the Quiché Maya residents of the Guatemalan mountain village of Chimel in 1959. That first month of the year found the dozen families of the tiny settlement awaiting the birth of a child. At last, on the sixth day of January 1959 the waiting ended. Juana Tum, wife of village founder Vicente Menchú, gave birth to a daughter. A week later the infant was taken to the nearby village of Uspantán and baptized Rigoberta Menchú Tum.

The prescient attention to the infant would prove well founded: Rigoberta Menchú's life story is as exemplary as it is astonishing. It tells of the determination of a marginalized young woman who persisted in obtaining an education despite numerous obstacles, including traumatic loss—and championed the right to an education for other Indigenous people. It tells of the international community's empowerment of a humble victim of persecution in such way that she went on to become an influential voice for human and Native American rights. Rigoberta was at first surprised, even amused, to find herself in the role of a paladin for human rights. Yet she accepted the difficult task, in the process becoming a figure of consideration and controversy in international forums.

Chapter 9

THE EARLY YEARS OF RIGOBERTA MENCHÚ: AN UNEVEN EDUCATION AND PERSISTENCE

As the years passed, little Rigoberta Menchú caught the attention of everyone living in the pioneer settlement of Chimel, in mountainous northwestern Guatemala. She was intelligent, had a sparkling personality, and delighted in exploring the tropical high-country cloud forest that surrounded the family farm. Her father approved of his newest child, the fourth of seven eventually born to the family. Vicente Menchú soon concluded that Rigoberta would receive the best education he could provide her because he badly needed the help of an educated family member. Although energetic and intelligent, an army veteran, and the founder of Chimel, Vicente Menchú was illiterate. This severely hindered him in a bitter land dispute with his in-laws, members of the large and prosperous Tum Cotojá clan. The battle over landownership had sent Vicente Menchú on many trips to file paperwork at the national land office in Guatemala City, paperwork he could not read and was forced to sign with an *X*. An educated child could help him better defend the family's land claim.

Rigoberta Menchú had an uneven elementary school education. Even before his favorite daughter reached school age, Vicente Menchú had two of Rigoberta's cousins tutor her. When she turned six, he sent her away to boarding school in Guatemala's third-largest city, Chichicastenango. But Rigoberta was so unhappy there that her father brought her home and enrolled her in a convent school in nearby Uspantán. It was a primitive place without electric lights or running water, where the teaching nuns were barely literate themselves. It was, however, close to home, permitting Rigoberta to spend weekends and holidays with her family. When at home in Chimel she occasionally took classes taught by two US Peace Corps volunteers who were stationed there. She was eighteen by the time she began high school.

In 1977 Rigoberta's father sent her away to study in Guatemala City at a high school operated by Belgian nuns of the Order of the Sacred Family. Soon the young Quiché Mayan woman became one of the nuns' favorite students. Although she worked to help pay her room and board and took a full slate of classes, Rigoberta could usually be found studying late into the night. She also excelled at sports, especially basketball, and was respectful and devout. Like all members of her family, Rigoberta Menchú was a Roman Catholic. On more than one occasion during her stay at the school she told her teachers that her goal in life was to become a teaching nun.

By her own account, Rigoberta Menchú learned more from her own people than she did at any of the schools she attended. Her trips home to Chimel were the high points of her early life. For her, vacations at home afforded her the ability to immerse herself in her Indigenous culture—this was simply not possible away from her village. Beyond her home she was surrounded by Hispanic culture and the ladinos, or mixed-blood and Hispanicized Guatemalans, who scorned their country's substantial Indigenous minority.

Guatemala's Spanish-speaking mestizos viewed their nation's Mayan peoples as unacculturated and primitive outsiders who insisted on speaking Quiché Mayan instead of Spanish. And they spoke not just one Quiché language but rather twenty-one mutually unintelligible dialects of it. Rigoberta Menchú, for example, spoke the Ixil dialect of Quiché Mayan. That was a fact she revealed to an anthropologist named Elisabeth Burgos when she was in her early twenties. She also made clear to Burgos that she disliked ladinos and everything about them. What she loved was Mayan culture, especially her people's rituals such as those surrounding birth, marriage, and death. In her conversations with Elisabeth Burgos, she spoke at length of the Mayan people's reverence for the land and for corn, and for the earth and all its living creatures. These values were integral to the millions of Mayan people spread across southern Mexico, Guatemala, and parts of Honduras.

Roman Catholicism was another powerful character-shaping force for Rigoberta Menchú. Her social conscience and impulse toward activism came in part through three church programs. The first was called Catholic Action. Promoted throughout Latin America in the 1960s and 1970s, Catholic Action sent priests and lay workers into the countryside to educate the poor and promote self-help programs. It offered field days featuring agricultural exhibits and lectures for adults, games for their children, and copious quantities of food. Rigoberta fondly recalled those events as another high point of her early life.

Liberation theology and community groups also influenced the young Mayan woman. A left-wing movement in Latin American Catholicism of the 1970s and 1980s, liberation theology taught that God was on the side of the oppressed, and that unjust "savage capitalism" must be instilled with a social conscience.[1] Priests of the movement organized campesino unions and political pressure groups throughout Latin America. In Guatemala the most important of these was the Committee for Campesino Unity (Comité para la Unidad Campesina), or CUC, established in southern El Quiché Department during the mid-1970s. Although it was mostly ladino in its leadership, it had significant Indigenous membership. The CUC was the third church-related program influencing Rigoberta Menchú Tum. It offered Guatemalan campesinos advice and assistance, and helped them organize subsidiary organizations following occupational lines. Through these groups rural dwellers learned how to improve their working conditions through job actions that included strikes. Rigoberta became an enthusiastic CUC member around 1978, when the organization proclaimed its intent to "unite all workers against traditional forms of exploitation."² Sadly, both for the CUC and Rigoberta Menchú, that was precisely when Guatemala's long-smoldering civil war caught fire.

Rigoberta was troubled when she returned home for the holidays in late November 1978. She had learned that disturbing events had taken place in Chimel and Uspantán just a few months before. Members of a guerrilla group called the Guerrilla Army of the Poor (Ejército Guerrillero de los Pobres) had come down from high mountains to the north and held rallies in both villages. They urged the people to join in helping them overthrow their dictatorial national government. Several years earlier the same group had passed through the region meting out revolutionary justice and executing an exploitative coffee plantation owner. When Vicente Menchú told his daughter of the guerrillas' visit, she saw fear in her father's eyes for the first time. As a military veteran, Menchú had seen Guatemala's military punish those unfortunate enough to live in areas where guerrillas were active.

When the new school year began in February 1979, the nuns told Rigoberta that she would not be continuing her education in Guatemala City, but rather at the order's *colegio* in nearby Chiantla. It was a school surrounded by high walls giving it the look of a fortress. The nuns correctly reasoned that the leftist daughter of campesino activist Vicente Menchú might soon find herself a target of government persecution.

A RURAL "DIRTY WAR": GUATEMALA'S KILLING FIELDS

Guatemala's civil war had its remote origins in Russia's Bolshevik Revolution of 1917, which set into motion revolutionary communism's challenge to globalized free-market capitalism. Marxism-Leninism posited violent, state-led redistribution of economic wealth, in sharp contrast to capitalism that was geared to minimal government interference with the creation and maintenance of private wealth. The United States encouraged Caribbean-basin nations to uphold capitalist principles and to oppose communism. It mattered little to the hemisphere's largest democracy that most of those countries were ruled by dictatorial right-wing military regimes and the economic elites who funded and supported them.

In immediate terms, Guatemala's civil war dated from 1959, the year Rigoberta was born and when Fidel Castro seized power in Cuba and launched a nationwide land reform program. US pressure led Castro to proclaim himself a Marxist-Leninist and to ally Cuba with the Soviet Union. Castro went on to support "Castroite" revolutionaries throughout Latin America. He trained and armed young revolutionaries dedicated to overthrowing their national governments and replacing them with Castro-style communist regimes. One who sought the Cuban leader's help was Guatemalan army veteran Aurelio Yon Sosa, who established a guerrilla group in the eastern part of the country in the early 1960s. In 1966, however, the Guatemalan army swept down on and destroyed Sosa's three-hundred-man force. In the process it also killed some three thousand unarmed civilians presumed to be guerrilla sympathizers. Yon Sosa fled to Chiapas, where in 1970 he was killed by a Mexican army patrol.

Not long after Yon Sosa's death the Castroite Guerrilla Army of the Poor, or EGP, established itself in mountainous northwestern Guatemala. Its area of activity was Ixil Triangle, extending from the Mexican border southward, through uninhabited high mountains and down through their lower elevations. Villages like Uspantán and Chimel lay squarely within its zone of operations. It was this group Vicente Menchú feared might bring the military into his region.

The EGP was founded by agronomist Rodrigo Ramírez, who had met Che Guevara in the Argentine embassy following the 1954 military coup against Jacobo Árbenz. Both men had worked in Árbenz's land reform program. Ramírez was reunited with Guevara in Cuba following Fidel Castro's takeover of the island. In Cuba he received training and weapons, and he returned to Guatemala to found and lead the EGP. The group's banner bore a likeness of Che Guevara. By the late 1970s the EGP passed freely through villages such as Uspantán and Chimel that placed Ixil Department and its people in the crosshairs of the Guatemalan army. Between 1975 and 1984 the military conducted a scorched-earth campaign throughout the hapless region. The army's stated goal was to exterminate the guerrilla fighters—and all accused, or even suspected, of being their sympathizers. Among those so charged were Rigoberta Menchú and other members of her family.

All of Central America became a tinderbox after Sandinista guerrillas overthrew Nicaragua's Somoza regime in mid-1979. Leftists in Guatemala and in neighboring El Salvador were inspired and excited by the Sandinista success. They believed they too would soon be leading triumphal marches into their own national capitals. The optimism of Guatemala's revolutionary community emboldened Rodrigo Ramírez and his followers to launch what they were sure was their definitive offensive against the government. The revolutionaries visited Chimel in April 1979 and again in August, hoping to recruit new members from the Ixil Mayan who made up the majority population. During their second visit they executed two ladino landowners, Horacio García and Eliu Martínez. Both men owned substantial properties neighboring Chimel and were said to be corrupt and avaricious. As the EGP stepped up activities, like-minded revolutionaries formed urban guerrilla cells in Guatemalan cities. They advertised for new recruits and began launching attacks on public buildings and military installations.

Meanwhile the country's military and its ally the United States were determined that Guatemala would not go the way of Cuba and Nicaragua. Guatemala's military took a page from the playbook of military regimes in Brazil and the Southern Cone and launched a bloody all-out offensive against the revolutionaries. They embraced a rural version of the strategy of "dirty war" practiced in southern South America. Dirty war featured extrajudicial kidnapping, torture, and murder of anyone suspected of being either a guerrilla or a guerrilla sympathizer. These atrocities were often carried out by "death squads" made up of off-duty police and military. The man who ordered Guatemala's anti-guerrilla operation was president and army general Romeo Lucas García. He had earned the nickname "Butcher of Zacapa" years earlier when he ordered soldiers to slaughter peasants protesting the theft of their land by friends of the government. During 1979–1980 Lucas García turned Guatemala into a killing field.

Rigoberta's younger brother, Petrocinio, was the first Menchú Tum to die. Relatives of the recently murdered landowners Horacio García and Eliu Martínez had accused Petrocinio of having EGP sympathies. Petrocinio was arrested by an army patrol in September 1979 as he walked down a country lane with his girlfriend. Rigoberta visited home not long after her brother's kidnapping and found her father preparing to lead a delegation of his neighbors to Guatemala City to argue Petrocinio's innocence and to demand his release. At the end of the year, when Vicente Menchú discovered that his son had been tortured and murdered by the army, he organized a second and more dramatic protest, one leading him to join a group occupying the Spanish embassy in Guatemala City. When Menchú and five supporters arrived in Guatemala City in January 1980, they unwisely joined forces with radical students from the University of San Carlos and with others from the left-wing activist community. It was those younger activists who persuaded Menchú and the other campesinos from Chimel to don ski masks and join them, machetes in hand, in occupying the Spanish embassy, taking hostages as they did so. Police answered by setting fire to the embassy, causing all but one of the protesters to die of smoke inhalation. Vicente Menchú was among the fatalities.

Six weeks after the embassy incident, the Guatemalan army attacked Chimel, by then known in military circles as a "guerrilla town." Rigoberta's mother Juana Tum was raped and murdered during the attack. The Guatemalan military next went in search of Rigoberta Menchú. Informers told officials that she had recently joined the Committee for Campesino Unity, now viewed as a subversive organization. The CUC slogan, "Clear head, caring heart, fighting fist of rural workers," appealed to her on a deeply personal level, and the nuns of her *colegio* became alarmed by some of her questions, such as, "What would happen if we rose up against the rich?"[3] When they noticed plainclothes police staked out across the street from their school, they decided it was time for Rigoberta Menchú to depart Guatemala. Sister Gertrudis, Mother Superior of the cloistered school, set into motion a plan to help her flee. She had the distraught young woman placed under watch to make sure she remained inside the *colegio*. She then got in touch with other members of the Order of the Sacred Family in Guatemala City and Mexico City, asking for their help in planning the young woman's escape. Late one evening in mid-1980, when no police seemed to be watching the high school, Mother Superior Gertrudis and Sister Gladis went to Rigoberta's room. They cut her hair, gave her ladino clothes to wear, and packed her colorful huipil (embroidered blouse) and other Indigenous clothing in a small suitcase. They led her to a waiting car that took her to the Guatemala City airport. There she and Sister Gladis boarded a plane and flew to Mexico City. Mexican nuns met them there and took them by car to San Cristóbal de las Casas, capital of the state of Chiapas and home of Bishop Samuel Ruiz Moreno—Mexico's leading advocate of liberation theology.

LIFE IN EXILE

"Chiapas," Rigoberta later wrote, "brought me back to life."[4] She was embraced by the family of Bishop Ruiz, especially by his sister Doña Lucha, who treated the Guatemalan orphan like her own daughter. Doña Lucha saw to it that Rigoberta received grief counseling by a local physician who prescribed a "sleep cure" for her. The treatment required a week's sleep interrupted only by meals, which were brought to her by Doña Lucha. Following Rigoberta's treatment, women of the bishop's household bought her new clothes in the style of the local Mayan peoples of Chiapas. Next, she was put to work at a nearby church school teaching first aid to refugee children from Guatemala. At the end of her first two months in southern Mexico, in late 1980, Bishop Ruiz took Rigoberta with him to a Latin American bishops' conference in Oaxaca. Gathered there were the region's leading proponents of liberation theology. Bishop Ruiz asked Rigoberta to address his colleagues. Wearing her huipil and *corte*, a traditional Mayan skirt, and her *peraje*, or scarf, on her head to hide her cropped hair, and speaking in broken Spanish, she told her tragic story to those assembled.

Not long after the bishops' meeting, during the Christmas holidays, Bishop Ruiz presented Rigoberta with the best of all possible gifts: her younger sisters Anita and Lucía. A relative had found the girls wandering in the countryside days after their mother's murder and had taken them to the Mexican border, where he entrusted them to priests working with the flood of refugees fleeing Guatemala.

The Menchú Tum sisters were so happy to be together that they decided to celebrate Christmas Eve in a distinctly untraditional way. They bought three bottles of rum and announced that "this Christmas we're going to get really drunk."[5] Their party left them with colossal hangovers and a determination never to touch rum again. Still, over the course of their celebration Anita and Lucía convinced Rigoberta that they were miserable in Mexico, surrounded by people speaking languages they did not understand. They also talked her into returning home and participating in the revolution against Lucas García and his government.

Going back to Guatemala at the height of bloody civil war was the worst decision the Menchú Tum sisters could have made. Yet that is what they did, putting their lives in mortal danger. They briefly became cadres of an umbrella revolutionary group made up of teachers, students, left-wing political parties, trade unionists, and others, calling themselves the Democratic Front against Repression (Frente Democrática contra la Represión). The girls' cadre was named in honor of their father—the Vicente Menchú Revolutionary Christian Guerrilla Front (Frente Guerrillera Cristiana Vicente Menchú). Working in central Guatemala City, Rigoberta, Anita, and Lucía delivered messages and helped transport flyers and revolutionary wall posters. Not long after taking up this work they made a mistake that nearly cost them their lives. While on the way to deliver a load of revolutionary flyers a bundle fell off their truck and scattered down the street. The truck driver and the Menchú Tum sisters panicked and fled the scene in different directions. Anita and Lucía eventually made their way northward to the Ixil Triangle, where they joined hundreds of displaced people living in high mountain camps called CPRs, or Communities of the Population in Resistance. They arrived there just as President Lucas García proclaimed "Operation Ashes" (Operación Ceniza) and deployed fifteen thousand soldiers to sweep through Guatemala's mostly Indigenous northwestern highlands. In that operation a few guerrillas and as many as ten thousand civilians died. The world looked on in horror, branding Guatemala's president the hemisphere's worst violator of human rights. Anita and Lucía eventually made their way back across the border into Mexico, to a camp in Chiapas full of Quiché Mayan refugees. They remained there for the following twelve years.

Rigoberta fled south, down the Pan American Highway on Guatemala's Pacific coast, eventually reaching Nicaragua's capital Managua. There she was welcomed by officials of the Sandinista regime who took her to the office of the United Nations High Commission for Refugees. Officials there issued her a passport identifying her as a UN-sponsored refugee. The Sandinistas also provided her with a plane ticket. May 1981 found Rigoberta Menchú once again in Mexico. Her career as a cadre for the guerrillas was at an end. So too was any hope for revolution in Guatemala. By late 1981 most of the country's leftists were either dead or in exile. In neighboring El Salvador an uprising led by that country's Faribundo Martí Front for National Liberation (Frente Faribundo Martí para Liberación Nacional, or FMLN), had also failed. And in Nicaragua a US-sponsored right-wing, counterrevolutionary force called the Contras was harassing and weakening that country's socialist government. Further revolutionary action anywhere in Central America was by then impossible.

Orphaned and driven from her home, Rigoberta's future looked dim. That, however, could not have been further from the truth. She spent most of 1982 back in San Cristóbal de las Casas teaching Indigenous refugee girls at a church-run school. At that time, her sisters were in hiding with EGP guerrillas across the border in Guatemala. Rigoberta had seemingly reached the dead end reserved for innocents caught up in great power struggles—but the young Quiché Mayan was about to enter a whirlwind that would carry her to global fame in a span of a mere ten years. Her spectacular rise was rooted in a relatively new concern in the world: sensitivity to human rights, and a wide-ranging desire in the Western world to protect those rights.

"I, RIGOBERTA MENCHÚ": FAME AND CONTROVERSY

Over the first half of the twentieth century, Western nations were horrified to find themselves fighting two world wars in the brief span of thirty-one years. When World War II ended, citizens of the victorious nations were further revolted by ghastly wartime atrocities committed throughout Europe by the Nazis and their sympathizers. These two events—two world wars and massive violations of human rights—moved world leaders to establish the United Nations in 1945 and soon thereafter to draft the Universal Declaration of Human Rights. The United Nations was tasked with maintaining world peace; the Universal Declaration of Human Rights spelled out individual freedoms not to be denied citizens of any nation. These interconnected developments in turn led to the creation of a host of groups known as nongovernmental organizations, or NGOs, many of them dedicated to lobbying members of the United Nations on human rights issues. Rigoberta Menchú began her rise through human rights NGOs.

Not long after her return to Mexico, after her brief stint as a guerrilla cadre, Rigoberta found herself being contacted by several NGOs interested in restoring peace in Guatemala. By that time, she was known to the Guatemalan exile community not merely as a victim of that country's genocidal violence but as a courageous activist willing to risk her life fighting against Guatemala's murderous government. These groups drew her into their circle. Once they did that, an interconnected web of NGOs combined to make her Guatemala's best-known peace activist.

Three NGOs set Rigoberta on her future course. The first was the loosely organized liberation theology coalition within the Roman Catholic Church. Her friend and benefactor Bishop Samuel Ruiz Moreno was the first to recognize her potential and to encourage her to speak out against the criminal acts of her government. Second among them was the Guerrilla Army of the Poor, whose secretariat was now housed in Mexico City. Its leaders had been defeated, driven from Guatemala, and reduced mostly to speaking out against the dirty war going on in their country. The third and most important of the groups was made up of some sixty Guatemalan exiles, most of them academics, lawyers, and professionals. They called themselves the Guatemalan Committee for Patriotic Unity (GCPU). In 1982 they prepared to send the group's leaders on a ten-nation European tour whose goal was to organize a Europe-wide Guatemalan solidarity network. When Rigoberta joined the GCPU, she became only its second Indigenous member. In 1983 the all-Guatemalan NGO conducted Rigoberta Menchú Tum on a whirlwind tour through western Europe.

A noted scholar and leader of the Guatemalans in exile, Arturo Taracena, greeted Rigoberta at the Paris airport in January 1983. Taracena took her under his wing and helped prepare her for the wintertime slog through European capitals. During her trip Rigoberta spoke little, focusing instead on trying to make sense of what she was seeing and attempting to understand the principles of human rights organizing across national boundaries. After returning to Paris, Taracena and others worked to help her improve her Spanish and quell her fear of speaking before groups of pale-skinned foreigners. As she recalled of the experience, "I learned a lot from all of them. They corrected my Spanish and altered the view I had of their ladino culture. Gradually they helped me learn to write Spanish and answer the telephone."[6]

Taracena then convinced Rigoberta to write about her experiences. The scholar spent two weeks interviewing her and transcribing her testimonial. Next, he delivered both Rigoberta and his notes to Venezuelan anthropologist Elisabeth Burgos-Debray, at the time living in exile in Paris. Married to Regis Debray, the famous Marxist writer and intimate of Ernesto Che Guevara,

Burgos was well known in European literary circles. She had agreed to read Taracena's transcription of Rigoberta's story and to spend an additional week interviewing her. They decided that Burgos would turn Rigoberta's testimony into a book-length manuscript and have it published. The resulting work appeared in 1984 in both Spanish- and English-language editions. Its English-language version, *I, Rigoberta Menchú: An Indian Woman in Guatemala*, became an international bestseller in both its English- and Spanish-language editions, going on to win Cuba's prestigious Casa de las Américas Award. It was instantly embraced as a text in colleges and high schools across the United States and Europe, and was read throughout Latin America. The book eventually played a role in helping Rigoberta Menchú Tum win the 1992 Nobel Peace Prize.

Despite the book's fame, it came under criticism soon after publication. Those familiar with Latin America and with Guatemala detected an unevenness and slightly surreal quality in the book. About half of its pages presented an idealized view of Quiché Mayan life purportedly as lived by the young Rigoberta. That portion of the work depicted her tribe and village as living isolated from Hispanic ladino Guatemala and following traditional ways much as Mayan people had lived from time immemorial. The book's second half portrayed teenage Rigoberta as having suffered every imaginable sort of abuse at the hands of evil ladinos. While Rigoberta was working as a housemaid for a wealthy family in Guatemala City, according to the book, "The mistress treated [her] not like a dog, because she treated the dog well."[7] Another chapter describes her life as a field hand, when she was sprayed with pesticides while working on a lowland sugarcane plantation, and how she later watched a younger brother die as a result of pesticide poisoning. The book also depicts the people of Chimel heroically resisting army incursions, and even killing a soldier in self-defense. None of these things actually occurred. They were whole-cloth creations of the book's editor, Elisabeth Burgos.

I, Rigoberta Menchú became at once influential and controversial. In 1999, fifteen years after the book's publication, anthropologist David Stoll published a meticulously researched account of Rigoberta's life, her family, and their tragic experiences during Guatemala's civil war. What Stoll's work reveals is that *I, Rigoberta Menchú: An Indian Woman in Guatemala* is fundamentally a work of fiction. Burgos had in fact written a fanciful account of Quiché Mayan life gleaned from anthropological studies. She falsely turned Rigoberta Menchú into not simply a victim of her country's civil war but a recipient of every conceivable form of abuse visited on Guatemala's Indigenous, poor, and working-class citizens by their country's exploitative ladino and White elites. When Burgos published the work in 1984 she had no inkling that her creation would become an international bestseller. Rigoberta Menchú, on the other hand, dismissed the work from the start. As she later recalled, while the work was still unfinished, she spent two months reading and attempting to understand it. At one point, Rigoberta was heard to remark that it was not her book but, rather, the creation of Elizabeth Burgos. Still, she never corrected the many untruths contained in it. She was justifiably angered that Burgos had copyrighted the book in her own name, won the Casa de las Américas Award for writing it, and had failed to share all the book's royalties with her.

Prior to her dealings with Elisabeth Burgos, and during her solidarity-building trip through Europe, Rigoberta Menchú experienced a life-altering experience. While visiting the UN Economic and Social Council housed in Geneva, Switzerland, she met representatives of the International Indian Treaty Council, the diplomatic arm of the US-based American Indian Movement, or AIM. As soon as the North American Indian leaders laid eyes on Rigoberta, decked out in full Mayan garb, they rushed to meet and befriend her. Tribal leaders like Kickapoo chief William Wahpepah saw in Rigoberta Menchú a link to Indigenous Latin America. Wahpepah and others understood that through her they could make their protest movement on behalf of Native American rights truly international. Rigoberta, similarly, saw her Indigenous brothers from North America as potential allies in helping her defend her own downtrodden people. Most important for her personally, the meeting in Geneva linked her to the North Americans at the level of ethnicity. As she later put it, "Our indigenous souls united." Rigoberta Menchú valued her tribal identity above all else, even to the extent that some have branded her an ethnic chauvinist. "I'm an Indianist, not just an Indian," she wrote. "I'm an Indianist to my fingertips and I defend everything to do with my ancestors."[8]

When the Guatemalan solidarity-building group departed Geneva, Rigoberta had in hand an invitation to attend a meeting of the International Council of Indian Treaties, to be held at Duke University in October 1983. She attended the meeting, and when it adjourned, she found herself named a member of the group's board of directors. Thanks to that she was eligible to appear before the United Nations and other international bodies as a credentialed lobbyist. That was pivotal to her rise as a noted lobbyist for the rights of Indigenous peoples.

Rigoberta took up her duties at a critical moment in the Indigenous rights movement. It was during the period 1982–1983 that the United Nations constituted its Working Group on Indigenous Peoples and its Indigenous Peoples' Center for Documentation, Research and Information. The aim of the latter was to archive all national records of native peoples around the world. Suddenly, then, the twenty-five-year-old Quiché Mayan woman from Guatemala found herself at the forefront of a global movement to protect the rights of First Americans throughout the Western Hemisphere. Rigoberta Menchú Tum had emerged as a pioneering figure in the global civil rights movement of Indigenous Americans.

Rigoberta Menchú's most important work at the UN involved promoting peace in Guatemala. When she appeared in Geneva as a lobbyist in late 1983, French jurist and member of the UN Human Rights Council Louis Joinet said the following, "Good, we've got a Mayan here at last; we've finally got a Guatemalan. It will be the first time Guatemala is discussed."[9] With these words Joinet consecrated Rigoberta Menchú as the UN lobbyist responsible for telling world leaders about Guatemala's ghastly civil war and convincing them it was their obligation to help end it.

Rigoberta soon learned that lobbying for a just cause is grueling, often discouraging work. UN diplomats do their best to avoid the lobbyists who swarm corridors and meeting rooms of United Nations buildings. Diplomats especially do not want to talk with human rights activists, in part because they know all too well that their own countries are guilty of human rights abuses to one degree or another. Nor do they see dealing with human rights to be their chief job. They are, after all, diplomats appointed by their governments to deal with other diplomats. Yet Rigoberta Menchú would not be brushed off. Between 1983 and 1987 she pursued UN officials with a tenacity that imprinted her image on everyone she encountered. Short in stature, dressed in tribal dress, and undeniably Indigenous, she buttonholed anyone who might be useful in helping bring peace to her homeland and social justice to her people. At times she did become discouraged, especially when she perceived that ethical issues were not high on the agendas of decision-makers. "I literally steam-rolled down corridors, battering down all doors," she recalled. "I used to say 'Oh my God, what a hard life!'"[10] Still, she persisted, even when other lobbyists grew frustrated and returned home.

SPEAKING OUT: RISKS AND REPERCUSSIONS

By the mid-1980s, conditions in Central America had begun to improve, a condition that aided the lobbying activities of Rigoberta and her colleagues. At last, the world's attention was focused on Central America and the Cold War–inspired suffering it had visited on the region's peoples. In 1986, Costa Rican president Oscar Arias had launched a successful effort to start peace talks among warring parties. A year later the Arias Peace Plan was signed. In October 1987 Arias was awarded the Nobel Peace Prize for his efforts. The year after that there was a democratic opening in Guatemala. The country elected its first civilian president in thirty-three years. That event played a significant role in helping Rigoberta and her colleagues achieve their greatest success in six years of intense lobbying. They were at last granted permission to speak about Guatemala before the General Assembly of the United Nations. Rigoberta delivered the address, beginning with the sentence, "Mr. President, in my country they speak twenty-two languages."[11] Guatemala's UN delegation reacted with shock. Standing before them was the notorious Quiché Mayan woman Menchú Tum, indicting their government for its decades of wrongdoing. They stormed out of the session. The following day, however, they returned and listened stone-faced as Rigoberta Menchú spoke of Guatemala's civil war, its attending human rights abuses, and her own personal loss. Afterward the General Assembly voted overwhelmingly to sanction the Guatemalan government for its behavior, to send observers to monitor future elections, and to investigate any future abuses committed by the country's armed forces. That marked the first time the United Nations had ever permitted a human rights advocate to speak against the government of Guatemala within its General Assembly. Rigoberta's response to the vote was typically understated: "We were amazed at what we had achieved. We were happy with our work."[12]

Encouraged by the success of her speech, Rigoberta decided to return to Guatemala for the first time in nearly seven years. Even though the head of the country's UN mission had invited her to return, and had assured her she would be safe, that turned out not to be true. As soon as Rigoberta set foot on Guatemalan soil she was arrested and hauled off to jail on charges of disturbing public order and threatening national security by voicing Marxist-Leninist ideas. Additionally, she was charged with aiding the Guerrilla Army of the Poor (EGP). These charges were based on the fact that she had planned to attend a meeting of left-wing organizations that included representatives of the EGP.

Rigoberta's arrest triggered an international outcry. Messages from abroad flooded into President Vinicio Cerezo's office, one of them from the president of France. Within six hours the charges were dropped and Rigoberta was released. Soon thereafter she left the country. The following year she again traveled to Guatemala, to attend a church-sponsored dialogue on spurring peace talks between the government and the guerrillas. Yet again she received death threats, and a bomb was discovered in a car parked near the house where she was staying. Once again, she departed Guatemala in haste, traveling to Italy to address that country's Socialist Party. While there the Italian parliament voted her a diplomatic seat in the body until she could safely return home.

In 1989, the Italian Socialists also nominated Rigoberta Menchú for the Nobel Peace Prize, but Costa Rican president Oscar Arias had received the award in 1987—and the prize committee was not inclined to give the prize to two Central Americans in two years. Still, Rigoberta's supporters continued to nominate her for the award. They knew the Nobel Prize Committee looked for both historical significance and personal uniqueness in candidates for the peace prize. Rigoberta Menchú stood high in the uniqueness category because no Indigenous American had ever received the award. And few recipients of the award possessed as dramatic and affecting a personal story as she. Nor did it hurt her chances that several members of the Nobel Committee had read her fanciful, ghostwritten testimonial *I, Rigoberta Menchú*. In addition, several committee members had met Rigoberta during one or more of her visits to Scandinavia. All these factors, and two others as well, made it nigh inevitable that Rigoberta Menchú Tum would become the recipient of the 1992 Nobel Peace Prize.

The first and most compelling was that 1992 marked the five hundredth anniversary of Christopher Columbus's arrival in America. While this event had been celebrated over many years throughout the Western world, little attention had been paid to the people whose lives were changed for the worse by the European invaders. Now, the Nobel Prize Committee could seize the opportunity to begin setting the record straight. They could for the first time recognize an Indigenous American, one who was widely recognized for her work at the United Nations. Second, the Nobel Committee had been influenced by the Native American civil rights movement that gained world attention during the 1970s and 1980s. Rigoberta Menchú had of course been one of the movement's early members, making it a truly international body. So, as the quincentennial celebration preparations moved apace, those sensitive to Native American issues seized on Rigoberta Menchú Tum as the single best representative of the First American experience of European colonization of their homeland.

In 1991 the United Nations invited Rigoberta Menchú to join a committee charged with arranging the body's celebration of the quincentenary of the discovery of America. She resigned from the committee when she understood that its chair, a Spaniard, intended to make the event a celebration of Spain's "civilizing" impact on the New World Americans. Upon her departure Rigoberta remarked, "Our people said there was nothing to celebrate."[13]

Native Americans organized numerous antiquincentenary events as the year 1992 approached. One of them was held in Colombia in 1989, with South America as its focus. The 1991 event, set in Guatemala's second-largest city, Quetzaltenango, highlighted North America and the Caribbean basin. There, in Guatemala's Indigenous heartland and near the birthplace of

Rigoberta Menchú, thousands attended the October 1991 event, titled "Five Hundred Years of Indigenous Popular Resistance." Dozens of organizations, including the World Council of Churches, the Catholic Church, and numerous Protestant denominations, NGOs, and private individuals funded the event. The Pan-Mayan Movement was much in evidence. Its leaders advocated the political and cultural equality of Mayan peoples living in Yucatán and southern Mexico, Guatemala, and Honduras. Rigoberta Menchú was lionized at the event: one attendee from the United States recalled that every time she appeared, "people screamed out her name. . . . Rigoberta is like a saint, a huge indigenous symbol."[14] The quincentennial protest of 1991 adjourned after nominating Rigoberta Menchú Tum for the 1992 Nobel Peace Prize.

In early 1992 Rigoberta's Argentine friend and 1980 peace prize laureate Adolfo Pérez Esquivel visited her in her small Mexico City office. Esquivel told Rigoberta that both he and fellow laureate Desmond Tutu had nominated her for that year's award and that she should prepare herself for victory. As the months passed, Rigoberta anxiously awaited the month of October, when the award winner would be announced. On October 9, 1992, she traveled to Guatemala City, where she was received at the airport by a large and enthusiastic crowd. By then she could travel freely around the country, even though official Guatemala continued to distrust her and many private citizens viewed her as too close to the guerrillas and other radical groups.

Rigoberta and her entourage were in the village of San Marcos on October 16 when she learned she was indeed the 1992 Nobel Peace Prize recipient. As she recalled the moment, "We were all at a loss for words. A priest at the church set off fireworks all over town. It was like a torrential rain falling. They rang the bells."[15]

A month later, Rigoberta traveled to Oslo, Norway, for the award ceremony. There she was given a medallion and a check for $1.2 million. She was lauded in a speech given by the chairman of the prize committee. In it he praised her work for reconciliation and peace in Guatemala, calling her 1984 testimonial "a uniquely potent symbol of a just struggle" and "an extraordinary human document." Along with her peace-related activities the Nobel Committee recognized her work for social justice "and ethno-cultural reconciliation based on the rights of Indigenous peoples." The chairman also informed those attending the event that she had received nominations from North American tribal leaders "who wanted to draw attention to the fact that the European discovery of America entailed the extermination and oppression of Indigenous populations."[16] Rigoberta responded in Spanish, with a simple yet moving address calling for peace in Guatemala and for recognition of the rights of Indigenous peoples around the world.

REMEMBERING THE PAST, REACHING FOR PEACE

In 1994, Rigoberta Menchú returned home for good. By that time the country she had fled in terror twelve years before was much changed. Political tensions had declined thanks to the end of the Cold War two years earlier. The Soviet Union had collapsed in December 1991, leaving its client state Cuba severely weakened. That in turn cut off Cuban support of Guatemalan guerrilla groups. The resulting slow return to peace meant that government executions of presumed leftist campesinos had declined. And when such incidents did occur, as in the 1995 Xamán massacre, they were swiftly investigated and those responsible punished. Rigoberta Menchú was on a speaking tour in the United States when word of the Xamán incident reached her. She rushed back home to assist in the investigation. As a result, a new NGO was created in Guatemala, the Alliance against Impunity (La Alianza contra la Impunidad). Another consequence of the Xamán massacre and Rigoberta Menchú's direct intervention in its investigation was passage of a new Guatemalan law making extrajudicial killing a statutory crime.

Upon her return to Guatemala, Rigoberta hurled herself into a flurry of activity. She purchased a spacious house in a suburb of Guatemala City and filled it with members of her family. She took in her half sister Regina and Regina's surviving child. She also took in her sister Anita and Anita's daughters Maya Rigoberta and Juana María. Anita and her children had spent most of the previous twelve years living in a Chiapas refugee camp. Within a few months of buying the house Rigoberta and her fiancé Ángel Canil were married. She had met her husband in 1991 at the quincentennial protest held in Quetzaltenango. They married in March 1995 and promptly adopted the infant son of an impoverished niece. They named him Mash Nawaljá, or Thomas Water Spirit. Soon they were calling him by a nickname, Kalito. Meanwhile a brother and sister of Ángel Canil also came to live with them.

In November 1995, while Rigoberta was busy helping arrange the wedding of a niece named Regina Menchú Tomás, Kalito was kidnapped by his biological father, a man named Manuel Velásquez. Kalito's father and his accomplices had left a ransom note demanding a large sum of money in exchange for the child. Police soon located the infant, returned him to Rigoberta, and arrested Velásquez, who subsequently served a seven-year prison term. Rigoberta ended the eventful year 1995 with a visit to Chimel. She was saddened to find the verdant upland rain forest of her youth degraded after decades of logging, slash-and-burn agriculture, and incessant planting of corn. Before returning to Guatemala City, she helped establish a cooperative for the twenty families living in Chimel. They named it the Sowing Peace

Cooperative. She also helped the destitute villagers defend claims to their farms from a neighbor who had falsely registered them in his name.

In 1996, the guerrillas and the Guatemalan government negotiated a seventeen-article peace agreement—without Rigoberta Menchú. The country's various guerrilla groups had united in an organization called the Guatemalan National Revolutionary Union (Unión Nacional Revolucionaria Guatemalteca). Rigoberta was not a member. As early as 1982 she had criticized this implicit racism of the guerrillas' ladino leadership. She also broke with the guerrillas because of their failure to include Indigenous leaders in any of their secretariats. Rigoberta Menchú, former cadre of the guerrillas, orphaned by the civil war, and Guatemala's most famous Indigenous activist, was not invited to participate in the final peace negotiations. Consequently, she refused to endorse the agreement despite the fact that it contained a provision guaranteeing Indigenous Guatemalans more equitable access to landownership.

Most Guatemalans admired Rigoberta Menchú for her extraordinary personal success. Others disliked her. Three factors help explain this. First, a great many non-Indigenous Guatemalans historically harbored deep prejudices against native peoples. Some of them reacted to Rigoberta Menchú's fame by making her the butt of jokes. One of them, both racist and sexist, is: "One day Rigoberta goes to heaven and knocks on the gate. 'Hey, Jesus,' Saint Peter calls out, 'the tortillas are here.'" Other Guatemalans disliked Rigoberta's leftist politics. Conservative Guatemalans laughed at the following joke: "What is Rigoberta's blood type? EGP-positive."[17]

The third reason some of her fellow citizens weren't entranced by Rigoberta Menchú lay in her own scorn for her country's mixed-blood ladinos. She had disparaged Hispanicized Guatemalans specifically for their *mestizaje*. As she put it, "The Spaniards raped our ancestors to breed a race of mestizos." She mocked ladino women who wore the huipil and otherwise affected an Indigenous look: "This shows they have no values of their own." For her, ladinos are people "who doubt their own identity," who "are often foreigners in their own land."[18] Many viewed such remarks as racist.

With her country's long civil war now ended, and her family ensconced in their rambling house in Guatemala City, Rigoberta Menchú was at last free to write an account of her life in her own words, not a spurious one larded with events that had never taken place. She spent much of 1997 working on her book *Crossing Borders*, which was published in 1998. Introduced as the second volume of her autobiography, it told of her flight from Guatemala in 1982, her years as a lobbyist before the United Nations, her receipt of the Nobel Peace Prize, and of events transpiring up to the time of the book's publication.

Hard on the heels of *Crossing Borders* came Richard Stoll's 1999 exposé of *I, Rigoberta Menchú*. Rigoberta's many detractors on the right read Stoll's book with glee. They used it to hold her up as both untrustworthy and not meriting her fame. Right-wing pundit Dinesh D'Souza was one of many who taunted the Quiché Mayan woman, titling his own his diatribe "Lier, Rigoberta Menchú." If Rigoberta was perturbed by this criticism she gave no sign of it. Rather, the new millennium found her as outspoken as ever in defending human rights, the rule of law, and the rights of Indigenous peoples. Following the September 11, 2001, terrorist attacks in the United States, she blasted US president George W. Bush for demanding that the world join him in his war against terrorism. Rigoberta Manchú responded to the US leader:

> We ... never had sympathy for terrorism since we were its victims. We ... who carry in our souls the pain of the genocide perpetrated against us ... are fed up with providing the dead for wars that are not ours. We cannot share the arrogance of your infallibility nor the single road onto which you want to push us when you declare that "Every nation in every region now has a decision to make: either you are with us or you are with the terrorists.[19]

From the time of her return home Rigoberta Menchú was active in Guatemalan political affairs (see figure 9.1). In 1995 she founded her own NGO, the Rigoberta Menchú Tum Foundation. Through it she launched voter registration campaigns in heavily Indigenous regions of the country. She stood as a presidential candidate in the 2007 election, and again in the 2011 contest. She lost badly in both contests. But in the process, she gave Indigenous Guatemala its own political party, called Encounter for Guatemala (Encuentro por Guatemala). Despite her failure to win her country's highest elected office, she took pride in the fact that in 2007 Indigenous candidates running for office under Encuentro por Guatemala banners won 129 of 332 mayoral contests held throughout the country. At the level of politics, the emergence of native peoples as a political force in Guatemala seemed nearly miraculous in a country that had historically abused its Indigenous peoples.

During the second decade of the new century Rigoberta Menchú oriented her public activities around her foundation. Within Guatemala the Rigoberta Menchú Tum Foundation promoted feminist initiatives in collaboration with the Union of Guatemalan Women. It helped members of that group liaise with kindred foreign organizations like the International Campaign to Stop Rape in Conflict and the Nobel Women's Initiative. She was cofounder of the latter entity, along with fellow peace prize laureate Wangari Maathai of Kenya. Rigoberta Menchú used her own foundation to promote citizen participation among Indigenous Guatemalans, working alongside the Council for Mayan Education, a group successful in helping Indigenous candidates win political office.

One of Rigoberta Menchú's most enduring legacies was in the area of ecological awareness. She shared native peoples' reverence for the natural world. Typical of her environmental statements was, "Listen, we want to have our say, because we love Mother Earth and we love life."[20] Such statements linked her to contemporary and cutting-edge environmental initiatives such as the Rights of Nature Movement and its goal to grant legal standing to the natural environment. In turn this environmental movement harmonizes with the culture of America's First Peoples as well as with that of Rigoberta Menchú.

EPILOGUE

Rigoberta Menchú had her detractors both at home and abroad. She had her prickly side and her prejudices. And she continued to pursue her goals with a doggedness that exasperated some and angered others. In the end she prevailed, drawing attention to her country's sins against its poorest and Indigenous citizens. In attempting to suggest the essence of Rigoberta Menchú Tum it is perhaps best to let Guatemala's first Nobel Peace Prize winner speak for herself: "After drip, drip, dripping in the same place, I begin to leave a mark, and I leave my mark on people's hearts."[21]

NOTES

1. For more on liberation theology, see Olivia Singer's "Liberation Theology in Latin America," which includes an annotated bibliography, in *Modern Latin America, 8th Edition Companion Website,* https://library.brown.edu/create/modernlatinamerica/chapters/chapter-15-culture-and-society/essays-on-culture-and-society/liberation-theology-in-latin-america/.

2. David Stoll, *Rigoberta Menchú and the Story of All Poor Guatemalans*, 2nd expanded ed. (Boulder, CO: Westview Press, 2008), 99.

3. Rigoberta Menchú Tum, with Dante Liano and Gianni Miná, *Crossing Borders*, translated and edited by Ann Wright (New York: Verso, 1998), 214.

4. Menchú, *Crossing Borders*, 100.

5. Menchú, *Crossing Borders*, 107.

6. Menchú, *Crossing Borders*, 113.

7. Elisabeth Burgos-Debray, *I, Rigoberta Menchú: An Indian Woman in Guatemala*, 2nd ed., trans. Ann Wright (New York: Verso, 2009), 111.

8. Burgos-Debray, *I, Rigoberta Menchú*, 194.

9. Menchú, *Crossing Borders*, 121.

10. Menchú, *Crossing Borders*, 129.

11. Menchú, *Crossing Borders*, 125.

12. Menchú, *Crossing Borders*, 133.
13. Menchú, *Crossing Borders*, 168.
14. Stoll, *Rigoberta Menchú*, 208.
15. Menchú, *Crossing Borders*, 14.
16. Francis Sejersted, "Award Ceremony Speech," transcript of speech delivered at Nobel Peace Prize Ceremony, Oslo, December 10, 1992, https://www.nobelprize.org/prizes/peace/1992/ceremony-speech/.
17. On the joking and stereotyping of Rigoberta Menchu, see, for instance, Diane M. Nelson, "Indian Giver or Noble Savage: Duping, Assumptions of Identity, and Other Double Entendres in Rigoberta Menchú Tum's Stoll/En Past," *American Ethnologist* 28, no. 2 (2001): 303–31.
18. Menchú, *Crossing Borders*, 222–23.
19. Rigoberta Menchú Tum, "Letter from Rigoberta Menchú to President George W. Bush," trans. Beth Baltimore, *Meridians* 2, no. 2 (2002): 277.
20. Menchú, *Crossing Borders*, 184.
21. Menchú, *Crossing Borders*, 166.

REFERENCES

Blachman, Morris, William M. Leogrande, and Kenneth Sharpe, eds. *Confronting Revolution. Security through Diplomacy in Central America*. New York: Pantheon Books, 1986.

Burgos-Debray, Elisabeth. *I, Rigoberta Menchú: An Indian Woman in Guatemala*. Translated by Ann Wright. New York: Verso, 2009. First published 1984.

D'Souza, Dinesh. "Liar, Rigoberta Menchú." *Boundless Webzine*, 1999.

Engle, Dawn Gifford, with Giacomo Buonafina. *Rigoberta Menchú: Daughter of the Maya*. Documentary film. Amazon.com, 2016.

Menchú Tum, Rigoberta. "Letter from Rigoberta Menchú to President George W. Bush, September 23, 2001." Translated by Beth Baltimore. *Meridians* 2, no. 2 (2002): 274–77. https://www.jstor.org/stable/40338528.

Menchú Tum, Rigoberta, with Dante Liano and Gianni Miná. *Crossing Borders*. Translated and edited by Ann Wright. New York: Verso, 1998.

Nelson, Diane M. "Indian Giver or Noble Savage: Duping, Assumptions of Identity, and Other Double Entendres in Rigoberta Menchú Tum's Stoll/En Past." *American Ethnologist* 28, no. 2 (2001): 303–31. http://www.jstor.org/stable/3094971.

Sejersted, Francis. "Award Ceremony Speech." Transcript of Speech delivered at Nobel Peace Prize Ceremony, Oslo, December 10, 1992. https://www.nobelprize.org/prizes/peace/1992/ceremony-speech/.

Singer, Olivia. "Liberation Theology in Latin America." *Modern Latin America, 8th Edition Companion Website*. Brown University: Center for Digital Scholarship. https://library.brown.edu/create/modernlatinamerica/chapters/chapter-15-culture-and-society/essays-on-culture-and-society/liberation-theology-in-latin-america/.

Stoll, David. *Rigoberta Menchú and the Story of All Poor Guatemalans*. 2nd expanded ed. Boulder, CO: Westview Press, 2008. First published 1999.

Woodward, Ralph Lee, Jr. *Central America, a Nation Divided*. 3rd ed. New York: Oxford University Press, 1999. First published 1979.

Chapter 10

Dilma Rousseff, 1947–

INTRODUCTION

Brazil was the only Latin American country that did not become a republic following independence. Instead, in 1822, when it declared its independence from Portugal it became a monarchy, ruled by Emperor Pedro I. He was succeeded by his son, who was crowned Emperor Pedro II in 1841 and ruled Brazil for the ensuing forty-eight years. In 1888, Princess Isabel, acting as regent for her father, signed the Lei Áurea, or Golden Law, which fully abolished slavery—much to the displeasure of the Brazilian landowning elite. Within a year, the military staged a bloodless coup d'état and deposed Pedro and his family from imperial rule. With Marshal Deodoro da Fonseca at the helm, coup leaders declared their country a republic and organized it as a federal presidential system similar to the systems of the United States, Argentina, and Mexico. Like its sister republics, Brazil created states headed by governors and bicameral legislatures. Following an initial false start, in 1894 it elected a president who served out his entire four-year term. From that time until 1930, Brazilians elected new chief executives with metronome-like regularity. This was known as the time of Brazil's "Old Republic." The few domestic disturbances taking place between 1894 and 1930 were put down easily by the nation's military.

Brazil's relatively peaceful political scene won it respect throughout the Americas and Europe. At a time when most Spanish-speaking nations were torn by civil war, Brazil quietly doubled its national domain. Its diplomats took boundary disputes to international courts of arbitration and prevailed in nearly every case. By the 1920s Brazil was Latin America's largest nation, having approximately the same territorial size as the United States.

During the Old Republic (1889–1930), Brazil played an important role in global commerce. It supplied sought-after commodities to the world, becoming the leading exporter of coffee, natural rubber, and cacao. Brazil was a significant exporter of cattle, sugar, and cotton as well. The country also exported a wide range of minerals. Brazil's export economy made some citizens wealthy. By 1930 the Brazilian playboy was a fixture among the international glitterati, from Monaco and the French Riviera to New York and Buenos Aires.

Brazil's benign outward appearance, however, masked a range of structural and human problems. For example, its democratic political system was a sham: by 1930, only one in five adult Brazilians was permitted to vote. Women were denied the franchise, as were the poor. A great many Brazilians were poor. A substantial number of them were descended from enslaved people liberated in 1888, only a year before the republic was established. Additionally, the country's two richest states, coffee and industrial hub São Paulo and dairy-producing Minas Gerais, dominated national politics through a cozy power-sharing arrangement known as "coffee with milk."

A rigged and exclusivist political system was not Brazil's worst structural problem. The rule of law had been weak throughout the country since its founding by the Portuguese in 1500. Its citizens had never been given a voice in formulating laws handed down to them, virtually all of which were aimed at funneling Brazil's wealth to Portugal. In response, the colonials adopted the strategy of evading or violating the law whenever possible. In most cases this had the effect of reducing local and regional politics to what amounted to "thugocracy." Local elites called "colonels" (*coronéis*) ignored legal niceties and employed private armies to enforce their will. Woe betide the poor man who homesteaded a piece of land on the coffee or cacao frontier hoping to cash in on the export boom. His land tenure, and possibly his life, were likely to be brief. The local *coronel* usually annexed the plot of improved land to his own plantation.

In Brazil, a country of profound complexity and contradictions, an idealistic, middle-class woman of European descent rose to the highest levels of political power only to plunge—or be plunged—into a mire of corruption and scandal. Yet the life story of Dilma Rousseff, Brazil's first and only female president, is a story of continuity and change, tradition and reinvention. Through her we can not only trace the historical arc of Brazil's challenges but also look to the long-held image of a rich, inclusive nation.

DILMA ROUSSEFF AND THE NEW REPUBLIC

"God is a Brazilian." This humorous and only partly cynical aphorism is a favorite of Brazilians, who feel that the deity always smiles on the country in times of crisis. This was the case in 1930, when the Great Depression brought economic collapse to Brazil, spreading unemployment and misery. Throughout the Americas and Europe democratic regimes fell, often to be replaced by dictatorships. That was most strikingly the case in Germany, Europe's leading nation at the time. Nothing of the sort happened in Brazil. Instead, a man named Getúlio Vargas rose to power and between 1930, when he was first elected president, and his death in 1954, the authoritarian-turned-populist leader implemented profound reforms. He turned Brazil away from the free-trade model that had falsely promised unending wealth through the export of commodities and raw materials. With world trade at a standstill, Vargas turned Brazil toward a protectionist economic policy.

Vargas also politically empowered the poor and middle classes, speaking directly to *os trabalhadores do Brasil*—the workers of Brazil.[1] Of a corporatist mindset, he gave working-class and white-collar workers left-populist political parties geared to their interests. For workers it was the Labor Party and for the middle class the Social Democratic Party. Both were linked to the government through legislation tailored to their particular constituencies. Most strikingly, Getúlio Vargas was the first leader in Brazilian history to reach out to the poor. A populist at heart, he aided the dispossessed by creating social welfare programs so effective as to earn him the nickname "the father of the poor." During his nearly quarter century at the helm he successfully piloted his country across seas made stormy by economic dislocation, world wars, and the Cold War. During those years he refused to allow either communism or fascism to gain a foothold in Brazil.

The three presidents who followed Vargas continued their mentor's statist brand of populism, giving ever greater voice to non-elite Brazilians. The third of these, João Goulart (1961–1965), went so far as to endorse the unionization of the army's enlisted ranks. That shocked conservative Brazilians and military commanders who viewed such a possibility as threatening both to their chain of command and to national security. In mid-1964 military leaders stepped in and removed Goulart from office. That ended the age of Getúlio Vargas and marked the beginning of twenty years of military rule.

The military takeover of Brazil made little impact on the family of sixteen-year-old Dilma Rousseff. In 1964 she and her family members were still mourning the death two years earlier of Pedro Rousseff, the father of Dilma and her siblings. Pedro Rousseff had been born Petar Rúsef in Bulgaria in 1900. There he earned a law degree and joined the country's Communist Party. In 1929 he fled Bulgaria when his party was outlawed and made his way to Brazil, where he latinized his name, becoming Pedro Rousseff. By the 1940s he was a successful businessman working for the German corporation Mannesmann and dabbling in real estate. Along the way he met and married schoolteacher and Rio de Janeiro native Dilma da Silva, going on to settle down with her in Belo Horizonte, the capital of Minas Gerais state. There they had three children, the second of whom was Dilma Vana Rousseff. She was destined to become Brazil's first female president.

Dilma grew up in a happy upper-middle-class household. She lived in a substantial house on a tree-lined street in one of the nicer neighborhoods of Belo Horizonte and attended school at Our Lady of Sion, a private institution whose faculty was made up of French nuns. There she and her younger sister Zana Lúcia were taught the things required of proper young ladies. Her first fifteen years passed in a tranquil and uncomplicated way. But all of that changed with the death of her father. Forced to economize, her mother moved her children from private to public school, enrolling them in Central High School located in downtown Belo Horizonte.

The change was profound for teenage Dilma. Our Lady of Sion was all female, calm, and sedate. Central High was coeducational, gritty, and noisy, and filled with students from middle- and lower-class families. Most of its teachers had middle-class origins and were politically on the left. One of Dilma's favorites was a Marxist social studies instructor named Apolo Heringer Lisboa. It was he who opened her eyes to class struggle and the oppression of the poor by the rich. One day Heringer assigned Rousseff a reading from *Capital*, by Karl Marx. The sixteen-year-old found the German philosopher's prose tough going. The next day in class she asked, "So Marx was for the workers, right?"[2] When Heringer assured her that Marx was indeed for the workers Dilma Rousseff decided to cast her lot with the proletariat about whom Marx wrote so passionately.

RADICAL REVOLUTIONARIES

Following high school, Rousseff enrolled in the Federal University of Minas Gerais in Belo Horizonte, majoring in economics—but learning economics was not to be her chief interest. Rather, revolutionary ferment on campus drew her in. Over the nearly three years following Brazil's military coup, the generals in charge had steadily tightened their grip on political life through a series of decrees termed Institutional Acts. Early in Rousseff's freshman year, General Humberto Castelo Branco announced the Third Institutional Act, which banned elections at the state level. The previous year he had banned political parties. These measures angered many Brazilians and infuriated the country's left-wing college students. A sophomore in 1966, Dilma Rousseff joined a group called Workers' Politics (Política Operária), a spin-off of the Brazilian Socialist Party. One of its leaders was her high-school mentor

Apolo Heringer. When Rousseff joined the party, it was divided between its left and right factions. Its more conservative members advocated calling a constituent assembly that would rewrite the national constitution in order to reduce the generals' power. The party's left wing advocated taking up arms and overthrowing the government outright. Dilma Rousseff endorsed the latter course of action and joined the militants in helping found a new party, the revolutionary National Liberation Command (Colina).

The events playing out in 1960s Brazil were functions of the global Cold War being fought between the United States and USSR, or Soviet Union. Communist revolutionary Dilma Rousseff and anti-communist General Humberto Castelo Branco represented the two faces of the conflict within Brazil. As the Cold War intensified everywhere in Latin America, Brazil's generals stepped up repression within their country. That in turn further radicalized revolutionaries like young Dilma. In 1966, when French revolutionary theorist Régis Debray published a how-to guide to guerrilla warfare, *Revolution within the Revolution*, the National Liberation Command of Belo Horizonte embraced its call for war to the death against enemies of the revolution. Apolo Heringer recalled that Debray's book "inflamed everyone, including Dilma."[3]

Belo Horizonte's revolutionary cell was lucky to have Dilma Rousseff as a member. She lived in an apartment owned by her family near the university campus, an ideal spot for meetings—and for the storage of weapons and munitions. This included her cell's most prized weapon, a Russian-made Kalashnikov machine gun.

Dilma Rousseff fell in love in her Belo Horizonte apartment. There she met journalist and fellow Colina member twenty-six-year-old Cláudio Galeano; Rousseff was nineteen when the two married in 1967 in a civil ceremony. It was Galeano who convinced his fellow revolutionaries not to let his nearsighted bride fire any of their weapons, this to protect them from being accidentally shot by her. Thus freed from military training, Rousseff took on the job of editing a revolutionary newsletter and distributing it around the city. As funds flowed in to Colina from several bank robberies, she also helped out by keeping track of the group's expenditures.

The years 1968–1969 proved pivotal for Brazil's revolutionary left. On December 13, 1968, General Arthur da Costa e Silva decreed the Fifth Institutional Act, which suspended all political rights and imposed strict censorship. Brazil was now a full-fledged dictatorship. The new Institutional Act opened the way for a ruthless pursuit of left-wing militants. Within a month of its proclamation, Colina's safe house in Belo Horizonte was raided by police. In the confusion of that January day in 1969 two police officers were shot dead. Colina members fled the city. Rousseff and her husband made good their escape, reaching Rio de Janeiro. There Dilma and a female colleague took up residence in a rooming house at the edge of the city. Cláudio Galeano traveled south to Rio Grande do Sul, where he took part in an airplane hijacking that allowed him to fly into exile in Cuba. Rousseff remained in Rio under deep cover.

Now separated from her husband, Dilma Rousseff took a leadership position in Colina. In early 1969 she was one of those representing the group in discussions leading to its merger with a dissident faction of the Brazilian Communist Party. The negotiations led to the formation of a larger and more ambitious revolutionary organization called VAR (Armed Revolutionary Vanguard) Palmares. The communists' leader was a lawyer named Carlos Araújo, a widely traveled and charismatic man in his early thirties. Araújo had spent time in the Soviet Union, had met Fidel Castro and Che Guevara, and, when he was a teenager, had fought with the communist peasant leagues led by the legendary Francisco Julião. When Dilma Rousseff met Carlos Araújo the sparks flew. She saw Araújo as a handsome man of action, an intrepid fighter for the rights of the people. For him the young, fiery *mineira* was "a very pretty woman." What they shared, Araújo later recalled, "was passion."[4] Rousseff and Araújo entered into a relationship destined to endure for the following thirty years.

Their joining of forces initially brought good luck to VAR Palmares. In late 1969 they mounted an operation involving the theft of a safe once owned by the recently deceased former São Paulo mayor, Adhemar de Barros. VAR Palmares knew the safe would yield rich pickings. After all, "he steals but gets things done" was how Paulistas characterized Barros when he was in office. Nor were the revolutionaries disappointed. When the safe was opened it yielded $2.5 million.

Shortly after that success, disaster struck VAR Palmares. In early 1970 Dilma Rousseff departed Rio for São Paulo to collaborate with the cell located in that city. Carlos Araújo traveled to his home state of Rio Grande do Sul to do work for the guerrilla group. Rousseff was the first to be arrested. On January 19 her colleague José Ribeiro was taken into police custody and confessed under torture that a VAR Palmares meeting was to take place the next day at a downtown São Paulo restaurant. Rousseff arrived late for the meeting, witnessed arrests taking place, and might have escaped had a policeman not searched her backpack and found her pistol. She and her colleagues were led away to Tiradentes Prison, named after Joaquim José da Silva Xavier, a precursor of Brazilian independence, who was housed and subsequently executed there 181 years before. Rousseff's arrest ended her career as an urban guerrilla.

Dilma Rousseff was tortured off and on for three weeks following her arrest with the aim of extracting information on other members of VAR Palmares. The questioning was punctuated by beatings, though from time to time her tormentors subjected her to more inventive forms of abuse. When her interrogations at last ended, Rousseff took satisfaction in the fact that she had given up no information on the whereabouts of Carlos Araújo or other colleagues.

At her trial, prosecutors tried to portray the young woman as a key leader of VAR Palmares. One of them referred to the slim, determined defendant, dressed in blue jeans and gazing myopically into the distance, as "the she-pope of subversion." That obviously rang hollow to the military tribunal sitting in judgment. Patriarchal Brazil was not known for placing extraordinary power in the hands of females. The prosecutors' hyperbole may in fact have embarrassed the judges. A photograph of the proceeding shows one member of the tribunal hiding his face behind his hands and another with his head on his desk. The sentence they handed down was relatively light: six years in prison, subsequently reduced to three. Additionally, Rousseff was deprived of her right to participate in political activity for sixteen years. Freed in late 1972, Rousseff traveled to Porto Alegre, where she waited for Carlos Araújo to complete a five-year prison sentence.

DILMA ROUSSEFF, STATE WORKER

While Dilma Rousseff was in jail, Brazil experienced a miracle, though not in a religious sense. Instead, the "Brazilian Miracle" was economic in nature. During each year from 1969 to 1973 the country enjoyed a sky-high 10 percent growth in GDP (gross domestic product), a rate of increase seen nowhere else in the world at the time. When viewed over a more extended period, Brazil's miracle years were merely a spike in exceptionally high economic growth reaching back to the mid-1930s—even as far back as the half century preceding the Great Depression. The country's economic growth, especially in the post–Getúlio Vargas era, sprang from national industrial planning, referred to as "statist" economic development.

Government-sponsored industrial growth had begun in the latter 1800s and involved a process that would become known as Import Substitution Industrialization (ISI). At first it involved national manufacture of products called "consumer nondurables"—products such as soap, toothpaste, cigarettes, and textiles. By the time Getúlio Vargas took power, Brazil was producing nearly 100 percent of its consumer nondurables and had moved far into manufacturing "consumer durables," items such as refrigerators, farm implements, and an infinity of other consumer products. At the time of Vargas's death, the country made almost all its consumer durables and was entering into manufacture of capital equipment—machines that make machines. From 1950 onward Brazil pushed in the direction of full industrialization. After the military coup of 1965 the country's leaders simply seized the baton handed them unwillingly by the nation's three democratically elected Varguista presidents, Juscelino Kubitshek, Jânio Quadros, and João Goulart. The generals pushed the process of industrialization toward completion.

President General Ernesto Geisel (1974–1978) was the most significant promoter of Brazilian industrialization during the military rule. During his term, seemingly limitless amounts of money were placed at his disposal by international bankers. Geisel responded by borrowing from them freely. He could hardly do otherwise. Oil shocks of the 1970s had sent a flood of petrodollars from the oil-rich Middle East into the world's banking capitals. The banks in turn lent the money to developing countries like Brazil at below-market rates. Geisel used the money to turn auto manufacture into Brazil's leading economic sector, permitting millions of Brazilians of the middle and upper classes to purchase Brazilian-made autos, thereby creating a virtuous cycle of economic expansion. Geisel also pushed Brazil to become the world's leading producer of ethanol because the country produced little petroleum, and the cost of imported oil was exorbitant. Meanwhile, Geisel ordered Brazil's national oil company Petrobras to step up its search for oil fields thought to exist off Brazil's Atlantic coast.

Dilma Rousseff's family benefited from this economic "miracle" and another policy President Geisel also set into motion: the process of removing the military from power and returning Brazil to democracy. He called this policy *distensão*, or "decompression." So when Dilma Rousseff left jail and arrived in Porto Alegre in early 1973, she was able to pick up her life as a college student without penalty. She entered the Federal University of Rio Grande do Sul, completed her bachelor's degree in economics, and paid for her expenses with the help of part-time jobs. Meanwhile, she divorced Cláudio Galeano. When Carlos Araújo was released from prison in 1975, the two married in a civil ceremony and in March of the following year welcomed the birth of their daughter, Paula Araújo.

In 1977 Rousseff began work as an intern at the Foundation of Economics and Statistics (FEE), a state agency of Rio Grande do Sul. Although she and her husband were banned from running for political office, both volunteered in the political campaign of Glênio Peres, a member of the leftist coalition Brazilian Democratic Movement Party who was running for a place on the city council of Porto Alegre. Not long after winning and taking his seat on the council, Peres delivered a speech denouncing the government's torture of political prisoners, a subject Rousseff and Araújo had doubtless discussed with him. The speech resulted in Peres's being expelled from the city council and Rousseff's losing her internship. The São Paulo newspaper *O Estado* learned of the incident and referred to Dilma Rousseff as a VAR Palmares militant who was "cohabiting with the subversive Carlos Araújo." The newspaper referred to Rousseff as one of "ninety-seven subversives" who had infiltrated the public administration of Rio Grande do Sul.[5]

Despite occasional blasts from the right, political tensions were rapidly cooling in Brazil. Sadly, that was far from the case in neighboring Argentina, where the 1970s found the country's police and military conducting a "dirty war" against the political left. Over that decade some ten thousand mostly young Argentines were dragged away to prisons where they were interrogated under torture and executed; their bodies were either buried in unmarked graves or hurled into the sea.[6] The same thing had happened a decade earlier in Brazil but to a lesser degree. A government agency later established that 379 leftist militants had been "disappeared" in Brazil during 1969–1970, a time in national history known as the "leaden years" (*anos de chumbo*).

Ernesto Geisel's decompression of Brazilian politics and his opening of the political system continued under his successor, General João Baptista Figueiredo (1979–1983). Figueiredo completed the country's return to democracy. When he entered office, the draconian Fifth Institutional Act was annulled, censorship lifted, and political rights restored to those deprived of them. That included Dilma Rousseff and Carlos Araújo. Brazilians who fled the country during the leaden years began returning home. Notable among them were leftist novelist Jorge Amado and anthropologist and left-economic theorist Fernando Henrique Cardoso.

Brazil's return to democracy under Geisel and Figueiredo, a process termed *abertura*, or "opening," permitted Dilma Rousseff and Carlos Araújo to become active in the state politics of Rio Grande do Sul. Now established in Porto Alegre, both became members of the Brazilian Labor Party (PDT), which was established by a left-wing populist named Leonel Brizola. Rousseff promoted her husband's political career, helping him win seats in the state legislature during the 1980s and 1990s. The couple's success in promoting Brizola's party won Rousseff a job advising the PDT caucus in the Rio Grande do Sul state legislature.

In the late 1970s civil society roared back to life in Brazil, and organized labor made a comeback. During 1978–1979 massive strikes took place in the country's industrial heartland of São Paulo state. A fiery and articulate labor leader named Luiz Inácio Lula da Silva emerged from the strikes. Having only an elementary-school education, Lula da Silva perfectly symbolized the mass of poor Brazilians the "Brazilian Miracle" had left behind. During the boom times of the 1960s and 1970s, the rich had gotten richer and the poor notably poorer. Now workers demanded their piece of the pie. Chief among their demands were calls for wage increases, union autonomy, and the right to collective bargaining.

In 1980, the first year new political parties were allowed to form, Lula da Silva joined with other labor activists, leaders of the Catholic liberation theology movement, academics, and intellectuals to form the Workers' Party (PT). It quickly emerged as the voice of Brazilian labor, with Lula da Silva its foremost leader. In 1986 voters in São Paulo sent Lula to the National Congress. In 1989, 1994, and 1998, Lula ran for president as the Workers' Party candidate. He lost all three elections, the last two to Fernando Henrique Cardoso, the man who tamed hyperinflation in Brazil.

As Luiz Inácio Lula da Silva and Fernando Henrique Cardoso were emerging as rising stars in Brazil's political firmament, Dilma Rousseff was becoming known as a political force in the left-leaning state of Rio Grande do Sul. After Dilma helped PDT leader Alceu Collares win the 1985 mayoral contest in Porto Alegre, Collares appointed her secretary of finances for the municipality. She qualified for the post thanks to her ongoing graduate study toward the PhD in economics, now at Brazil's prestigious Campinas State University. The appointment meant that at last Rousseff and her family were financially secure. She and her husband had also outgrown criticism of their radical backgrounds. In short, both had returned to the upper-middle-class lifestyles in which they had been reared. Carlos Araújo had, with the help of his wife, made himself a respected member of the political establishment of Rio Grande do Sul.

CHANGE IN THE AIR: LULA AND THE RISE OF THE WORKERS' PARTY

Unfortunately for Rousseff, Araújo, and all Brazilians, just as things were starting to look up, they suddenly found themselves confronting a fearsome foe: hyperinflation. During the period 1986–1989 inflation in Brazil rose to 1,600 percent per year and reached a staggering 2,400 percent in 1993. On many days prices in stores doubled between the time they opened in the morning and the time they closed in the evening. This was especially devastating to the poor and those living on fixed incomes. Brazil's hyperinflation was merely one aspect of a complex of economic ills afflicting the country. For the first time since the Great Depression, Brazil's economy contracted, producing a ghastly condition known as "stagflation." The shocking one-two punch of economic stagnation and sky-high inflation led Brazilians to label the 1980s their "lost decade." Free-spending generals had saddled Brazil with the world's largest foreign debt, leading the country into default in 1983. Brazil had become unable to pay even the interest on the debt. Some Brazilians prayed for help from above as others joked, "Not even God can pay Brazil's foreign debt."

Economic nationalism also contributed to Brazil's economic malaise. Decades of protectionism had saddled the country with overstaffed and sometimes unproductive nationally owned companies. Brazilians' reluctance to tax wealth was also to blame. So too were extremely generous pensions paid to white-collar workers who could legally retire at age fifty-five. Government bonds indexed to inflation became a fiscal nightmare as the government struggled to meet interest payments. All the while the state doled out fat subsidies to industry. Journalist Michael Reid writes that as of the 1980s, Brazil possessed an economy that was at once inflationary, unfair, and skewed in the direction of entrenched economic interests.

Brazil's sorry economic state was not helped by the poor quality of the first four presidents elected following the end of military rule. The first of them was Tancredo Neves, a man so elderly that he had been a cabinet officer under Getúlio Vargas, who served as president from 1930 to 1945 and from 1951 to 1954. Neves died in 1985, before taking office, and was succeeded by his vice president, José Sarny. Sarny, in turn, was a weak leader unable to tame the inflation that rose to 2,000 percent in 1988—his last year in office. Conditions grew even worse under his successor, Francisco Collor de Mello. After running on an anti-corruption platform, Collor was found guilty of corruption, impeached, and removed from office. His vice president, Itmar Franco, a bumbling former senator, succeeded him. Brazilians despaired of ever finding a leader who was both competent and honest.

Fortunately for all, in May 1993 Itmar Franco appointed Fernando Henrique Cardoso his minister of finance. Cardoso proved to be a godsend. Within two years he and a team of young economic advisers brought inflation down from a peak of 2,400 percent to zero. His Real Plan combined economic reforms that opened the economy to foreign imports and investment, with a program that amounted to putting the bloated state on a diet. One of the plan's most innovative features was its creation of a virtual currency that allowed for gradual de-indexing of government debt without damaging the new national currency, the real. As inflation plummeted Cardoso's popularity soared. By 1994 it was clear that he would be Brazil's next president. In that year's election Cardoso won 54 percent of the vote. The Workers' Party candidate Lula da Silva managed to win just 24 percent.

Rio Grande do Sul's left-wing political establishment was disheartened by Lula's electoral shellacking. At the same time, everyone living there was grateful to Fernando Cardoso for slaying the inflation dragon. Meanwhile, Dilma Rousseff's reputation as a competent administrator continued to grow. In 1993, her patron Alceu Collares, then state governor, appointed her secretary of energy, a post she held until Collares left office a year later. Rousseff then returned to the state economic and statistical bureau where she had previously served as an intern. Now she edited its monthly journal, *Economic Indicators*. She also resumed her seemingly never-ending graduate study at Campinas State University.

In 1994 Dilma Rousseff was betrayed by her closest friend and political adviser, her husband. That year she discovered not only that Carlos Araújo had a mistress but that the woman was pregnant with his child. The episode crippled the quarter-century love relationship of Rousseff and Araújo. Although they continued to cohabit for several years more, their breakup became permanent in 2000. Rousseff, now in her fifties, moved out on Araújo, divorced him, and established her own household. She remained single thereafter.

In 1998 there was little doubt that the new governor of Rio Grande do Sul, Olívio Dutra, a member of Lula da Silva's Workers' Party, would name Dilma Rousseff the state's secretary of energy. At millennium's end the former revolutionary had remade herself into one of Brazil's leading experts in the field of hydroelectric energy management. During her second stint as state energy czar she oversaw a 46 percent increase in energy generation at a moment when Brazil at large was entering a time of drought and corresponding energy cutbacks. Rousseff's extraordinary success was owed in part to the fact that she had accepted the argument that public-private cooperation on energy generation yielded better results than did outright state ownership of electric utilities. This represented a sharp revision of her youthful Marxist belief that Brazil's means of production should be owned and controlled by the state. Her change of mind in turn attracted the attention of President Fernando Henrique Cardoso, who sought Rousseff's advice on handling the rolling power outages caused by the widespread drought. Thanks to Rousseff's leadership Rio Grande do Sul had experienced no outages.

In 2000 the energy minister of Rio Grande do Sul changed her party affiliation and thereby her political future. She left Leonel Brizola's populist Democratic Labor Party (PDT), which Rousseff accused of having moved too far to the right, and joined the Workers' Party (PT) of Luiz Inácio Lula da Silva. Her change of party angered her old copartisans. But it had the effect of placing her in the political party of Brazil's next president.

Brazil's energy crisis extended into the last years of Cardoso's presidency, leading him to continue his consultations with Dilma Rousseff. The two had known each other for more than twenty years, from the time Cardoso returned from exile and Rousseff was an intern at the Foundation of Economics and Statistics of Rio Grande do Sul. One of the young intern's tasks had been to handle local arrangements for Cardoso's speaking engagements in Porto Alegre. At the time both were Marxists. But by the 1990s each had moved away from Marxism to acceptance of the neoliberal premise that privately owned utilities could operate synergistically with publicly owned ones.

Neoliberalism was persuasive even in statist, protectionist Brazil. Fernando Henrique Cardoso, who assumed the presidency in 1995, was convinced by neoliberal arguments despite his early sympathy for Marxist ideas. Over his eight-year presidential term he sold 119 state-owned companies and opened other state-owned enterprises to private-sector competition. Cardoso's reforms had painful side effects. Tens of thousands of people lost jobs as newly privatized firms fired workers deemed to be less than cost effective. Such layoffs were especially prevalent in industrialized São Paulo state.

Cardoso's neoliberalism was sharply criticized by Lula da Silva and other members of the Brazilian left. Yet when Cardoso left office at the end of 2002 it was clear that his reforms had brought good results. Inflation remained low, productivity increased, and, miracle of miracles, the country experienced a fiscal surplus. Brazil had achieved a pleasant combination of economic stability and growth. Yet Cardoso had not become a doctrinaire economic liberal. He never lost his sensitivity to the plight of the poor, and to the state's obligation to help them. Over his eight years in office he gave special attention to improving public education. Brazilian public schools, being tuition free, were where poor and lower-middle-class families sent their children to be educated. Cardoso raised teachers' salaries and improved primary and secondary education generally. Notable as well was his cash grant program called the Family Shopping Basket (Bolsa Família). Pioneered earlier in labor-friendly states such as Rio Grande do Sul, Bolsa Família paid cash stipends to heads of family who earned less than the minimum wage. Cardoso extended the program nationwide.

Throughout Cardoso's time in office his most significant opposition came from the left, particularly from Workers' Party leader Luiz Inácio Lula da Silva. When Cardoso's popularity declined during 2001–2002, it became clear that the party of Brazil's poor and middle class would come to power. The man who led it was one of their own. Lula was born in 1945 in the poor northeastern state of Pernambuco. When he was seven his mother moved him along with his six brothers and sisters south to Santos, the port of São Paulo state. During his early twenties he worked as a lathe operator in an automobile assembly plant. In 1980, at the age of thirty-five, he helped organize the Workers' Party, going on to become its perennial presidential candidate. Lula's wait ended in 2002 when he decisively won both the general and runoff elections. In both contests he trounced José Serra of Cardoso's Social Democratic Party.

It was a new, moderate Lula da Silva who prepared to take power in what would lengthen to two presidential terms extending from January 2003 to January 2011. In the heat of the campaign Lula had published a "Letter to the Brazilian People" in which he assured moderates and conservatives that not only had he come to terms with Fernando Cardoso's neoliberal reforms but that he would stand behind them. This helps explain why, in selecting members of his cabinet, his thoughts turned to Dilma Rousseff, who, similarly, had come to terms with public-private cooperation.

DILMA ROUSSEFF ON THE NATIONAL STAGE

Rousseff was surprised in mid-2001 when presidential candidate Lula da Silva invited her to a meeting on national energy policy. At the meeting she stuck out like the proverbial sore thumb, first because she had never completed her doctorate, unlike the other attendees, and second, because she was female. Despite these drawbacks the political appointee from Rio Grande do Sul impressed everyone present. Working from her laptop computer, she competently and persuasively helped attendees grapple with the issues raised, even in debate with nuclear engineer Luiz Pinguelli Rosa, the odds-on favorite for the post of energy minister in a Lula da Silva administration. As the meeting progressed Lula watched Rousseff with growing approval. As he later recalled, "There appeared a comrade with a little computer in her hand. . . . When we started debating I saw she had a different approach from the others. . . . It occurred to me, 'I think I've found my minister.'"[7] When Lula appointed Rousseff minister of energy and mines in the first week of his first term, no one could tell who was more surprised—Dilma Rousseff or Luiz Pinguelli Rosa. Later events underscored the wisdom of Lula's selection.

Lula's appointment of a woman to a signally important cabinet position was almost as remarkable as his own rise from poverty to the presidency: no female public figure in modern Brazil had risen as high as Dilma Rousseff in public life. Brazil is an intensely patriarchal country where women of good families rarely enter politics, unlike in Spanish America. As of the twenty-first century, numerous Spanish-speaking countries in Latin America had elected female heads of state, Argentina and Chile being leading examples. Colombia is a hemispheric leader in the number of women elected to congress. Even landlocked Paraguay claims the revered Irish-born Eliza Lynch as pivotal to its political history. But as of 2002, no such figure had previously appeared in the Brazilian republic. Shortly after Dilma Rousseff's appointment as energy minister a friend from the elite private school she attended as a child told her that she was virtually the only one in her class who had undertaken a career outside the home.

While Dilma Rousseff is a feminist, that is not her defining feature. She is also a competent and skilled public servant who is not afraid to speak her mind. Her greatest qualities are her organization, energy, and understanding of the task at hand, traits that earned her the respect of the men with whom she worked. During her years as energy minister, she repeatedly clashed with the head of the gas and energy department of Petrobras, Ildo Sauer. Rousseff rejected Sauer's extreme statist position so resolutely that Lula had to repeatedly step in to mediate between them. Rousseff occasionally shouted at committee meetings, although according to a colleague, "It's her way. It's not personal. In five minutes, it's OK."[8] Men outside Rousseff's political circle invariably spoke and wrote of the upstart politician in negative and sexist ways. Off-color jokes aside, political opponents tarred the middle-aged progressive administrator as short-tempered and bossy, unattractive and frumpy. Rousseff was forbearing in the face of such criticisms and rarely responded to them. As the rare woman working surrounded by Brazilian men, she tended to be philosophical: "When you are a woman in authority," she once remarked, "they say you are hard, dry, and insensitive, while a man in the same position is strong, firm, and charming."[9]

Rousseff's challenges as a Brazilian woman who presided over a group of opinionated men was put to the test between 2003 and 2010, when she served as Lula da Silva's appointed chair of Petrobras. It was there that she forcefully advanced the position that the state oil company must not betray the country's statist and protectionist stance by rushing to embrace neoliberalism's free-trade capitalism. At issue was the Petrobras board's majority position that private companies should take the lead in developing the rumored offshore oil fields. Such transnational corporations, they argued, would do the job in a cost-effective way. While Rousseff agreed that was indeed the case, she insisted that if Brazil developed the fields, thousands of new jobs would be created for Brazilians. Additionally, by imposing domestic content requirements on oil rigs and drilling equipment, technology transfer would occur. All of this, argued economic nationalist Rousseff, was worth the added expense of Brazil-led oil extraction. Her protectionist argument carried the day.

The importance of Dilma Rousseff to the Lula administration and to Brazil increased significantly in 2007, early in Lula's second term. Brazilian geologists at last confirmed the existence of world-class oil and natural gas fields under the Atlantic Ocean floor within the country's territorial waters. As Petrobras board chair, Rousseff was tasked with drawing up a legal framework for exploiting the fields. The thoroughly statist document she and her colleagues produced proclaimed the oil deposits property of the state, and Petrobras the entity charged with developing them.

When Lula da Silva learned of the oil discovery, he exulted that Brazil had won the lottery and called the oil and gas fields "a gift from God."[10] That good news was just one aspect of the country's economic boom times. Lula's second term, from 2007 to 2010, was a time of explosive growth in the country. Its BRIC (Brazil, Russia, India, China) sister nation China poured billions of dollars into the economy in exchange for Brazilian soybeans, sugar, and other agricultural products, and for an array of raw materials. In 2008, when a financial crisis pushed the United States and Europe into sharp recession, Brazil emerged relatively unscathed. Lula mocked the 2008 recession as being caused by "blue-eyed people who previously seemed to know everything and reveal they know nothing."[11] Dilma later recalled that "people said we didn't know how to govern, that we just got lucky.... But when this crisis happened, much more serious than in 1929, we showed enormous managerial competence and an ability to react with daring."[12] About that same time, international credit-rating agencies announced Brazilian government bonds to be investment grade. In January 2008 the country became a net creditor. Brazil was riding high. Lula's approval ratings soared, making him the most popular president in the country's history.

What could go wrong? The answer was: plenty. As Lula da Silva and Dilma Rousseff danced political samba in a carnivalesque atmosphere, the rumble of thunder could be heard in the distance. As every moviegoer knows, that meant the happy times were about to end.

PETROBRAS AND THE *LAVA JATO* SCANDAL

Corruption brought both Lula da Silva and Dilma Rousseff down—this, and a spirit of impunity, are as old as Brazil itself. Those in positions of political power are often found to be corrupt to some degree. And levels of corruption grow in proportion to the quantity of money at hand. In modern times dominant political parties have accepted as a normal operating procedure the bribing of partners in Congress in exchange for their votes; such partners cause the government headaches when they don't receive anticipated payoffs. And bribery is merely one of numerous illegal practices employed to lubricate Brazil's political machinery.

In mid-2005, for example, the manager at a federal post office was secretly filmed receiving a suitcase stuffed with bribe money destined for a political ally of Lula da Silva's named Roberto Jefferson. Furious at being humiliated by the exposé, Jefferson called a press conference at which he exposed the government's practice of making such payments to Workers' Party allies. Jefferson referred to the money as the *mensalão*, or "big monthly payment." He went on to say that such payments often ran to 30,000 reais ($12,500). The *mensalão* scandal ensnared Workers' Party president José Dirceu, Lula's chief of staff. Disgraced and facing criminal charges, Dirceu resigned from both his party and government posts. Lula replaced him with Dilma Rousseff, relying on her reputation for honesty to calm public outrage. In Brazil the position of presidential chief of staff is similar to that of prime minister in parliamentary systems. With her promotion Dilma Rousseff became the second-most powerful figure in Brazilian politics.

Brazilians eventually put the *mensalão* scandal behind them. This was largely because Lula da Silva and his new chief of staff had not protected the guilty. They let justice run its course, with the result that numerous politicians served prison sentences of up to eleven years. Dilma Rousseff did not mince words on the subject of corruption. "Corruption offends and embarrasses workers, harms businesses, and offends both men and women of good will and diminishes the importance of honest work."[13]

Despite scandals that tarnished Lula's time in office, he remained popular thanks to Brazil's burgeoning economy. In late 2006 he was reelected by a landslide 61 percent of the vote. During Lula's second term he gained international recognition for greatly expanding the Family Shopping Basket program. Public officials everywhere, even in leading nations, noted that recipients of the Brazilian cash stipends were required both to send their children to school and to have them vaccinated.

When Lula's presidency drew to an end in 2010, he selected Dilma Rousseff to succeed him. Relatively new to the Workers' Party, she was not besmirched by the scandals tainting senior party leaders. Accordingly, Lula announced the candidacy of his chief of staff in good PT fashion, at the inauguration of a government-sponsored project for the poor: a cable car extending up to a mountaintop favela in Rio de Janeiro. The cable car spared favela dwellers an arduous thousand-step climb up to their homes at the end of a long workday, often following a commute lasting two hours or more. At the event Lula heaped praise on Rousseff, his way of telling Brazilians that she was to be the PT candidate in that year's presidential contest.

To prepare herself for the presidential race Rousseff gave herself a new look. She changed her hairstyle, got rid of her glasses in favor of contact lenses, and had a face-lift. The new Dilma Rousseff made her appearance just before the election. When Lula da Silva saw her, he gushed, "I'm going to change my name and I will be called Dilma Rousseff."[14] Dilma Rousseff won the presidency in a run-off contest, with 56 percent of the vote (see figure

Figure 10.1. Official photo of President Rousseff at Alvorada Palace on January 9th, 2011, Palácio do Planalto. This image was produced by the Press Secretary of the Presidency of the Federative Republic of Brazil

10.1). A few days later she said: "It is not by chance that after this great man, Brazil can be governed by a woman—a woman who will continue the Brazil of Lula, but who will do so with the soul and heart of a woman."[15]

Progressives everywhere in the Americas celebrated her victory. US president Barack Obama sent his secretary of state, Hillary Rodham Clinton, to represent him at Rousseff's inauguration. Regional presidents who attended included Hugo Chávez of Venezuela and Juan Manuel Santos of Colombia. Once in office, Rousseff appointed eleven women to her cabinet of thirty-seven. Over her first term as Brazil's first female chief executive, her popularity soared to 79 percent. She was lauded for her legislative achievements, especially in the area of rural electrification. Her Light for All program brought electricity to some 2.5 million rural households. Over their combined terms in office Lula da Silva and Rousseff reduced chronic poverty in Brazil by 75 percent.

In 2014 Dilma Rousseff won a second presidential term thanks to a heavy vote in her favor from the country's impoverished northern and northeastern states. Poor residents there had benefited notably from the Family Shopping program. However, Brazilians in the better-off southern states failed to give her a majority vote, revealing that Brazil was growing ever more politically divided. Many people in better-off parts of the country concluded that Workers' Party presidents focused so much on helping the poor that slightly better-off Brazilians like them were not having their needs met. They felt increasingly that they had been left out of the country's vaunted progress.

An early sign of popular unhappiness manifested in 2012 in the protests that first flared up against an increase in bus fares. Public demonstrations against the fare increase started in São Paulo and quickly spread to the rest of the country. The protests continued well into Rousseff's second term in office. Political analysts attributed the anger to average Brazilians' struggle to hang on to middle-class status all the while being poorly served by a dysfunctional system of public health, shabby public transportation, and substandard public schools. Discontent was further fanned by the lavish expenditure of public monies on the 2014 World Cup and the 2016 Rio Olympics. The usual corruption scandals, centering on kickbacks and bribes, accompanied the expenditures. A sharp economic downturn was another contributing factor.

Most sobering of all were rumors of staggering corruption around the deepwater oil fields being developed by Petrobras—the prime source of the shocking fall of both Dilma Rousseff and Luiz Inácio Lula da Silva. The Petrobras scandal was by far the worst in the history of Brazil, routinely rated as one of the world's most corrupt developing nations.[16] Dilma Rousseff, who was not charged with corruption in the scandal swirling around Petrobras, became a victim of national revulsion against politics and politicians.

The tsunami of corruption first came to light in Europe in 2013, when a lawyer for the Dutch corporation SBM Offshore exposed his company's lavish bribery of Petrobras officials and members of the Brazilian Congress. SBM Offshore, a manufacturer of deepwater drilling platforms, knew of Brazilians' susceptibility to bribery and acted accordingly to ensure its slice of the oil bonanza pie. So too did all other companies—domestic and foreign—that stood to gain from the oil boom. Bribery was most flagrant in Brazil's lower house of Congress. There the feeding frenzy sank to the level of burlesque when members of Congress were seen at night lined up at ATMs near the legislative building. They were laundering bribe money handed out to them for approving contracts awarded to companies with which they connived. Because the most popular of these ATMs was outside the Tower Gas Station and Car Wash (*lava jato*), Brazilians labeled it the *lava jato* scandal.

The president of Brazil's Chamber of Deputies, Eduardo Cunha, was the *lava jato* king of corruption—and his reign, or network, extended far and wide. Over fifteen months between February 2015 and May 2016, he accepted ninety-six million reais ($40 million) in bribes and kickbacks, some of which were connected to the 2016 Rio Olympics. Cunha was also president of the Brazilian Democratic Party, a coalition ally of Dilma Rousseff's Workers' Party. An evangelical Christian, Cunha laundered his payments through the bank of an evangelical megachurch in Rio. Marcelo Odebrecht, the owner of Brazil's largest construction company, paid bribes not only within Brazil but also internationally. Venezuela's president Hugo Chávez and Panama's president Ricardo Martinelli were among the prominent foreigners accepting bribes from Odebrecht.

The only saving feature of *lava jato* was that justice was ultimately served. Some one hundred politicians and businessmen were found guilty of corruption and packed off to prison. Eduardo Cunha received a fifteen-year sentence. Marcelo Odebrecht was sentenced to nineteen years in jail. A sad footnote to the *lava jato* scandal was that it slammed the door on twenty-one years of progressive reform in Brazil stretching back to the presidency of Fernando Henrique Cardoso. It also ended Rousseff's presidency.

Rousseff's impeachment came quickly. Brazilians could not forget that she had once chaired the board of directors of Petrobras. Demands for her ouster began in late 2015 and intensified over the year that followed. Rousseff was charged with illegally transferring funds from one government agency to another in order to cover growing deficits. In March 2016 thousands demonstrated in Brasília demanding her impeachment. The former speaker of the lower chamber of Congress, Eduardo Cunha, helped direct the demonstrations from his prison cell. It was the payback exacted by a corrupt public official against another public official who was not corrupt. In Cunha's eyes the president's "crime" was that she had failed to protect him from justice. Congress wasted no time in acting, though no crime ever came to light. Rousseff was impeached and removed from office in August 2016. An ironic twist is that a significant number of the congresspeople who voted her out of office were soon to be incarcerated for accepting dirty money.

EPILOGUE

How had Dilma Rousseff, Lula's stalwart former minister and handpicked presidential successor, fallen so far out of favor? Some Brazilians continued to investigate through the media. Dilma appealed her impeachment charges in 2019, the year of the successful release of Brazilian filmmaker Petra Costa's *The Edge of Democracy*, an award-winning documentary that investigated the downfall of Dilma and a democratic Brazil in peril. In his review of the film, Jon Lee Anderson zooms in on potential answers:

> In her film, Costa, in a quest to comprehend these events, asks several politicians their reasons for impeaching Dilma. One of them tells her that Dilma had not "bonded" well with the political class in Brasília, that she was cold and had never "given hugs." Another veteran says, gnomically, "I can also say that Dilma was honest. But a good cook is not one who cooks to her own taste—she cooks to please those who will be eating."[17]

One might view Dilma Rousseff in terms of her ultimate failure. Similarly, it could be concluded that Brazil is a failed democracy condemned to frustrated mediocrity by its people's ingrained tradition of lawbreaking. Both these judgments would be incorrect. Dilma Rousseff was an idealist who rose to prominence by unswervingly working to improve the lot of her fellow citizens. At this writing the former president remains politically active. The year 2019 found her appealing the charges leading to her impeachment. She, her political party, and her mentor Lula da Silva, charged that judge Sérgio Mora, who sent Lula to prison, was in league with the president at the time, Jair Bolsonaro, who styled himself the "Brazilian Donald Trump." Yet Rousseff's removal from office neither dampened her social commitment nor ended her political career.

The saga of Brazilian politics continues, and the colorful panorama of political life there changes constantly, kaleidoscopically, entertainingly. The most recent past president Jair Bolsonaro (2019–2022), who ran on an anti-corruption campaign, was soon under investigation for corruption and for illegally protecting his son Flávio from money-laundering charges. Lula da Silva marked his first year in prison by giving an interview in which he opined that "Brazil is governed by lunatics and US lackeys."[18] Lula later emerged from prison to become president once again in 2023. Brazilian politics is perhaps best contemplated while sipping a glass of cachaça while sitting down to enjoy a fine meal of feijoada with all the trimmings. In 2018, Dilma Rousseff ran for Senate as a Workers' Party candidate for the state of Minas Gerais; she did not win. One might muse on internationally renowned composer and musician Tom Jobim's remark to a student of the country, Michael Reid: "Brazil is not for beginners."[19] But Dilma Rousseff, ever the student, is surely taking notes.

NOTES

1. Michael Conniff, "Getúlio Vargas: 'Workers of Brazil! Here I Am at Your Side!'" in *Problems in Modern Latin American History: A Reader*, ed. John Charles Chasteen and Joseph S. Tulchin (Wilmington, DE: Scholarly Resources, 1994), 115–17.
2. Luiz Maklouf Carvalho, "'Arms and the Men: The Political and Affective Education of Dilma Rousseff.' Interview with Apolo Heringer Lisboa." *Piauí* 32 (April 2009): 22, http://revistapiauí.estado.com.br/edicao-31/vueltas-da-republica-armas-e-os-varones.
3. Maklouf, "Arms and the Men," 14.
4. Maklouf, "Arms and the Men," 21.
5. Maklouf, "Arms and the Men," 30.
6. To this day, the Argentine Madres de la Plaza de Mayo regularly protest the loss of their sons and daughters.
7. Luiz Maklouf Carvalho, "Seas Never Before Sailed: How and Why Dilma Rousseff Became the Candidate for President and Successor of Lula," *Piauí* 34 (July 2009): 34, https://piaui.folha.uol.com.br/materia/mares-nunca-dantes-navegados/.
8. Maklouf, "Seas Never Before Sailed," 30.
9. Joe Leahy, "Dilma Rousseff: 'A Woman in Authority Is Called Hard, While a Man Is Called Charming,'" *Financial Times*, December 8, 2019, https://www.ft.com/content/cd5c2b24-bc05-11e6-8b45-b8b81dd5d080.
10. Michael Reid, *Brazil: The Troubled Rise of a World Power* (New Haven, CT: Yale University Press, 2014), 153.
11. Reid, *Brazil*, 155.
12. Reid, *Brazil*, 155.
13. "A corrupção significa democratizar o poder," *Vermelho: A esquerda bem informada*, March 18, 2015, https://vermelho.org.br/2015/03/18/combater-a-corrupcao-significa-democratizar-o-poder-afirma-dilma/.
14. Luiz Inácio Lula da Silva, "Me llamaré Dilma Rousseff," *El Mundo* (Buenos Aires), June 14, 2010, https://www.Pagina12.com.ar.diario/elmundo/4-147-2010-06-14.html.
15. Lula da Silva, "Me llamaré Dilma Rousseff."

16. Transparency International, a nongovernmental watchdog organization that rates nations in terms of corruption, routinely awards Brazil a profound F. By contrast, the world's least corrupt countries, usually Scandinavian ones, come away with B+ ratings. The United States rates a C-.
17. Jon Lee Anderson, "The Fracturing of Brazil in 'The Edge of Democracy,'" *New Yorker*, December 13, 2019, https://www.newyorker.com/culture/culture-desk/the-fracturing-of-brazil-in-the-edge-of-democracy.
18. Luiz Inácio Lula da Silva, "Brazil Governed by 'Lunatics' and US 'Lackeys,' Says Ex-President Lula," *Guardian*, April 27, 2019, https://www.theguardian.com/world/2019/apr/27/brazil-governed-by-lunatics-and-us-lackeys-says-ex-president-lula.
19. Reid, *Brazil*, 22.

REFERENCES

"A corrupcão significa democratizar o poder." *Vermelho: A esquerda bem informada*, March 18, 2015. https://vermelho.org.br/2015/03/18/combater-a-corrupcao-significa-democratizar-o-poder-afirma-dilma/.
Amado, Jorge. *Gabriela: Clove and Cinnamon*. New York: Alfred A. Knopf, 1962.
———. *The Violent Land*. New York: Alfred A. Knopf, 1991. First published 1945.
Anderson, Jon Lee. "The Fracturing of Brazil in 'The Edge of Democracy.'" *New Yorker*, December 13, 2019. https://www.newyorker.com/culture/culture-desk/the-fracturing-of-brazil-in-the-edge-of-democracy.
Baumgarten de Bolle, Monica. *Como matar a borboleta-azul: Uma crônica da era Dilma*. Rio de Janeiro: Editorial Intrínsica, 2016. Digital edition.
Brazilian Ministry of Foreign Affairs. *Discursos selecionados da Presidente Dilma Rousseff*. Club de Autores, 2017. Digital edition.
Conniff, Michael. "Getúlio Vargas: 'Workers of Brazil! Here I Am at Your Side!'" In *Problems in Modern Latin American History: A Reader*, edited by John Chasteen, Charles and Joseph S. Tulchin, 115–17. Wilmington, DE: Scholarly Resources, 1994.
Costa, Petra. *The Edge of Democracy*. Busca Vida Filma, 2019. https://www.netflix.com/title/80190535.
Crandall, Britta H. "Brazil: The Politics of Elite Rule." In *Latin American Politics and Development*, 9th ed., edited by Harvey Kline, Christine J. Wade, and Howard J. Wiarda, 123–39. Boulder, CO: Westview Press, 2018.
Debray, Regis. *Revolution Inside the Revolution*. New York: Grove Press, 1967. First published 1966.
Leahy, Joe. "Dilma Rousseff: 'A Woman in Authority Is Called Hard, While a Man Is Called Charming.'" *Financial Times*, December 8, 2019. https://www.ft.com/content/cd5c2b24-bc05-11e6-8b45-b8b81dd5d080.
Lula da Silva, Luiz Inácio. "Brazil Governed by 'Lunatics' and US 'Lackeys,' Says Ex-President Lula." *Guardian*, April 27, 2019. https://www.theguardian.com/

world/2019/apr/27/brazil-governed-by-lunatics-and-us-lackeys-says-ex-president-lula.

———. "Me llamaré Dilma Rousseff." *El Mundo* (Buenos Aires), June 14, 2010. https://www.pagina12.com.ar/diario/elmundo/4-147564-2010-06-14.html.

Maklouf Carvalho, Luiz. "'Arms and the Men: The Political and Affective Education of Dilma Rousseff.' Interview with Apolo Heringer Lisboa." *Piauí* 31 (April 2009): 11–31. https://piaui.folha.uol.com.br/materia/as-armas-e-os-varoes/.

———. "Seas Never Before Sailed: How and Why Dilma Rousseff Became the Candidate for President and Successor of Lula." *Piauí* 34 (July 2009): 28–33. https://piaui.folha.uol.com.br/materia/mares-nunca-dantes-navegados/.

Reid, Michael. *Brazil: The Troubled Rise of a World Power*. New Haven, CT: Yale University Press, 2014.

Roett, Riordan. *Brazil: Politics in a Patrimonial Society*. 5th ed. Westport, CT: Praeger, 1999.

Rousseff, Dilma. "A corrupção significa democratizar o poder." April 17, 2018. http://www.blogdadilma13.

Schwarcz, Lilia M., and Heloisa M. Starling. *Brazil: A Biography*. New York: Farrar, Straus and Giroux, 2018. First published 2015.

Serbin, Kenneth. *From Revolution to Power in Brazil: How Radical Leftists Embraced Capitalism and Struggled with Leadership*. Notre Dame, IN: University of Notre Dame Press, 2019.

Skidmore, Thomas E. *Brazil: Five Centuries of Change*. 2nd ed. New York: Oxford University Press, 2009.

Glossary

abertura	opening; refers to Brazil's transition to democracy (1974–1988)
alegría	joy, happiness
anos de chumbo	era of military repression, political violence, and censorship in Brazil (1968–1974); literally, the "leaden years"
bolos	aspiring, freelance Cuban musicians and actors
cabecitas negras	pejorative term for Argentine migrant workers and laborers; literally, "small black-haired people"
campesino/a	farmer; country person; agricultural laborer
científico	mid-nineteenth century official who followed the Positive principles of Auguste Comte, including the practical use of the scientific method as applied to finance, industrialization, and education
claves	hand-held percussion instrument consisting of rounded pieces of wood struck together
colegio	high school
corregidor	a district administrator in the Spanish-American colonies, whose administrative district was termed a *corregimiento*
corte	traditional Mayan skirt
criollo/a	(creole) Spanish Americans of European descent
cusqueño/a	person from Cusco, Peru
descamisados	Argentinian term for laborers meaning "shirtless ones"; term adopted and popularized by Eva Péron (Argentina)

Glossary

despedida	farewell celebration
diktat	an order or decree imposed without popular consent by a government or ruler
encomienda	grant of indigenous labor awarded by the king to early settlers in Spanish America
enganche	practice of enticing indigenous people to leave their communities and work on the properties of creoles (Whites)
feijoada	Brazil national dish, a black bean and pork stew often topped with farofa, toasted cassava flour.
gamonalismo	the manipulation of, typically, indigenous and mestizos by rural political bosses
huipil	loose, elaborately decorated blouse worn by Mayan women in Central and South America
kuraka	indigenous leader, Andean region
ladino/a	mixed descent, Hispanicized Spanish Americans
ladrona	thief (Spanish)
lava jato	car wash; term given for the corruption scandal that derailed the presidency of Dilma Roussef
limeño/a	person from Lima, Peru
mambí	Cuban patriot or rebel during the wars for independence against Spain
manigua	densely forested tropical uplands in Cuba's mountainous Oriente province
mazombo	Brazilian-born person of European descent living in Brazil (colonial era)
mensalão	parliamentary vote-buying scandal in Brazil (2005)
mestiza de vasca	woman of Indian and Basque descent
mestizaje	mixing of ethnic and cultural groups, particularly European and Native American
mestizo/a	Spanish American of European and Indigenous descent
mit'a	forced labor draft of Peruvian Indigenous people imposed by the Spanish during the colonial era
obraje	workshop
orishá	African tribal deities
patiloca	footloose
paulista	a person from the Brazilian state of São Paulo
peraje	scarf worn by Mayan women
pistoleros	gunmen
pongo system	on-demand labor system for small plots of land

real, reais	Brazilian currency
reducción	indigenous settlement by Jesuits, dating from early colonial ties in Spanish America
reinoís	Portuguese-born living in Brazil (colonial era)
ronda	rounds of chorus
salseros	those who dance the salsa
Te Deum	from Latin, a religious hymn in of praise to God
tertulia	social gathering, usually to discuss literature
tradicciones	a semi-historical Peruvian literary genre
transnationalism	globalization leading to the connecting of peoples, states, and cultures
unidades básicas	women's clubs foundational to the Peronist Women's Party
velada	musical and literary social gathering, usually held in the evening
yerba mate	tea widely consumed in southeastern South America, particularly in Paraguay and Argentina

Index

abertura (opening, democratic), 223, 239
abolition of slavery, 36–37, 39–40, 215
abortions, 135
advertisements, 175
Africans, enslaved, 35, 169. *See also* slavery
Afro-Brazilian/s, 19–20
Afro-Cuban/s, 8, 170–89
agriculture, 39, 57, 87, 163, 209
Aguirre Cerda, Pedro, 107–8, 119
AIM. *See* American Indian Movement, US
alcoholism, 117
alegría (joy), 143, 239
Alessandri, Arturo, 117
Alfonso, Catalina "Ollita," 171, 185
Algeria, 57
Ali, Muhammad, 182
Alliance against Impunity (La Alianza contra la Impunidad), Guatemala, 209
Amado, Jorge, 223
American Bible Society, 95
American Indian Movement (AIM), US, 204
amputation, 147
Anacaona (band), 172–73
Los Andes (weekly publication), 92–93

Andrada e Silva, José Bonifácio de, 24
anos de chumbo ("leaden years"), 223, 239
Anti-Imperialist League, Mexico, 131
Araújo, Carlos, 220–23, 226
Araújo, Paula, 222
Árbenz, Jacobo, 147, 177, 192–93, 197
architecture, 127
Arequipa, Peru, 88
Arévalo, Juan José, 192–93
Argentina, 3–4, 56, 85, 215, 223; classes in, 153–54, 156–58, 160; economy of, 163, 165–66; Matto de Turner in, 93–95; military, 154–57, 163–64, 223; Paraguay and, 59, 68–69; Peronist Party, 155–58, 160–67; poverty in, 153, 160, 166–67; radio in, 8, 151–52, 154–56, 164 ; US and, 118, 158. *See also* Buenos Aires
Argentine Institute for the Promotion of Trade, 163
Arias, Oscar, 205, 207
Armed Revolutionary Vanguard Palmares (VAR), 220–21, 223
Arnaz, Desi, 169
arrests, 71–72, 142, 159, 164; Menchú Tum, R., 206; of Rousseff, D., 220
arsenic poisoning, 118–19

243

art/artists, 128; Kahlo, F., as, 130–41, 143–45
Asencio, Don Ascencio de, 40, 42–43
assassination, 4, 85, 142
Asturias, Miguel Ángel, 101
Asunción, Paraguay, 55, 61–63, 65–67, 70–72, 74–77
Austria, 13–15, 20
authoritarian, 55, 68, 217
authors/writers, Latin American, 80, 84–87, 91–92, 95–96, 101–3, 108
auto manufacturing/automobiles, 125, 221–22
Aves sin nido (*Birds without a Nest*, Matto de Turner), 91–92, 96
Ávila, Amelia Robles, 4–5, 10n9

bananas, 191–92
Banco Central, 163
Barros, Adhemar de, 220
Bastidas, Micaela, 81, 83
Bates, Margaret, 122
Batista, Fulgencio, 175–76, 193
Battle of Cascorro, 48
Battle of Cerro Corá, 73–74
Battle of Lomas Valentinas, 72
Battle of Tuyutí, 70
Battles of Curuzú and Curupayty, 70
Bautista Gill, Juan, 74–75
Bay of Pigs invasion, 177
Beecher Stowe, Harriet, 91
Belzú, Manuel Isodoro, 85
Berggruen, Heinz, 142–43
"Big Stick" diplomacy, 191
bilingual, 55
Billboard magazine, 185
biracial, 38
Birds without a Nest (*Aves sin nido*, Matto de Turner), 91–92, 96
Black Rob (musician), 184
Black Virgin of Regla (saint), 183
Blazing Mulatto Women (Las Mulatas de Fuego), 173
boarding houses, 112

Bocetos al lápiz de americanos célebres (Matto de Turner), 91, 95
Bohus, Irene, 142
Bolívar, Simón, 39, 80
Bolivia, 85, 87
bolos (aspiring artists), 172
La Bolsa (newspaper), 89–90
Bolsa Família (Family Shopping Basket), Brazilian policy, 220, 222–23, 227, 231, 233
Bolshevik Revolution (1917), 131, 196
Bolsonaro, Jair, 235–36
Bonaparte, Mathilde, 58
Bonaparte, Napoleon, 13, 15–16, 21, 58
Borges, Jorge Luis, 101
Bourbon reforms, 81
Boyle Crooke, William, 57
bozales (enslaved peoples), 37
Braganza (imperial family), 2, 6–7, 13–17, 23
Bramuglia, Juan Atilio, 164
Brazil, 13, 56, 118–19, 163, 198; Afro-Brazilians, 19–20; corruption, 216, 225, 230–31, 233–36, 237n16; democracy/democracies, 215–16, 222–24, 235; economies, 215–17, 221, 224–27, 229–31; elections, 222, 224–25; FEE, 222, 226–27; independence of, 2, 6–7, 13–14, 22, 26–28, 215; ISI, 221–22; middle-class, 215, 217–18, 222, 227, 233; military, 115, 215, 217–22; Paraguay and, 59, 68–74; PDT, 223–24, 226; Portugal and, 13–32, 215–16; PT, 224, 226–28, 231, 233; revolutionary left, 218–21, 223; slavery in, 20, 215–16; women in, 216, 221, 228–29, 233. *See also* presidents, Brazilian
Brazilian Democratic Movement Party, 222–23
Brazilian Labor Party (PDT), 223–24, 226
"Brazilian Miracle," 221, 223–24

Brenner, Anita, 137–38
Breton, André, 139–41
bribes/bribery, 230–31, 233–34
BRIC (Brazil, Russia, India, China) countries, 230
Britain, 2, 13, 16, 20, 57, 60
Brizola, Juan José, 60
Brizola, Leonel, 223, 226
The Broken Column (painting), 144
Brown, James, 182
The Buena Vista Social Club (film), 186
Buenos Aires, Argentina, 4, 67, 153–59, 164–65; Matto de Turner in, 81, 93–95
Bulgaria, 217
Burgos-Debray, Elisabeth, 195, 202–4
Bush, George W., 211

cabecitas negras ("small black-haired people," pejorative), 158, 239
Cabrales, María, 42–44
Cáceres, Andrés Avelino, 79, 88, 93, 95
Las cachuchas (social clique), 128–31
Calcott, Maria, 24–25
Calderón, Matilde, 126
California, 134–35, 142–43
Câmara, José Antônio Correia da, 73
*campesino/a*s (farmers), 114, 117, 239; Guatemalan, 198–99, 209
Canary Islands, 183
cancer, 122, 165–67, 185–87
Canil, Ángel, 209
Capital (Marx), 218
capitalism, 125–26; free-trade/market, 22, 196, 229
Caracas, Venezuela, 172–73
Cárdenas, Lázaro, 138, 147
Cardoso, Fernando Henrique, 223–27, 234
Carnegie Hall, New York City, 178
Carrillo, Juana, 66
car wash (*lava jato*, Dilma Rousseff corruption scandal), 230–31, 233–35, 240

Caso, Antonio, 128
Castelo Branco, Humberto, 218–19
Castilla, Ramón, 83
Castro, Domitila de, 28–32
Castro, Fidel, 193, 196–97, 220; Cruz, C., and, 8, 175–77, 184, 186
Catholic Action (program), 195
Catholicism, Roman, 1–2, 21, 56, 84, 127, 183, 194–95; in Chile, 105–6; corruption and, 7–8, 80, 91–93; in Cuba, 171; Paraguay and, 61, 76–77; in Peru, 80, 82, 91
cattle ranchers/production, 163, 165
Celia and Johnny (album), 181–82
Central Intelligence Agency (CIA), US, 146, 177, 193
Cerezo, Vinicio, 206
Céspedes, Carlos Manuel de, 43, 45
Chaplin, Charlie, 143, 146
Chávez, Hugo, 233–34
Chiapas, Mexico, 9, 197, 199–200
Chile, 4, 8, 87–88, 103–7, 116–19, 121–22, 228
Chimel, Guatemala, 193–98, 203, 209–10
China, 37, 230
Chinese laborers, 37
cholera, 70
Christianity, 55, 234
CIA. *See* Central Intelligence Agency, US
científico (mid-nineteenth century official), 84, 239
cimarrones (runaway slaves), 37, 39
citizenship, 4, 40, 161, 164, 182
civil rights, 205, 207
civil war, 2, 72, 117; Guatemalan, 196–99, 203–6, 210; Peruvian, 79, 89
classes: Argentine, 153–54, 156–58, 160; upper, 20, 65, 125, 222; Upper-middle-, 162, 218, 224; working, 156–58, 217. *See also* middle-class
claves (percussion instrument), 169, 239

Clinton, Bill, 183–84, 185
Clinton, Hillary Rodham, 233
CMQ (Cuban radio station), 172–73
Coelho Netto, Henrique, 92
Cold War, 209, 217, 219
colegio (high school), 127–29, 171, 194, 196, 199, 239
Collares, Alceu, 225–26
Colle, Pierre, 140
Collor de Mello, Francisco, 225
Colombia, 101–2, 183–84
colonialism, 1–6, 13, 81, 84, 87, 207–8; Cuba and, 35–37, 42–51; Paraguay and, 55, 71; by Portugal, 215–16
Columbus, Christopher, 1, 207
Committee for Campesino Unity/Comité para la Unidad Campesina (CUC), 195–96, 198–99
communism, 8, 125, 138, 146, 196–97, 217
Communist Party, 131, 133; Brazilian, 220; Guatemalan, 192
Communities of the Population in Resistance (CPR), Guatemala, 200
Comte, Auguste, 84, 95
Congressional Medal of the Arts, US, 183
Congress of Vienna, 15
Constitution, Brazil, 29
Constitution (1917), Mexico, 4–5, 126
Contras (Nicaragua), 201
Copeland, Aaron, 136
coronéis ("colonels"), 216
corregidor (district administrator), 83, 239
corruption, 80, 91–93, 152; Brazilian, 216, 225, 230–31, 233–36, 237n16; Guatemalan, 197
corte (Mayan skirt), 199, 239
Costa, Petra, 235
Costa e Silva, Arthur da, 219
Costa Rica, 191, 205
Cours de philosophie positive (Comte), 84
COVID-19, 9n4

CPR. *See* Communities of the Population in Resistance, Guatemala
"Cradle Songs" (poems), 111–12
Crimean War (1853–1856), 58
criollo/a (creole, Spanish Americans of European descent), 81–83, 93, 177, 239; in Cuba, 40–43
Crossing Borders (Menchú Tum, R.,), 210–11
Cruz, Celia, 7–8, 170–77, *174*, 184, 186–88
Cruz, Simón, 170–73
Cruz, Sor Juana Inés de la, 107
Cuba, 50–52, 113, 196, 198, 220; Afro-Cubans, 8, 170–89; colonialism and, 35–37, 42–51; Guatemala and, 209; *manigua*, 44, 46–47, 240; music from, 169–80; race/racism in, 35–40, 42–51; slavery in, 35–49, 171; Spain and, 7, 35–37, 42–51; sugar, 35, 39, 42, 45, 48; US and, 177, 179, 182, 184, 186, 188
Cuban Revolution, 43–51, 175–80, 185
cubism, 131
CUC. *See* Committee for Campesino Unity/Comité para la Unidad Campesina
Cunha, Eduardo, 234–35
cusqueño/a (person from Cuszco, Peru), 239

Dana, Doris, 121–22
dance music, 170
Darío, Rubén, 101, 106–7
Darwinism, social, 84
death/s, 22–25, 126, 129, 143, 152, 196, 218–20; assassination as, 4, 85, 142; colonialism and, 81, 87; of Cruz, C., 182, 187–88; in Cuban conflicts, 39–40, 51; in "dirty wars," 197–98, 200–201, 223; executions as, 2, 39, 46–47, 71–72, 74, 176, 209; of Francia, 55–56; of Godoy, J., 118–22; of Gorriti, 86; from the Great Hunger, 57; of Kahlo, F., 147;

of Leopoldina, 30, 32; of López, C., 67; of Marcos, M., 45–46; Matto de Turner on, 82, 88; of Mistral, 122; of Neves, 225; of Perón, E., 152, 166–67; in Peruvian Civil War, 79; of Solano López, 73–74; of Trotsky, 142; of Vargas, 217, 222; during War of the Triple Alliance, 68, 70–74
"death squads," 198
Debray, Regis, 202–3, 219
Debret, Jean-Baptiste, 18, 28, 32
debt, 26, 224–25
décima (poetry), 181, 189n14
Delpar, Helen, 134
La Democracia (newspaper), 164
democracy/democracies, 22, 29, 196, 217; Brazilian, 215–16, 222–24, 235; Guatemalan, 192–93, 206
Democratic Front against Repression (Frente Democrática contra la Represión), Guatemalan, 200
descamisados ("shirtless ones," laborers), 158, 239
Desolación (Mistral), 113, 115, 121
despedida (farewell celebration), 112, 240
Detroit, Michigan, 135
DeVree, Howard, 139
diabetes, 119
"Diagnóstico" ("Diagnosis," song), 188–89
Díaz, Isadora, 70
Díaz, Porfirio, 3, 127
dictatorships, 3, 151, 217, 219
Diego and I (painting), 145
diktat (order/decree without popular consent), 240
Dirceu, José, 231
"dirty war," 196–99, 223
"disappeared"/political disappearances, 223, 236n6
distensão ("decompression" from military rule), 222
The Distribution of Arms (mural), 131

divorce, 141 85
Dodero, Alberto, 159, 163
Dominican Republic, 183
Dom João VI (king), 16–18
Dream of a Sunday Afternoon in the Central Almeda (mural), 146
D'Souza, Dinesh, 211
Duarte, Elisa, 153
Duarte, Eva. *See* Perón, Eva
Duarte, Juan, 152–53
Duarte, Juancito, 164
Duchamp, Marcel, 140
Dutra, Olívio, 226

earthquakes, 155
Economic Indicators (journal), 226
economies, 2–3, 125, 196, 230; Argentine, 163, 165–66; Brazilian, 215–17, 221, 224–27, 229–31; Cuban, 35; Peruvian, 83
The Edge of Democracy (documentary), 235
education, 82–83, 84, 113, 125, 223–24, 227; *colegio* (high school), 127–29, 171, 196, 199, 239; of Cruz, C., 171; elementary school, 171, 194; of Kahlo, F., 127–29; Matto de Turner on, 80, 95–96; of Menchú Tum, R., 193–96; of Mistral, 103–9; of Perón, E., 153–54; rights, 3–4, 79–80, 95–96; of Rousseff, D., 218, 222, 224
EGP. *See* Ejército Guerrillero de los Pobres
Einstein, Albert, 125, 136
Eisenstein, Sergei, 135
Ejército Guerrillero de los Pobres (Guerrilla Army of the Poor, EGP), Guatemala, 196–98, 202, 206
elections, 164–66; Brazilian, 222, 224–25; Guatemalan, 192–93, 206
elementary school, 171, 194
Eloesser, Leo, 136, 142, 144
El Salvador, 191, 197
encomienda (grant of indigenous labor), 240

Encounter for Guatemala (Encuentro por Guatemala) party, 87, 211
Ender, Thomas, 17
energy minister, Brazil, 228–29, 233
energy/power policies, 226–29
enganche (enticement of indigenous people), 82–83, 240
England, 2, 13, 16, 20, 57, 60
English (language), 179, 182, 203
environmentalism, 212
La Equitativa (press), 79–81, 92–93
Espinosa Medrano, Juan de, 90
Esquivel, Adolfo Pérez, 208
ethanol, 222
Europe/European, 95, 114, 163, 201, 217, 230, 234; colonization by, 87, 207–8; immigrants, 126, 158; Menchú Tum, R., in, 202; Mistral in, 115–21; Paraguay and, 55. *See also specific countries*
Eva Perón Foundation, *160*
executions, 2, 39, 46–47, 71–72, 74, 176, 209
exile, 15, 40, 131, 164, 180, 193, 220; of Cruz, C., 175–80, 188; of Lynch, E., 74–76; of Matto de Turner, 8, 79–81, 93–95; of Menchú Tum, R., 199–202
exports, 2–3, 19, 23, 35; Brazilian, 215–17
Exposition and Protest (Lynch, E.,), 75

Family Shopping Basket (Bolsa Família), Brazilian policy, 227, 231, 233
famine, 7, 57
Fania All-Stars (band), 180–84
Fanning, Ronan, 76
Faribundo Martí Front for National Liberation (Frente Faribundo Martí para Liberación Nacional, FMLN), Guatemala, 201
farmers. *See campesino/as* (farmers)
Farrell, Edelmiro J., 155–57
fascism, 118, 154

FEE. *See* Foundation of Economics and Statistics, Brazil
feijoada (Brazilian national dish), 240
Feliciano, José, 185
feminism, 3–4, 7–8, 80, 92, 95–96, 161–62, 167, 211, 229
Fernández, Fernando, 129
Fernández, Francisco, 63
Fernando VII (king), 35
fertilizer, 87–88
Fidel Suárez, Marco, 101–2
Figueiredo, João Baptista, 223
Figueredo, Félix, 49–50
Firestone, Sigmund, 142–43
firing squads, 2
Florida, 178, 185–86, 187
FMLN. *See* Faribundo Martí Front for National Liberation
Fonseca, Marshal Deodoro da, 215
footloose (*patiloca*), 240
Ford, Edsel, 135
Foundation of Economics and Statistics (FEE), Brazil, 222, 226–27
The Frame (painting), 138, 140–41
France, 57–60, 116, 118–20, 140–41, 163; Lynch, E., in, 74–76
Francia, José Gaspar Rodríguez de, 55–56, 64, 68–69
Francis II (Emperor), 14
Franco, Francisco, 118, 163
Franco, Itmar, 225
free Cubans of African descent, 35–40
free-trade/market capitalism, 22, 196, 229
French (language), 1, 24, 57, 70
Frente Democrática contra la Represión/ Democratic Front against Repression, Guatemalan, 200
Frente Faribundo Martí para Liberación Nacional (Faribundo Martí Front for National Liberation, FMLN), Guatemala, 201
Frente Guerrillera Cristiana Vicente Menchú (Vicente Menchú Revolutionary Christian Guerrilla Front), Guatemala, 200

Galeano, Cláudio, 219–20, 222
gamonalismo (manipulation of indigenous and mestizos), 82–83, 240
gangrene, 49, 146
García, Horacio, 197–98
Gaviria, César, 184
GCPU. *See* Guatemalan Committee for Patriotic Unity
GDP. *See* gross domestic product
Geisel, Ernesto, 222–23
genocide, 8, 202, 211
Germany, 2, 87, 126–27, 217
Gift of the heart (*Regalo del alma*) album, 187
Goddard, Paulette, 142
Godoy, Jerónimo, 103–4
Godoy, Juan Miguel, 116, 118–22
Godoy Alcayaga, Lucila. *See* Mistral, Gabriela
Goldberg, Whoopi, 185
Golden Law/Golden Law, Brazil, 215
Gómez, Francisco E., 51
Gómez, Máximo, 45, 48–50
Gómez Arias, Alejandro, 5, 128–31, 139
González de Calderón, Isabel, 126
Gorriti, Juana Manuela, 80–81, 85–86, 88
Goulart, João, 217, 222
Graham, Maria, 24–25, 28, 30
Grajales, Mariana, 6–7, 35–51, *36*
Grammy awards, 182, 185–86
Great Depression, 134, 216–17, 221
Great Hunger, Irish, 57
Great War, Paraguayan, 7, 64, 66, 68–74, 76
Grito de Ipiranga, 28
Grito de Yara, 43
gross domestic product (GDP), 221
guano, mining, 87–88
Guaraní Indians, 55–56, 65–66, 68
Guatemala: *campesinos*, 198–99, 209; Chimel, 193–98, 203, 209–10; civil war, 196–99, 203–6, 210; EGP, 196–98, 202, 206; elections, 192–93, 206; guerrillas, 196–201, 209–10; Indigenous people from, 193–205, 207–8, 210–11; land reforms, 193, 197; military, 197–98, 206; US and, 191–92
Guatemalan Committee for Patriotic Unity (GCPU), 202
Guatemalan National Revolutionary Union (Unión Nacional Revolucionaria Guatemalteca), 210
Guerrilla Army of the Poor (Ejército Guerrillero de los Pobres), Guatemala, 196–98, 202, 206
guerrillas, 3–4, 7; Guatemalan, 196–201, 209–10
Guevara, Ernesto "Che," 193, 197, 202–3, 220
Guillén, Palma, 113–14, 116, 118–19, 122
Guinness Book of World Records, 183
guitar, 169
gunman (*pistoleros*), 241

Haiti, 22
Hapsburg (royal family), 2, 13–17, 28
Harlow, Larry, 180–81
Havana, Cuba, 170–76
health, 119, 121; cancer and, 122, 165–67, 185–87; of Kahlo, F., 127, 129–31, 135–36, 142–47; of Leopoldina, 31–32
Henry Ford Hospital (painting), 135
Herencia (Matto de Turner), 93
Heringer Lisboa, Apolo, 218–19
Herrera, Hayden, 129
high school (*colegio*), 171, 194, 196, 199, 239; for Kahlo, F., 127–29
hijo de la chingada (son of a whore), 240
Hima-Sumac (play), 89
Hommy (song), 181
Honduras, 191
huipil (Mayan blouse), 199, 210, 240
human rights, 4, 193, 200–202, 205–6
"Hymn to the Tree" (poem), 110–11

hyperinflation, 224–25

I, Rigoberta Menchú (Burgos-Debray), 201–5, 207, 211
Ibáñez, Carlos, 115
Ibarbourou, Juana de, 117
Ibarguren, Juana, 152–54, 159
illiteracy, 194
I Love Lucy (television show), 169
Imbert, Aníbal Francisco, 154–55
immigrants, European, 126, 158
impeachments, 158, 234–35
imports, 163, 222
Import Substitution Industrialization (ISI), Brazil, 221–22
indentured servants, 37
independence, 1, 6–7, 39, 80, 84, 89, 191; of Brazil, 2, 13–14, 22, 26–28, 215; Cuban, 44–52; of Haiti, 22; of Mexico, 127; of Paraguayans, 55–56, 59
Indigenous people, 8–9, 105, 111, 117, 169, 195; Guatemalan, 193–205, 207–8, 210–11; labor of, 80, 82, 87, 240; Matto de Turner supporting, 79–80; Mexican, 133–34; Paraguayans, 55–56; Peruvian, 2, 80–89, 92–93; rights, 91, 193, 204–5, 207–8, 211–12. *See also specific Indigenous groups*
industrialization, 87; of Brazil, 221–22
inequality, 82, 125
inflation, 224–27
Insfrán, Juliana, 72
Institutional Acts, Brazilian, 218–19, 223
International Campaign to Stop Rape, 211
International Council of Indian Treaties, 204
Irala, Domingo Martínez de, 56
Ireland, 7, 57
Isabel (Princess), 215
ISI. *See* Import Substitution Industrialization, Brazil

Italy, 118, 122, 154, 163, 206–7
Ixil dialect, Quiché Mayan, 195

Jabón Radical, 154
Jamaica, 50
Jefferson, Roberto, 230–31
Jobim, Tom, 236
Joinet, Louis, 205
joy (alegría), 143, 239
Juegos Florales (Chilean poetry contest), 108–9
Julião, Francisco, 220

Kahlo, Frida, 4–5, 7–8, 10n9, 126–36; health of, 144–47; Rivera and, 128–29, 131–32, *132*, 136–47
Kahlo, Wilhelm/Guillermo, 126–27, 133
Kandinsky, Wassily, 140
kidnappings, 198, 209
King, B. B., 182
Knight, Pedro, 178–80, 182–83, 185–87
Kubitshek, Juscelino, 222
kuraka (Andean indigenous leader), 240

labor, Indigenous, 80, 82, 87, 240
labor draft (*mita*), 81
Labor Party, Brazil, 217
labor unions, 155–58, 161, 223
ladino/a (Hispanicized Spanish Americans), 195, 197, 199, 203, 210, 240
ladrona (thief), 240
Lagar (Wine Press, Mistral), 120
Lamarque, Libertad, 174–75
landownership, 37–38, 48, 194, 210
land reforms: Cuban, 175–76, 196; Guatemala, 193, 197
languages, 101, 200, 202; bilingual, 55; English, 179, 182, 203; French, 1, 24, 57, 70; Guaraní, 55–56; Lucumí, 173; Portuguese, 1, 18, 68; Quechua, 82, 85, 91, 95–96; Quiché Mayan, 195, 211
Latin America. *See specific topics*
Latin Grammy Awards, 186

lava jato (car wash; Dilma Rousseff corruption scandal), 230–31, 233–35, 240
"leaden years" (*anos de chumbo*), 223, 239
Lei Áurea/Golden Law, Brazil, 215
Lenin, Vladimir, 125, 136
Leopoldina (of Austria), 2, 6–7, 13–32, *19*
lesbianism, 114, 121, 129, 137
Levy, Julien, 139–40
Liberal (O Liberal, newspaper), 3–4
liberation theology, 195, 199, 202
Light for All, Brazilian program, 233
Lillis, Michael, 76
Lima, Peru, 80, 85, 90–91
Lima e Silva, Luiz de Alves de, 70
Limantour, José, 127
limeño/a (person from Lima, Peru), 93, 240
literature, Latin American, 5–6, 80, 84–87, 91–92, 95–96, 102–3, 108; poetry in, 101, 104–18, 122
The Little Deer (painting), 145
"The Little One-Armed Girl" (poem), 116
"Little War," 50–51
Live from the Cheetah (album), 181
Lloyd, Maud, 75–76
Lloyd Crooke, Eliza, 57
Lloyd Lynch, Jane, 57
López, Benigno, 62, 66
López, Carlos Antonio, 55, 59, 63, 66–67
López, Encarnación, 4
López, Francisco "Panchito," 61–62
Lopez, Jennifer, 185
López, Miguel Mariscal, 69
Los Andes, Chile, 107–8, 110
"lost decade," Brazilian, 224–25
Los Toldos, Argentina, 153
The Love Embrace of the Universe (painting), 145
Lucas García, Romeo, 198, 200
Lucha (Doña), 199

Lucumí (Cuban dialect), 173
Lula da Silva, Luiz Inácio, 9, 223–31, 233–36
"The Luminous Circle" (poem), 111
Lynch, Eliza, 6–7, 57–73, *69*, 228; exile of, 74–76
Lynch, John, 57, 62

Maathai, Wangari, 211
Maceo, Antonio, 7, 44–50
Maceo, José, 49, 51
Maceo, Marcos, 38–46
Maceo, Rafael, 44, 50–51
mambí (Cuban patriot), 46–47, 49–50, 240
Managua, Nicaragua, 200–201
Man at the Crossroads (mural), 136
manigua (forested tropical uplands in Cuba), 44, 46–47, 240
Marín, Lupe, 128
Márquez, Gabriel García, 101
marriage, 15, 42, 128–29, 131; of Cruz, C., 178; of Grajales, 40; of Kahlo, F., 133, 136–44; of Leopoldina, 16–19, 22, 26; of Lynch, E., 57–58; of Matto de Turner, 83, 85; of Menchú Tum, R., 209; of Perón, E., 157; of Rousseff, D., 219
Martí, Jose, 51–52
Martinelli, Ricardo, 234
Martínez, Eliu, 197–98
Martínez, Francisco, 72
Martínez, Rogelio, 174–75, 177
Martínez de Irala, Domingo, 55
Marx, Karl, 125, 146, 218
Marxism, 226–27
Marxism-Leninism, 131, 177, 196
Marxism Will Give Health to the Sick (painting), 146
Masonic lodges, 41–44
mass communication/media, 152, 158, 164
Masucci, Jerry, 180–81
Mato, Ramón, 82

252 Index

Mato Usandivaras, Grimanesa Martina. *See* Matto de Turner, Clorinda
matriarchy, 55–56
Matto de Turner, Clorinda, 82, 87–88, 91–92, *94*; exile of, 79–81, 93–95; positivism of, 83–86; on reforms, 7–8, 89–90
mazombo (Brazilian-born person of European descent), 20, 240
McMahon, Martin T., 72–73, 76
Mella, Julio Antonio, 131
memory, 103–4, 118, 121
Memory (painting), 137
Menchú, Vicente, 193–94, 196, 198
Menchú Tum, Petrocinio, 198
Menchú Tum, Rigoberta, 7–9, *192*, 197–98, 202–12; education of, 193–96; exile of, 199–201
mensalão (Brazilian vote-buying scandal), 230–31, 240
Mercader, Ramón, 142
Mercado, Ralph, 181
Mercante, Domingo, 157, 164
mestizaje (mixing of ethnic and cultural groups), 56, 210, 240
mestizo/a (Spanish American of European and indigenous descent), 105, 111, 117, 195, 240
metaphysics, 84
Methuen Treaty (1703), 13
von Metternich, Klemens, 15
Mexican Communist Party (PCM), 131, 133, 146
Mexican Revolution (1910–1920), 3–4, 125–27, 134
Mexico, 1, 127, 131, 151, 191, 215; capitalism and, 125–26; Chiapas, 9, 197, 199–200; Constitution (1917), 4–5, 126; Guevara in, 193; of Menchú Tum, R., in, 9, 199–202; Mistral in, 113–18
Mexico City, Mexico, 177–79, 181, 186–87, 199; Kahlo, F., in, 4–5, 137–39, 141, 143, 147; Kahlo, W., in, 126; "Tragic Ten Days" in, 127

Miami, Florida, 178, 185–86, 187
middle-class, 2–3, 125; Argentine, 153; Brazilians, 215, 217–18, 222, 227, 233; Cubans, 170–71; Mexican, 126
Middle East, 222
militaries, 59–61; Argentine, 154–57, 163–64, 223; Brazilian, 215, 217–22. 115; Guatemalan, 197–98, 206; Paraguayan, 69–73; Spanish, 35–37, 42–51; United States, 191
military rule/coups: Argentinian, 151, 154–57, 165; Brazilian, 217–22, 225; Chilean, 115; Guatemalan, 197
mining guano, 87–88
Ministry of Labor and Welfare, Argentina, 160–62
Miranda, Miguel, 163
Miró, Joan, 140
misanthropy, 121–22
miscarriages, 21, 32, 135
Mistral, Gabriela, 5, 7–8, *102*, 103–12, 121; in Mexico, 113–18; as a teacher, 105–7, 110, 113–15, 119, 122
mit'a (Peruvian forced labor draft), 81, 240
Mitre, Bartolomé, 66
modernity/modernization, 2–3, 58, 65, 84
Modotti, Tina, 131–33
monarchy, 2, 13, 29, 215
Monroy, Guillermo, 143
Montañez, Andy, 184
Montegrande, Chile, 103–5, 122
Mopié, Halia, 186
Mora, Sérgio, 235
Morales, Ed, 181
Morrow, Dwight, 133–34
"Mourning" (Luto, poem), 120
Las Mulatas de Fuego (Blazing Mulatto Women), 173
Mulhall, M. G., 67
Munchausen syndrome, 144
Muray, Nickolas, 140–41
Murillo, Gerardo, 147
Museum of Modern Art, 135

music, Latin American, 169–80
Mussolini, Benito, 154
My Birth (painting), 135
My Dress Hangs There (painting), 136
My Mission in Life (La razón de mi vida, Perón, E.,), 157, 159–60, 165–67

La Nación (newspaper), 164
Napoleon III (Emperor), 58
National Democratic Union Party, Argentina, 158
nationalism, 26, 37; Argentine, 158; Brazilian, 225
National Liberation Command (Colina) party, Brazil, 219–20
National Preparatory School/ Preparatoria, Mexico, 4–5, 127–29
Native American rights, 193, 204–5, 207–8
Nawaljá, Mash "Kalito," 209
Nazis, 118, 142–43, 201
La negra tiene tumbao (The black lady's got party) album, 186
neoliberalism, 227, 229
Neruda, Pablo, 101, 112
Nervo, Amado, 106, 107
Neves, Tancredo, 225
New Jersey, 187
New Spain, 81–82, 191
newspapers, 89–92, 95, 106, 115–16, 158, 164
New York City, 8, 122, 174–75, 179–81, 186–88; Kahlo, F., in, 5, 135–37, 139–41, 143
New York Times, 139
Neyra, Rodney, 173
NGOs. *See* nongovernmental organizations
Nicaragua, 191, 197–98, 200–201
nitrate conflicts, 87–88
Nobel Peace Prize, 203, 205, 207–8, 210, 212
Nobel Prize in Literature, 5, 8, 101, 106, 119

Nobel Women's Initiative, 211
Noguchi, Isamu, 137
nongovernmental organizations (NGOs), 201–2, 209
North Africa, 57
Norway, 208
Nueva Trova movement, 184

Obama, Barack, 233
obrajes (workshops), 82–84, 87, 240
Ocampo, Victoria, 117
Odebrecht, Marcelo, 234
O'Donnell, Leopoldo, 39
O Estado (newspaper), 223
oil/natural gas, 222, 229–30, 233
O'Keeffe, Georgia, 137, 139
Old Republic, Brazil, 215–16
oligarchy, 159
Olivares, Adelaida, 104
Olympics (2016), 233–34
Onís, Federico de, 113, 121
open marriages, 136–37, 145
"Operation Ashes" (Operación Ceniza), Guatemala, 200
orishá (African tribal deities), 240
Orozco, José Clemente, 128, 134
Ortiz Rubio, Pascual, 134–35

Pacheco, Johnny, 180–82, 185, 187
Pact of San Carlos (1859), 66
Pact of Zanjón, 50
painkillers, 146
Palacios, Manuel Antonio, 71
palenques (settlements of runaway slaves), 39, 46
Palma, Ricardo, 80, 86
Panama, 113, 191
Pan-Mayan Movement, 208
Paraguay, 4, 228; Argentina and, 59, 68–69; Asunción, 55, 61–63, 65–67, 70–72, 74–77; Catholicism and, 61, 76–77; colonialism and, 55, 71; Great War, 7, 64, 66, 68–74, 76; independence of, 55–56, 59; presidents, 55, 59–60, 64, 66–67,

74–75; War of the Triple Alliance, 7, 68–74
Partido Civil, Peru, 83
"Patagonian Landscapes" (poem), 109
patiloca (footloose), 113, 115, 240
patriarchy, 56, 221, 228
paulista (person from São Paulo), 240
PCM. *See* Mexican Communist Party
PDT. *See* Brazilian Labor Party
peace, 114, 208–10
peasants, 57; Guatemalan, 193, 198; Mexican, 126. *See also campesino/as* (farmers)
Pedro I (Emperor), 2, 7, 13–19, *19*, 21–32, *27*, 215
Pedro II (Emperor), 7, 32, 70, 72–73, 215
peraje (Mayan scarf), 199, 241
Peres, Glênio, 222–23
Perón, Eva, 7, *8*, 151–66, *160*
Perón, Juan Domingo, 118, 151–52, 155–59, 165–67
Peronist Party, Argentine, 155–58, 160–67
Peru, 4, 79; Catholicism in, 80, 82, 91; Indigenous people from, 2, 80–89, 92–93; Lima, 80, 85, 90–91; Matto de Turner on reforms, 7–8, 89–90; suppression in, 81–83
El Perú ilustrado (newspaper), 90–92
Peruvian Civil War (1894–1895), 79
Petrobras, 222, 229–30, 233–35
photography, 126–27
Picasso, Pablo, 140
Piérola, Nicolás, 79, 93
Pinguelli Rosa, Luiz, 228
pistoleros (gunman), 241
Platine War (1851–1852), 59
"Poem of the Son" (poem), 109
poets/poetry, Latin American, 101, 104–18, 122
police, 157; Guatemalan, 198–99
polio, 127
pongo system (on-demand labor system), 241

populism, 67, 166; Brazilian, 217; Mexican, 125–26
Portugal, 2, 5–6, 117; Brazil and, 13–32, 215–16; music from, 169
Portuguese (language), 1, 18, 68
positivism, 80, 82–86, 96
potato famine, 7, 57
poverty/poor people, 38, 57–58, 125; in Argentina, 153, 160, 166–67; in Brazil, 216–17, 223–24, 227, 233; in Cuba, 175–76; in Guatemala, 196, 203
power, 14, 79–80; of Castro, 196–97; of Perón, E., 8, 159–64, 166–67; of Perón, J., 155–56; of the United States, 191
Prado, Pérez, 169
pregnancies, 21, 25–26, 29–31, 40, 61, 66, 70
La Prensa (newspaper), 164
presidential chief of staff, Brazilian, 103, 231
Presidential Medal of the Arts, Colombia, 183
presidents, 45, 69; Argentine, 155–57, 165–66; Chilean, 107, 117, 119; Colombian, 102; Guatemalan, 192–93, 206; Mexican, 134–35, 138, 157; Paraguayan, 55, 59–60, 64, 66–67, 74–75; Peruvian, 79, 83, 88, 95–96; US, 183, 186, 191
presidents, Brazilian, 9, 222–23, 225–26; Fonseca as, 215; Lula da Silva as, 227–31, 236; Perón, J., as, 158–59; Rousseff, D., as, 216, 218, 231, *232*, 233; Vargas, 217
private school, 218
privatization, 227
propaganda, 155–56, 161, 165
protectionism, 217, 225, 229–30
pseudonyms, 84–85, 107
PT. *See* Workers' Party, Brazilian
public schools, 218, 227
Puente, Tito, 169, 179–80
Puerto Ricans, 181

Puff Daddy (musician), 184
Punta Arenas, Chile, 108–12

Quadros, Jânio, 222
Quatrefages, Xavier, 57–58, 61
Quechua (language), 82, 85, 91, 95–96
Quevedo, Miguel Ángel, 176
Quiché Mayan (language/culture), 195, 211

Rabel, Fanny, 143
race/racism, 1, 19–20, 38, 104–5, 119, 176–77, 210; in Cuba, 35–40, 42–51; in Peru, 81–84
radio: Argentine, 8, 151–52, 154–56, 164 ; Cuban, 170–74
Radio Belgrano (Argentina), 154, 156, 158, 164
Radio City Music Hall, New York City, 178, 180
"Rainbow Tour" by Perón, E., 163
Ramírez, Rodrigo, 197
Ramos, Delores, 171
rape, 193
La razón de mi vida (My Mission in Life, Perón, E.,), 157, 159–60, 165–67
Readings for Women (Mistral), 114
El Recreo de Cusco (magazine), 85, 87–89
reduccíon (indigenous settlement by Jesuits), 65–66, 241
Regalo del alma (Gift of the heart) album, 187–89
Regüeyferos, Fructuoso, 38
Reid, Michael, 225, 236
reinoís (Portuguese-born living in Brazil), 20, 241
religion, 71, 91–93, 105–6, 194–95. *See also specific religions*
Remembrance of an Open Wound (painting), 138–39
repression, 81–83
republics, sovereign, 68, 191. *See also specific republics*

revolutionary left: Brazilian, 218–21, 223; Guatemalan, 200–201
Revolution within the Revolution (Debray), 219
Reyes, Cipriano, 155, 164
Reyes, Neftalí, 112
Reymundo, Ana Cristina, 186–87
"Ríe y llora" (song), 188
rights, 166; citizenship, 4, 40, 161, 164, 182; civil, 205, 207; to education, 79, 86, 193; human, 4, 193, 200–202, 205–6; Indigenous, 91, 193, 204–5, 207–8, 211–12; voting, 161–63, 165, 216; for women, 3–4, 86, 161–63, 165
Rights of Nature Movement, 212
Rigoberta Manchú Tum Foundation, 211
rituals, 169, 195
Rivera, Diego, 8, 128–29, 131–32, 136–47
Rodig, Laura, 113–14
Rodríguez, Antonio, 49
Rodríguez, Silvio, 184
rondas (rounds of chorus), 111, 121–22, 241
Rondón, Juan Bautista, 43–44
Roots (painting), 144
Rosas, Juan Manuel de, 59
Rousseff, Dilma, 9, 218–24, 226–30, 232, 236; *lava jato* corruption scandal and, 230–31, 233–35, 240
Rousseff, Pedro, 217–18
Roxas y Andrada, Lázaro de, 66
Ruin (painting), 145
Ruiz Moreno, Samuel, 199–200, 202
runaway slaves (*cimarrones*), 37, 39
Russia, 15, 58, 131, 151, 196. *See also* Soviet Union

Sackville West, Lionel, 75
Salavarieta, Policarpa, 2
salon culture, Parisian, 58
salsa music, 169, 180–88
salseros (salsa dancers), 184, 241

Saltpeter War. *See* War of the Pacific (1879–1883)
Sánchez, Nicasio, 193
sanctions, 206
San Francisco, California, 134–35, 142–43
San Martín, José de, 84
Santana (musician), 184
Santería, 173, 183
Santos, Eduardo, 115
Santos, Juan Manuel, 233
Sarmiento, Escuela, 4
Sarny, José, 225
Sauer, Ildo, 229
Schaffer, Jorge, 17
Schapiro, Mary, 137
secretary of energy, Brazil, 226
secularism, 127
SEECO Records, 174–75, 180
Self-Portrait on the Borderline between Mexico and the United States (painting), 135–36
self-portraits, 8, 130, 135–36, 138–39, 144–45
Self-Portrait with Thorn and Hummingbird (painting), 144
Serra, José, 227–28
sexism, 161, 210
sexuality/sexual intercourse, 5, 129, 136–37, 142, 145
Shakira (musician), 186
Siegel, Sidney, 174–75, 179–80
Siete Partidas (legal code), 71
"El Silencio" (brotherhood), 47
Silva, Dilma da, 217–19
Silva Castro, Raúl, 121
Silva Paranhos, José María da, 63, 74
silver, 81
Siqueiros, David Alfaro, 128, 134, 138, 142, 147
Sister Sledge (musician), 182
slavery, 68–69, 169; abolition of, 36–37, 39–40; in Brazil, 20, 215–16; in Cuba, 35–49, 171
"slavocracy," 37–41

"small black-haired people" (*cabecitas negras*, pejorative), 239
Smithsonian Institute, 183
Social Aid Foundation, Argentina, 160–61
social Darwinism, 84
Social Democratic Party, Brazil, 217
Socialism, 158, 177, 207
Socialist Party, Brazilian, 218
social reforms, 3–5, 91, 126
social welfare, 160–63, 217
Sociedad de Beneficencia (organization), 159–60
Solano López, Francisco, 7, 55, 58–63, 65–77
soldaderas (free Black woman in Cuban wars), 37
Somoza, Anastasio, 191
"Sonnets of Death" (poems), 106–7
Sonora Matancera (band), 173–80, *174*
Soviet Union (USSR), 177, 188, 219, 220
Sowing Peace Cooperative, 209
Spain, 1–2, 5–6, 13, 80, 88, 163, 169, 207; Cuba and, 7, 35–37, 42–51; Mistral and, 116–18; Napoleon and, 15
Spanish Revolution of 1820, 22
"stagflation," 224–25
Stalin, Joseph, 133, 138, 142
Standard (periodical), 67
Stoll, David, 203, 211
Storni, Alfonsina, 109, 117
Stroessner, Alfredo, 76
suffrage, 161
sugar, 3, 87, 176, 203, 216, 230; Cuban, 35, 39, 42, 45, 48
suicide, 106, 117, 147
Sun and Life (painting), 145
Sun Sun Ba Baé (Pretty hummingbird of dawn, show), 173
Sur (magazine), 117
surrealism, 8, 139–41

Tagore, Rabindranath, 105–6

Taiping Rebellion (1850–1864), 87
Tala (*Havoc/Felling,* Mistral), 117–18
Taracena, Arturo, 202
taxes, 81, 161, 225
teachers/educators, 105–7, 110, 113–15, 119, 122
technology, 125, 151–52, 164
Te Deum (religious hymn), 72, 241
Tehuana Indians, 133–34
Telemundo, 183, 185–86
telethons, 185–86
Temuco, Chile, 112
Ten Years' War, 7, 37, 43
Ternura (Tenderness, poetry collection), 115, 121
terrorism/terrorist attacks, 186, 211
tertulia (social gathering), 85–86, 241
theosophy, 105–6
The Two Fridas (painting), 141
thief (*ladrona*), 240
Thinking of Death (painting), 144
Thompson, George, 68
Tico Records, 179–80
El Tiempo (newspaper), 115
Tinta, Peru, 83, 85
Tiradentes Prison (Brazil), 220
Toledano, Vicente Lombardo, 128
torture, 37, 71–72; in Guatemala, 198; of Rousseff, D., 221–23
Toward a Better Future (radio series), 156
tradicciones (Peruvian literary genre), 241
Tradiciones (Palma), 80
Tradiciones cuzqueñas (Matto de Turner), 89–90
"Tragic Ten Days," Mexico, 127
transgender people, 10n9
transnationalism, 241
treason, 71
Treaty of Ancón, 88
Tree of Hope (painting), 144–45
Trotsky, Leon, 138–39, 141–43
tuberculosis, 32
Tum, Juana, 193, 199

Tupac Amaru II, 2, 81, 83
Turner, José, 83
Tutu, Desmond, 208
Two Fridas (painting), 145
Two Nudes in a Forest (painting), 137
Two Women (painting), 133–34

Uncle Tom's Cabin (Beecher Stowe), 91
unidades basicas (women's clubs), Argentine, 162, 241
Unión Nacional Revolucionaria Guatemalteca (Guatemalan National Revolutionary Union), 210
United Fruit Company, 192–93
United Nations, 2–5, 205, 209; Economic and Social Council, 204; High Commission for Refugees, 200–201
United States (US), 1, 8, 20, 114, 196, 215, 233, 237n16; Argentina and, 118, 158; CIA, 146, 177, 193; Cruz, C., in, 178–79, 181–88; Cuba and, 177, 179, 182, 184, 186, 188; Guatemala and, 191–92, 198; Kahlo, F., in, 134–37, 139–41; Latin American music in, 169; Mistral in, 115, 120–22; Peru and, 88; presidents, 183, 186, 191; recession in, 230; terrorist attacks in, 186, 211; USSR and, 219
Universal Declaration of Human Rights, UN, 201
upper class, 20, 65, 125, 222
upper-middle-class, 162; Brazilian, 218, 224
Ureta, Romelio, 105–6
Urquiza, Justo José, 66
Uruguay, 4, 68–69, 184–85
US. *See* United States
US Peace Corps, 194

Valdés Pereira, Fidelia, 109
El Valle de Andorra (production), *63*
VAR. *See* Armed Revolutionary Vanguard Palmares

Varela, Hector, 76
Vargas, Getúlio, 217, 222, 225
Vasconcelos, José, 110, 113–15, 127–28
veladas (musical, literary social gathering), 85–86, 89, 241
Velasco, Adela de, 119
Velásquez, Juan Moreno, 181
Velásquez, Manuel, 209
Venezuela, 39, 172–73
Viaje de recreo (*Travel for Pleasure*, Matto de Turner), 95
Vicente Menchú Revolutionary Christian Guerrilla Front (Frente Guerrillera Cristiana Vicente Menchú), Guatemala, 200
voting, 161, 165, 211, 216. *See also* elections

wage laws, Argentine, 161–62
Wahpepah, William, 204
war criminals, 74
War of the Pacific (1879–1883), 86–89, 96
War of the Triple Alliance, 7, 64, 66, 68–74, 76
Washburn, Charles A., 70
weapons, 219
What the Water Gave Me (painting), 139
wheelchair, 146
White Cubans, 35, 37–40, 42
Wine Press (*Lagar*, Mistral), 120
Without Hope (painting), 144
Wolfe, Ella, 145
womanizers, 20, 62, 133, 137, 179
women, 1–6, 9n4, 84, 112–17, 135, 163, 195; Brazil and, 216, 221, 228–29, 233; Guaraní, 55–56; Matto de Turner supporting, 79, 85–86, 93–95; Paraguayan, 64–65, 73; pregnancies and, 21, 25–26, 29–31, 40, 61, 66, 70; rights for, 95–96, 161–63, 216; *soldaderas*, 37–38. *See also specific women*
Women's Congress, First International, 4
Women's Party, Peronist, 161–62, 167
Workers' Party (PT), Brazilian, 224, 226–28, 231, 233
Workers' Politics (Política Operária) party, Brazil, 218–19
working-class, 217; Argentine, 156–58
workshop (*obraje*), 240
World Cup (2014), 233
World Salsa Festival (1997), 184
World War I, 151, 201
World War II, 143, 151
Wyclef Jean (musician), 184

Xamán massacre (1995), Guatemala, 209

Yankee Stadium, New York City, 181–82
Yegros, Rómulo, 60
yerba mate (tea), 65, 241
Yon Sosa, Aurelio, 197
Yoruba people, 173
Young Communist League, Mexico, 131

Zapata, Emiliano, 4, 126, 166

www.ingramcontent.com/pod-product-compliance
Lightning Source LLC
Chambersburg PA
CBHW051806230426
43672CB00012B/2651